Programming in C#: Exam 70-483 (MCSD) Guide

Learn basic to advanced concepts of C#, including C# 8, to pass Microsoft MCSD 70-483 exam

Simaranjit Singh Bhalla
SrinivasMadhav Gorthi

BIRMINGHAM - MUMBAI

Programming in C#: Exam 70-483 (MCSD) Guide

Commissioning Editor: Pavan Ramchandani
Acquisition Editor: Shriram Shekhar
Content Development Editor: Ruvika Rao
Senior Editor: Afshaan Khan
Technical Editor: Ketan Kamble
Copy Editor: Safis Editing
Project Coordinator: Prajakta Naik
Proofreader: Safis Editing
Indexer: Pratik Shirodkar
Production Designer: Deepika Naik

First published: October 2019

Production reference: 1311019

Published by Packt Publishing Ltd.
Livery Place
35 Livery Street
Birmingham
B3 2PB, UK.

ISBN 978-1-78953-657-7

www.packt.com

Subscribe to our online digital library for full access to over 7,000 books and videos, as well as industry leading tools to help you plan your personal development and advance your career. For more information, please visit our website.

Why subscribe?

- Spend less time learning and more time coding with practical eBooks and Videos from over 4,000 industry professionals

- Improve your learning with Skill Plans built especially for you

- Get a free eBook or video every month

- Fully searchable for easy access to vital information

- Copy and paste, print, and bookmark content

Did you know that Packt offers eBook versions of every book published, with PDF and ePub files available? You can upgrade to the eBook version at www.packt.com and as a print book customer, you are entitled to a discount on the eBook copy. Get in touch with us at customercare@packtpub.com for more details.

At www.packt.com, you can also read a collection of free technical articles, sign up for a range of free newsletters, and receive exclusive discounts and offers on Packt books and eBooks.

Contributors

About the authors

Simaranjit Singh Bhalla is currently working as a technical architect manager for KPMG. He previously worked as a solutions architect with SMS Management and Technology in Sydney, Australia. He also worked with Microsoft Global Services for a period of three and a half years.

He has around seven years of experience in C#. He has extensive experience in the development of the Microsoft technology stack. He has performed multiple successful engagements in C#, .NET, Azure, JavaScript, and CRM. He has completed certifications in .NET 4.0 Framework, .NET 4.5 MVC, programming in C#, Windows Azure and Web Services, and others.

SrinivasMadhav Gorthi is a multi-skilled senior consultant with over nine years' experience in Microsoft Dynamics CRM implementations with the expertise to architect, design, and implement end-to-end solutions and business outcomes. Madhav has more than 17 years' experience in Microsoft technologies. He is currently working as a Solutions Architect in Sydney, Australia. Madhav has worked in Microsoft gold partner companies, including Velrada and Accenture. He has also delivered many end-to-end Microsoft applications using C#, ASP.NET MVC, Azure, and JavaScript.

About the reviewers

Aidan Temple is an experienced software engineer with a history of working in the gaming industry. He holds both a master's of professional practice in games development from Abertay University, and a Bachelor of Science degree in games software development from Glasgow Caledonian University. He has over 8 years' experience working with C# and C++.

Jasvinder Singh completed his Bachelor of Technology in IT from IIIT-Allahabad in 2008. His home town is Unnao, Uttar Pradesh, and he is currently based in Bangalore, India. He has around 11 years' IT experience in total and is currently working with Flipkart. He began his career by joining Microsoft as a software development engineer and has an abundance of experience of working in the product development domain industry.

His expertise lies in problem solving using algorithms and in AI. Apart from playing with his 3-year-old son, Avraj, he likes to travel and watches sci-fi films and documentaries.

Packt is searching for authors like you

If you're interested in becoming an author for Packt, please visit `authors.packtpub.com` and apply today. We have worked with thousands of developers and tech professionals, just like you, to help them share their insight with the global tech community. You can make a general application, apply for a specific hot topic that we are recruiting an author for, or submit your own idea.

Table of Contents

Preface

The MCSD 70-483 exam is an entry-level Microsoft certification exam for C# developers that is widely used to measure their expertise in the field of C# programming. This book is a certification guide to prepare you for the skills that are evaluated in the certification exam and also promotes building problem-solving acumen with C#. Every chapter in the book has been designed as preparation material for the Microsoft MCSD 70-483 exam.

For those who don't have much experience of working in C#, we have added some chapters at the start of the book that will provide basic knowledge about C# programming. This knowledge will not only help you to pass the certification but will also help you to become a better C# developer.

Who this book is for

The book is designed for both experienced developers and people new to C# who are intending to undertake the 70-483 Programming in C# certification exam in the near future. The book provides extensive knowledge of all the topics that are evaluated in the exam. To drive better understanding, each chapter in the book is accompanied by code examples along with assessment questions.

To make the path of learning C# easier for beginners, we have also tried to address the basics of C# and .NET Framework in the first three chapters of the book. To get the most value out of the book, you are expected to have a fair understanding of any programming language; for example, C, C++, or C#.

What this book covers

Chapter 1, *Learning the Basics of C#*, focuses on the basics of the C# language. In this chapter, you will learn about the underlying .NET Framework architecture and how all the components, such as the garbage collector, common language runtime, base libraries, and so on, interact with each other. We will analyze the similarities between C# and other programming languages such as C++ and C. We will also look at features that make C# different than C++ and C. Finally, using a very basic Hello World program, you will learn about the different components of a C# program, such as classes, namespaces, assemblies, and so on.

Chapter 2, *Understanding Classes, Structures, and Interfaces*, expands on the first chapter and covers some more basics of a C# application. In this chapter, you will learn about the different access modifiers available in a C# program, and also how they can be used to achieve code structure and reduced complexity. We will also look at the different primitive data types available in C#. While looking at the class and struct variables, we will see the difference between a reference type variable and a data type variable. We will then look at inheritance, which is an important aspect of C# programming. We will cover how inheritance is implemented in C# and how it differs from the implementation of an interface.

Chapter 3, *Understanding Object-Oriented Programming*, focuses on the four pillars of **Object-Oriented Programming (OOP)**. Using examples, you will learn how each of those pillars – encapsulation, polymorphism, abstraction, and inheritance—is implemented. While looking at inheritance, we will expand on the learning of Chapter 2, *Understanding Classes, Structures, and Interfaces*, and look at some other critical aspects, such as method overriding, virtual methods, and sealed and abstract classes. While looking at polymorphism, we will learn how we can implement both compile/static and runtime polymorphism in C# programs.

Chapter 4, *Implementing Program Flow*, focuses on how a developer can manage program flow in C#. In other words, this chapter helps you to understand how to control the program and make decisions using the statements available in C#. We will cover various Boolean expressions such as if/else and switch, which control the flow of code based upon conditions. This chapter also provides an overview of various operators, such as the conditional operator and the equality operator (<, >, and ==), which govern the flow of code. Apart from operators and decision-making statements, this chapter helps you gain an understanding of iterating through collections (for loop, while loop, and so on) and explicit jump statements.

Chapter 5, *Creating and Implementing Events and Callbacks*, focuses on events and callbacks in C#, which are important and give more control over the program. You'll learn about the publish/subscribe model using events and callbacks, and focus on delegates. Then, we will move on to different ways of initiating delegates and lambda expressions. We will also spend some time on a new operator called the lambda operator, which is used in Lambda expressions.

Chapter 6, *Managing and Implementing Multithreading*, focuses on handling responsiveness in long-running programs and how we can keep the user notified about their progress. We'll also look at how we can use the multi-core processing power that comes with every computer effectively. We will spend time looking at threads, thread properties, and how to use tasks and perform multithreaded operations.

`Chapter 7`, *Implementing Exception Handling,* focuses on understanding how to structure your program in a way that helps it to run in all scenarios; how we can handle unhandled exceptions; how to use the `try`, `catch`, and `finally` keywords and clean up resources once execution is completed. After reading this chapter, you will understand exceptions and how to use them in your program. You'll also be able to create custom exceptions.

`Chapter 8`, *Creating and Using Types in C#,* focuses on the different types of variables available in C#. In `Chapter 2`, *Understanding Classes, Structures, and Interfaces,* we introduced users to the reference and data type variables available in C#. In this chapter, we will expand on that knowledge and learn how both variable types are maintained in memory. We will look at the managed heap memory structure, which is used for saving reference type variables. We will also look at the use of variable types pointer types in C#. Using pointers, we can implement memory-related operations that are otherwise considered unsafe in C#. We will also look at some important features in C#, such as properties, named arguments, and optional arguments, which are available in C# programming. We will look at how we can convert value-type variables to objects using boxing and similarly use unboxing to convert the object back to a value-type variable. We will then look at the different operations that are possible on a string representation in C#. We will also look at how we can use `stringbuilder` to optimize the performance of a C# program.

`Chapter 9`, *Managing the Object Life Cycle,* focuses on how the garbage collector manages the allocation and release of memory in .NET Framework. In this chapter, you will learn the difference between managed and unmanaged code in C#. We will look at mark-compact algorithms, used by garbage collectors for the allocation and release of memory. We will look at the possible ways we can manage the memory allocated to unmanaged code. We will also look at how we can implement finalization in a C# application and the performance implications of doing so. We will introduce the IDisposable interface and understand its differences from a `finalize` block. We will also look at code examples, in which we will combine both the IDisposable interface and a `finalize` block to achieve the best possible memory management for a C# application. Finally, we will look at the use of the `using` block in a C# application.

`Chapter 10`, *Find, Execute, and Create Types at Runtime Using Reflection,* focuses on understanding how .NET Framework allows us to read/create metadata and how we can use reflection to read metadata and process it during runtime. We will focus on using attributes, creating custom attributes, and how we can retrieve attribute information at runtime. We'll also cover how we can use reflection to create types, access properties, and invoke methods.

Chapter 11, *Validating Application Input*, focuses on validating input from the different kinds of users who'll access your application and how we can avoid the application crashing based on user input. The purpose of this chapter is to understand the importance of validating input data in your application, the different validation techniques available in .NET Framework, and ways to validate JSON data and XML data.

Chapter 12, *Performing Symmetric and Asymmetric Encryption*, focuses on how to keep information secure, what measures we can take while transmitting information over the internet, and understanding cryptography to encrypt and decrypt plain text. After reading this chapter, you will understand how to encrypt and decrypt text and be familiar with the different algorithms available in .NET Framework to perform such exercises.

Chapter 13, *Managing Assemblies and Debugging Applications*, focuses on how to manage .NET assemblies, debugging applications, and how to use tracing. This chapter covers validation techniques we have already learned and exception handling for those scenarios, as well as monitoring code blocks. We'll also look at Visual Studio features or tools for debugging an application. After that, we'll look at the versioning of assemblies and how we can have the same assembly side by side, as well as how we can distribute those assemblies without impacting others.

Chapter 14, *Performing I/O Operations*, focuses on how I/O operations are performed in a C# application. In this chapter, we will look at the different operations possible in C# to access data in I/O files as well as operations coming from external web services. Using code examples, you will see how we can use the System.IO helper class to read/write data from a file. We will also look at the helper classes of File and FileInfo provided in C# for performing I/O operations. We will then look at the WebRequest and WebResponse helper classes, which help us to interact with data coming from external services/applications. Finally, we will look at how we can execute these operations asynchronously in an application.

Chapter 15, *Using LINQ Queries*, focuses on how LINQ queries are implemented in C#. In this chapter, you will be introduced to the basics of a LINQ query, gaining an understanding of the different components and how they are constructed in .NET Framework. We will then look at the features in C# that help with the implementation of LINQ queries. Some of those features are necessary while some of them help us to get the best outcomes from LINQ queries. Using code examples, you will come to understand the implementation of implicitly typed variables, object initialization syntax, Lambda expressions, extension methods, and anonymous types. We will then look at the different operations available in LINQ queries. Using code examples, you will learn about the different scenarios in which you can use each of these operators. Finally, we will look at how you can use LINQ queries to perform operations on an XML file.

`Chapter 16`, *Serialization, Deserialization, and Collections*, focuses on different serialization and deserialization approaches, such as XML serialization, JSON serialization, and binary serialization, available in .NET Framework. We will also look at how we can define data contracts in web services so that data can be exchanged between different applications. We will then look at different collection objects, such as arrays, lists, dictionary, queues, and stacks, available in C# and understand how they can be used to store and consume data.

To get the most out of this book

To get the best possible outcome from this book, it's advisable for you to have the following:

- A basic understanding of software development
- A basic understanding of any common programming language, such as C, C++, or C#

For the entirety of this book, we will be going through different code examples in C# and will be using Visual Studio 2017 Community Edition for the code examples. The following hardware requirements are essential for Visual Studio:

- Operating system:
    - Windows 10 or higher
    - Windows Server 2016: Standard and Datacenter
    - Windows 8.1
    - Windows Server 2012 R2: Essential, Standard, and Datacenter
    - Windows 7 SP1
- Hardware requirements:
    - Minimum 2 GB of RAM
    - 1.8 GHZ or faster processor
- Additional requirements:
    - Administrative rights of the system
    - .NET Framework 4.5 or higher
- Visual Studio: All of the code examples in this book have been compiled on Visual Studio Community Edition 2017 (you can also use a higher version of Visual Studio). It's available for installation at `https://www.visualstudio.com/downloads/`.

For better understanding, it's advisable that readers go through all the assessments at the end of each chapter as well as the mock tests available at the end of the book.

It's also advisable for readers to go through the code examples available for each of the chapters and do the self-practice after each chapter.

Download the example code files

You can download the example code files for this book from your account at www.packt.com. If you purchased this book elsewhere, you can visit www.packtpub.com/support and register to have the files emailed directly to you.

You can download the code files by following these steps:

1. Log in or register at www.packt.com.
2. Select the Support tab.
3. Click on Code Downloads.
4. Enter the name of the book in the Search box and follow the onscreen instructions.

Once the file is downloaded, please make sure that you unzip or extract the folder using the latest version of:

- WinRAR/7-Zip for Windows
- Zipeg/iZip/UnRarX for Mac
- 7-Zip/PeaZip for Linux

The code bundle for the book is also hosted on GitHub at https://github.com/PacktPublishing/Programming-in-C-Sharp-Exam-70-483-MCSD-Guide. In case there's an update to the code, it will be updated on the existing GitHub repository.

We also have other code bundles from our rich catalog of books and videos available at https://github.com/PacktPublishing/. Check them out!

Download the color images

We also provide a PDF file that has color images of the screenshots/diagrams used in this book. You can download it here: https://static.packt-cdn.com/downloads/9781789536577_ColorImages.pdf.

Conventions used

There are a number of text conventions used throughout this book.

CodeInText: Indicates code words in text, database table names, folder names, filenames, file extensions, pathnames, dummy URLs, user input, and Twitter handles. Here is an example: "By default, a method by the name of `Main` will also be added to the class."

A block of code is set as follows:

```
using System;
using System.Collections.Generic;
using System.Linq;
using System.Text;
using System.Threading.Tasks;
```

Bold: Indicates a new term, an important word, or words that you see onscreen. For example, words in menus or dialog boxes appear in the text like this. Here is an example: "To create a new project, click on **File** | **New Project** and select **Console App (.NET Framework)** as the project type."

Warnings or important notes appear like this.

Tips and tricks appear like this.

Get in touch

Feedback from our readers is always welcome.

General feedback: If you have questions about any aspect of this book, mention the book title in the subject of your message and email us at `customercare@packtpub.com`.

Errata: Although we have taken every care to ensure the accuracy of our content, mistakes do happen. If you have found a mistake in this book, we would be grateful if you would report this to us. Please visit www.packtpub.com/support/errata, selecting your book, clicking on the Errata Submission Form link, and entering the details.

Piracy: If you come across any illegal copies of our works in any form on the Internet, we would be grateful if you would provide us with the location address or website name. Please contact us at copyright@packt.com with a link to the material.

If you are interested in becoming an author: If there is a topic that you have expertise in and you are interested in either writing or contributing to a book, please visit authors.packtpub.com.

Reviews

Please leave a review. Once you have read and used this book, why not leave a review on the site that you purchased it from? Potential readers can then see and use your unbiased opinion to make purchase decisions, we at Packt can understand what you think about our products, and our authors can see your feedback on their book. Thank you!

For more information about Packt, please visit packt.com.

Learning the Basics of C# 1

In simple terms, programming is the art of writing a set of commands that instruct a computer to execute a particular task. In the early days, programming capabilities were limited due to memory and speed restrictions. Due to this, programmers wrote crude and simple tasks that did elementary jobs. With time and with more enhancements, people started writing programs in procedural languages such as COBOL.

Although the languages did the work, the programs had some limitations. There was not much scope for writing reusable components or design patterns that could be used in different places in the application. Hence, the applications were difficult to maintain and scalability was a challenge.

As a result, efforts were made to develop high-level programming languages that could overcome all such challenges faced by procedural languages. With time, many different programming languages were devised. C was developed between 1972 and 1973. At the time, it was a low-level procedural language that depended upon the underlying platform, such as Linux or Windows. C also did not fully utilize the concept of object-oriented programming (which we will go through in `Chapter 3`, *Understanding Object-Oriented Programming*).

C++ was introduced in 1998, and provided programmers with the ability to effectively use the concepts of object-oriented programming while still retaining the machine-level programming features provided by C. In this book, we will go through the different aspects of programming in C#. While retaining the OOP capabilities of C++, C# allows us to write programs independent of the underlying hardware implementation.

In this chapter, we will go over the basics of C#. We will review its underlying fundamentals and dive deep into the .NET Framework architecture. We will learn how common language runtime works to translate the application code to machine-level code. We will learn how C# is both different and similar to other languages, such as C and C++. We will then learn about the different components in a C# program, such as classes, namespaces, and assemblies. And, as a common tradition for any new language, we will look at the implementation of a `Hello World` program.

This chapter consists of the following topics:

- Comparing C# with C and C++
- .NET Framework
- .NET Framework release versions
- Visual Studio for C#
- Basic structure of C#
- Creating a basic program in C#

Technical requirements

For a better understanding of the chapter, you require the following knowledge:

- A basic understanding of software development
- A basic understanding of common programming languages: C, C++ and C#

For the entirety of this book, we will be going through different code examples in C# and will be using Visual Studio 2017 Community Edition for the code examples. The following hardware requirements are essential for Visual Studio:

- **Operating system**:
    - Windows 10 or higher
    - Windows Server 2016: Standard and Datacenter
    - Windows 8.1
    - Windows Server 2012 R2: Essential, Standard, and Datacenter
    - Windows 7 SP1
- **Hardware requirements**:
    - Minimum 2 GB of RAM
    - 1.8 GHz or faster processor
- **Additional requirements**:
    - Administrative rights of the system
    - .NET Framework 4.5
- **Visual Studio**: All code examples in this book have been compiled on Visual Studio Community Edition 2017. It's available for installation at: `https://www.visualstudio.com/downloads/`.

Sample code for this chapter can be found on GitHub at `https://github.com/PacktPublishing/Programming-in-C-sharp-Exam-70-483-MCSD-Guide/tree/master/Chapter01`.

Comparing C# with C and C++

In this section, we will explore how C# compares against other programming languages, such as C and C++. We will look at aspects that make C# similar, and also areas in which it differs from these languages.

C# versus C

If you have done some previous development on C# and C , you will realize that they follow similar code syntax, such as the use of semi-colons, and similar declarations of methods; the two languages are very different from one another. Just like in C, we can declare data variables with the same type, such as `Char`, and `Integer`. The following features make C# different from C:

Feature	C#	C
Object-oriented programming	Object-oriented programming is the main essence of any high-level programming language, and C# allows us to utilize the capabilities of OOP using the four main pillars of encapsulation, polymorphism, inheritance, and abstraction. In `Chapter 3`, *Understanding Object-Oriented Programming*, we will look at this in detail.	C as a programming language does not support polymorphism, encapsulation, and inheritance. It does not provide features such as function overloading, virtual functions, and inheritance.
Exception handling	Exception handling is the process of handling runtime errors that occur during the execution of the application. C# provides us with exception handling features that help us handle these scenarios in a better way. In `Chapter 7`, *Implementing Exception Handling*, we will look at this in detail.	C also does not provide any exception handling features.

	Every variable declared in a program has a type. In a typical type-safe language during the program compilation stage itself, the compiler will validate the values being assigned to variables and raise a compile time error if an incorrect type is assigned to it. C# is a type-safe language. However, in Chapter 8, *Creating and Using of Types in C#*, we will learn that it also allows you to use pointers using a keyword, UnSafe.	C language implements type safety, albeit with some exceptions. There are certain in-built functions such as printf that do not enforce that only character strings are passed to them.
Type safety		

Let's now look at how C# compares against another language, C++. After exploring the comparison between C# and C++, we will also explore how the .NET Framework makes C# a platform-independent language compared to C and C++.

C# versus C++

In most programming scenarios, C++ can be classified as an extension of C and can execute all the code that was written in C. It provides all the features of object-oriented programming while retaining the functionalities provided by C. There are several features that are common between C# and C++. Just as in C#, we can implement object-oriented programming, exception handling, and type safety in C++. However, there are also certain things that make C# different to C++ and more similar to Java.

Before we look at the differences and similarities between C# and C++, we must understand some key concepts pertaining to object-oriented programming.

The languages that implement object-oriented programming are classified in two categories:

- Fully object-oriented languages
- Pure object-oriented languages

A language is classified as a fully object-oriented programming language if it implements at least the four core pillars of *Abstraction*, *Encapsulation*, *Polymorphism*, and *Inheritance*.

On the other hand, a language can be defined as a pure object-oriented programming language when, apart from being fully object-oriented programming, it only contains classes and objects. This means that all methods, properties, and attributes declared must be inside a class and also should not have any predefined data types, such as char and int.

In the case of C#, we can have predefined data types. In Chapter 2, *Understanding Classes, Structures, and Interfaces*, we will look into those predefined data types in detail. This makes C# a *fully object-oriented language* and not a *pure object-oriented language*.

On the other hand, in the case of C++, we can define methods that are not part of any class. This, too, makes it a *fully object-oriented language*.

Now, let's look at some of the similarities and differences between C# and C++:

Feature	C#	C++
Object-oriented programming	As described previously, C# is a fully object-oriented language.	Similar to C#, C++ is also a fully object-oriented language.
Memory management	C# has got an inbuilt garbage collector that manages the allocation and deallocation of memory. In Chapter 9, *Managing the Object Life Cycle*, we will understand memory management in C# in detail.	C++ does not have a built-in garbage collector. Due to this, developers are responsible for handling the allocation and deallocation of memory.
Inheritance	C# does not support multiple inheritance. In Chapter 2, *Understanding Classes, Structures, and Interfaces*, we will learn what it means; however in simple terms, it means that a class can only inherit from one class at a time.	Compared to C# , C++ allows us to implement multi-level inheritance.
Use of pointers	Although C# allows us to use pointers in our code, we need to declare the code with a snippet of UnSafe. We will look into this in detail in Chapter 8, *Creating and Using of Types in C#*.	C++ allows us to use pointers anywhere without any implicit declaration in the code.

In the previous two sections, we saw how C# compares to both C and C++. However, there is one important difference that we haven't yet explored. That feature is platform independence and was one of the main reasons C# was introduced by Microsoft. When working with C and C++, we need to compile the code in accordance with the underlying platform features, such as the operating system.

Suppose we write an application in C or C++ and compile it. During the compilation stage, the compiler translates the code into a native language code that is only compatible with the underlying platform. This basically implies that an application in C++, developed and compiled on a Windows machine, will just be compatible with a Windows machine. If the compiled bits are used on a different system, such as Linux, it will not work there.

This difference is caused due to the varying nature of compilers and their compatibility with underlying operating systems, such as Linux and Windows. These are some of the common compilers in Linux and Windows that are available for C and C++:

- **Linux**: GCC, Failsafe C, and SubC
- **Windows**: Microsoft Windows SDK, Turbo C++, and SubC

Before C# was developed, this platform dependence issue was a major disadvantage compared to some of the other programming languages, such as Java. In Java, when an application is compiled, it's not directly converted into machine code. Instead, it's converted into an intermediate language known as **ByteCode**. The ByteCode is platform-independent and can be deployed on different platforms.

When Microsoft introduced C#, they inculcated the same principle in the language. When an application written in C# is compiled, instead of being converted to the native code compatible with the machine, the application is first translated to an intermediate language commonly known as **IL code**.

After the IL code is generated, the **Common Language Runtime** (**CLR**) comes into effect. CLR is a runtime environment that sits in the memory of the underlying machine and converts the IL code to the native code, which is specific to the machine. This process is **Just-In-Time** (**JIT**) compilation. In the next section, we will look at the underlying platform of the .NET Framework, which handles all this for a C# application.

.NET Framework

.NET Framework is a software development framework on which we can write a number of languages such as C#, ASP.NET, C++, Python, Visual Basic, and F#.

 Microsoft released the first version of .NET 1.0 in 2002. The current version of .NET Framework is 4.8. The code written in this book will be based on this version of .NET Framework 4.7.2.

.NET Framework provides language interoperability across different programming languages. Applications written in .NET Framework execute in an environment or a virtual machine component known as CLR.

The following diagram illustrates the different components in .NET Framework:

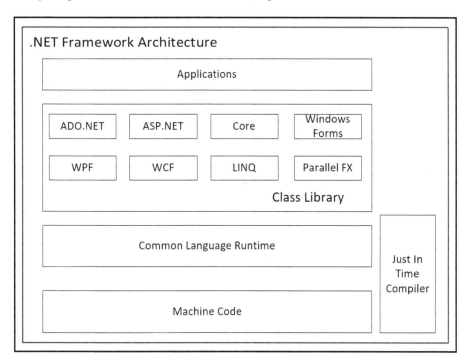

In the previous diagram, note the following:

- At the top of the hierarchy, we have applications or the program code that we write in .NET. It could be as simple as a `Hello World` console application program, which we will create in this chapter, or as complex as writing multi-threaded applications.
- The applications are based upon a set of classes or design templates, which constitutes a class library.
- The code written in these applications is then acted upon by CLR, which makes use of the **Just in Time (JIT)** compiler to convert the application code into machine code.
- The machine code is specific to the underlying platform properties. So, for different systems, such as Linux or Windows, it will be different.

For further information on .NET Framework, please refer to the official docs from Microsoft: `https://docs.microsoft.com/en-us/dotnet/framework/get-started/overview`.

In the next section, we will the .NET Framework in detail learn how interact with each other.

Languages/applications

Languages indicate the different types of applications that can be built in .NET Framework. If you are new to .NET Framework, you may not be familiar with some of the applications listed here:

- **ADO.NET**: In an ADO.NET application, we write programs to access data from sources such as SQL Server, OLE DB, and XML sources.
- **ASP.NET**: In an ASP.NET application, we write programs to build web apps such as websites and services using C#, HTML, CSS, and so on.
- **CORE**: In .NET Core applications, we write programs that support cross-platform functionality. The programs could be web apps, console applications, or libraries.
- **Windows Forms**: In Windows Forms applications, we write programs that provide client-side applications for desktops, tablets, and mobile devices.
- **WPF**: In WPF or Windows Presentation Foundation, we write programs that provide user interfaces in Windows-based applications. It runs only on Windows-supported platforms, such as Windows 10, Windows Server 2019, and Windows Vista.
- **WCF**: In WCF or Windows Communication Foundation, we write programs that provide a set of APIs, or in simpler terms, services, to exchange data between two distinct systems.
- **LINQ**: In LINQ, we write programs that provide data querying capabilities on .NET applications.
- **Parallel FX**: In Parallel FX, we write programs that support parallel programming. It involves writing programs that utilize the CPU's capabilities to the fullest by executing several threads in parallel to complete a task.

The class library

The class library in .NET Framework consists of a collection of interfaces, classes, and value types on which the applications are built.

These collections are organized in different containers known as **namespaces**. They are a set of standard class libraries that can be used for different purposes in an application. Here are some of the namespaces:

- `Microsoft.Sharp`: This contains a type that supports compilation and code generation for C# source code, and the type that supports conversion between Dynamic Language Runtime and C#.
- `Microsoft.Jscript`: This contains classes that support compilation and code generation using JavaScript.
- `Microsoft.VisualBasic`: This contains classes that support compilation and code generation for Visual Basic.
- `Microsoft.VisualC`: This contains classes that support compilation and code generation for Visual C++.

Common Language Runtime (CLR)

CLR is a runtime environment that sits in the memory of the underlying machine and converts the IL code to native code. The native code is specific to the underlying platform in which the code is running. This provides a platform independence feature in a typical application made on .NET Framework. Some of the other features provided by CLR are mentioned here:

- **Memory management**: CLR provides automatic allocation and release of memory across the application. Due to this, developers do not need to explicitly write code to manage memory. This eliminates issues that can lead to degradation of application performance due to memory leaks. CLR manages the allocation and removal of memory using a garbage collector, which manages the memory allocation in the following manner:
  - **Allocating memory**: When an application is executed in CLR, it reserves a continuous space of memory for its execution. The reserved space is known as a managed heap. The heap maintains a pointer to the memory address where the next object defined in the process will be allocated.

- **Releasing memory**: During the runtime execution of the program, the garbage collector runs at scheduled times and examines whether the memory allocated in heaps are still in scope of program execution or not.
- It determines whether the program is still using the memory on the basis of roots or the collection of memory objects are still in the scope of the program. If any memory allocation is not reachable as per the collection in the root, the garbage collector determines that the memory allocated in that memory space can be released.
- We will look into memory management in detail in `Chapter 9`, *Manage the Object Life Cycle*.

- **Exception handling**: When an application is being executed, it may result in certain execution paths that could generate some errors in the application. Some of the common examples are as follows:
  - When an application tries to access an object such as a file that is not present in the specified directory path.
  - When an application tries to execute a query on the database but the connection between the application and the underlying database is broken/not open.
  - We will look into exception handling in detail when we go through `Chapter 7`, *Implementing Exception Handling*.

In the next section, we will look at the release history of .NET Framework and its compatibility with different versions of CLR and C#.

.NET Framework release versions

The first version of .NET Framework 1.0 was released in 2002. Just like .NET Framework, there are different versions of CLR and C# as well. The different versions of .NET Framework are compatible with some particular versions of both CLR and C#. The following table provides a compatibility mapping between the different .NET Framework versions and its compatible versions of CLR:

.NET Framework	CLR version
1.0	1.0
1.1	1.1
2.0/3.0/3.5	2.0
4.0/4.5/4.5.1/4.5.2/4.6/4.6.1/4.6.2/4.7/4.7.1/4.7.2/4.8	4

The following table matches the different versions of .NET Framework with its compatible C# version, and lists some of the important programming features that were released in that version of C#:

Version	.NET Framework	Important features in C#
C# 1.0/1.1/1.2	.NET Framework 1.0/1.1	First release of C#
C# 2.0	.NET Framework 2.0	Generics anonymous methods, Nullable types, and Iterators
C# 3.0	.NET Framework 2.0/3.0/3.5/4.0	Query expressions, Lambda expression, and Extension methods
C# 4.0	.NET Framework 2.0/3.0/3.5/4.0	Dynamic binding, Named/optional arguments, and Embedded interop types
C# 5.0	.NET Framework 4.5	Asynchronous members
C# 6.0	.NET Framework 4.6/4.6.2/4.7/4.7.1/4.7.2	Exception filters, String interpolation, `nameof` operator, and Dictionary initializer
C# 7.0/7.1/7.2/7.3	.NET Framework 4.6/4.6.2/4.7/4.7.1/4.7.2	Out variables, Pattern matching, Reference locals and returns, and Local functions
C# 8	.NET Framework 4.8	Read-only members and Default interface members

In the next section, we will look at Visual Studio, an IDE tool provided by Microsoft for building applications with .NET Framework, and some of its built-in features that can help us during the development phase.

Visual Studio for C#

Microsoft Visual Studio is an **Integrated Development Environment** (IDE) tool used by developers worldwide to develop, compile, and execute their .NET Framework applications. There are several features provided in the tool that help developers not only improve the quality of the application developed, but also greatly reduce the time of development.

Some of the key features of Visual Studio are mentioned here:

- It uses Microsoft software development platforms such as Windows API, Forms, WPF, and Silverlight.
- While writing code, it provides IntelliSense code-completion features, which help the developers write code efficiently.
- It also provides a forms designer for building GUI applications, a class designer, and database schema designer.
- It provides support for different source control systems, such as GitHub and TFS.

The current version of Visual Studio is 2017. For development purposes, Microsoft provides a Community Edition of Visual Studio, which is free of cost and can be used for non-commercial activities.

It's essential that before using the Community Edition, we go through the terms and conditions of use as well: `https://visualstudio.microsoft.com/license-terms/mlt553321/`.

In the next section, we will do a walk-through on the basic syntax involved in writing a basic C# application.

Basic structure of C#

In this section, we will go over a basic programming syntax of a C# application, namely: classes, namespaces, and assemblies.

As C# is an object-oriented language, and at the basic level it contains building blocks known as **classes**. The classes interact with one another, and as a result, provide functionality at runtime. A class consists of two components:

- **Data attributes**: Data attributes refer to the different properties defined in the class object.
- **Methods**: Methods indicate the different operations that are to be executed in the class object.

As an example, we will look at the representation of a car as an object in C#. At a very basic level, a car will have attributes such as the following:

- **Make**: For example Toyota, Ford, or Honda.
- **Model**: For example Mustang, Focus, or Beetle.
- **Color**: Color of the car, such as Red or Black.
- **Mileage**: Distance covered per liter of fuel consumed.

Please note that a car can have more attributes, but as this example is just being used for the sake of explanation, we have included these basic attributes. While writing a C# application, all of these will be captured as attributes for the Car class.

Similarly, to make sure the Car class achieves all of the desired features, it will need to implement the following operations:

- StartEngine: This function represents how the car starts moving.
- GainSpeed: This function represents how the car accelerates.
- ApplyBrake: This function represents how the car applies brakes to slow down.
- StopEngine: This function represents how the car stops.

While writing any application in C#, the starting point is always to capture all the actors/objects that are interacting with each other. Once we identify the actors, we can then identify the data attributes and methods that each of them must have so that they can exchange the required information with each other.

For the Car example being discussed, the following would be the definition of the Car class. For the sake of explanation, we have just assumed that the attributes will be of type String; however, when we go through Chapter 2, *Understanding Classes, Structures, and Interfaces*, we will go over some more data types that can be declared in a class. For the car example, the following syntax would be a representative program in a C# application:

```
class Car
{
    string Make;
    string Model;
    string Color;
    float Mileage;
    void StartEngine()
    {
        // Implement Start Engine.
    }

    void GainSpeed()
```

```
    {
        // Implement Gain Speed.
    }

    void ApplyBrake()
    {
        // Implement Gain Speed.
    }
    void StopEngine()
    {
        // Implement Gain Speed.
    }
}
```

In any application, there can be some classes that are related to one another. They can be based in terms of similar functionality, or they could be dependent on each other. In C#, we handle such a segregation of functionality via **namespaces**. For example, we can have a namespace for handling all operations related to reading/writing logs in the file directory. Similarly, we can have namespaces for handling all operations related to capturing user-specified information from inputs.

When our applications continue to evolve and we have several namespaces, we may have a need to group related namespaces under one umbrella. This ensures that if any class changes under any particular namespaces, it will not affect all the classes defined in the application. This structuring of namespace is done via **assemblies** in C#. Assemblies are also known as DLLs, or dynamically linked libraries. Depending upon how we structure our code, when an application is compiled, it results in multiple DLLs.

Creating a basic program in C#

Now we will look at how to create a basic program in C#. For the sake of explanation, we will work on the Console Application project:

1. To create a new project, click on **File | New Project** and select **Console App (.NET Framework)** as the project type:

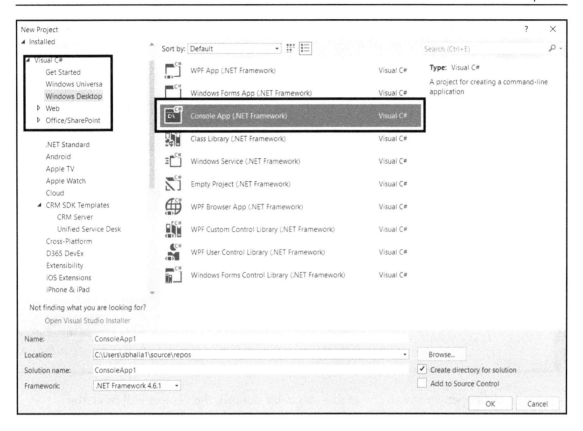

After giving the solution an appropriate name and path, click on **OK**. Check that the solution has been created. At this point, you should see the Solution Explorer. By default, a `.cs` file, `Program.cs`, should be added to the solution. By default, a method by the name of `Main` will also be added to the class. This method is the first entry point when this application is executed.

Please note that for a console program, it's not possible to change the default method, which would be the first entry point for the application.

2. Let's open `Program.cs` at this stage. By default, the project will have the following `using` expressions for the following namespaces:

```
using System;
using System.Collections.Generic;
using System.Linq;
using System.Text;
using System.Threading.Tasks;
```

A `using` statement basically signifies that the program can use the classes and methods defined in those namespaces for any execution. In further chapters, we will go over namespaces in detail and learn how to use them.

3. Now, have a look at the program structure. By default, each class needs to be associated with a namespace. The namespace expression present in the `Program.cs` class indicates the namespace this class is part of:

```
namespace ConsoleApp1
{
    class Program
    {
        static void Main(string[] args)
        {
        }
    }
}
```

 Please note that C# is a case-sensitive language. This basically means that if we change the name of the method from `Main` to `main`, CLR will not be able to execute this method.

Each method in C# consists of two parts:

- **Input parameters**: This is a list of variables that will be passed to the function when it's executed.
- **Return type**: This is the value that will be returned by the function to the caller when the function finishes its processing.

In the case of the `Program` function declared previously, the input variable is a collection of arguments. The output variable is void; in other words, it does not return anything. In the forthcoming chapters, we will go over functions in more detail.

Now, let's write a program syntax to execute the famous `Hello World` output. In a console application, we can do this using `Console.Writeline`:

1. The code implementation for this program is as follows:

```
using System;
using System.Collections.Generic;
using System.Linq;
using System.Text;
using System.Threading.Tasks;
namespace ConsoleApp1
{
```

```
class Program
{
    static void Main(string[] args)
    {
        Console.WriteLine("Hello World");
    }
}
```

2. At this stage, we have finished the program and are ready to execute it. Click on **Build | Build Solution**. Check that there are no compile time errors:

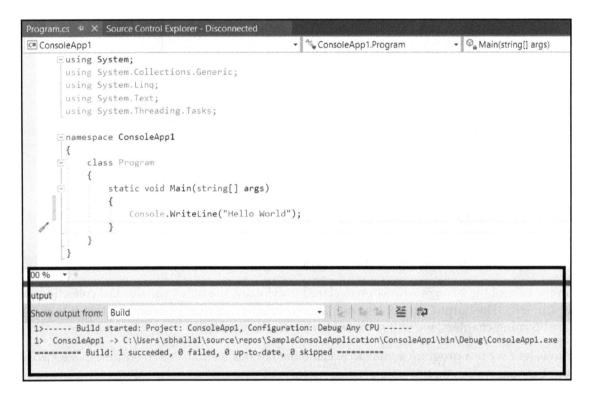

3. At this stage, internally, Visual Studio should have created an .exe application for the project:

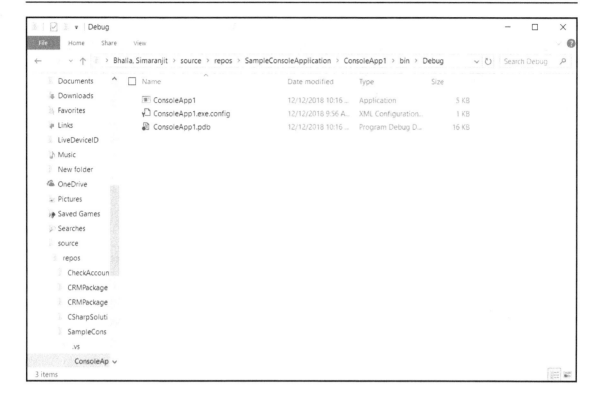

4. Open Command Prompt and navigate directly to where the `.exe` file has been created. Execute the `.exe` file and check that the desired output of `Hello World` appears in Command Prompt.

Summary

Before we move to the next chapter, let's summarize what we have learned during this chapter. We had a brief recap on the building blocks of C#. We had a walk-through of the .NET Framework architecture and visited the different components in it. We also analyzed what makes C# different from programming languages such as C and C++. We went over the functioning of CLR and how it implements garbage collection in C#. We then wrote our first program, *Hello World*. By now, you should have a good awareness of what C# is and the features it contains.

In the next chapter, we will go over some more basic principles of C# programming. We will analyze the different possible access modifiers in C#. Access modifiers make sure that the properties and methods present in a class are only exposed to the relevant modules in an application. We will learn the behavior and implementation of value and reference type data variables in C# programming. We will go over inheritance and interface, and how they are implemented in a C# application. We will discuss the differences between inheritance and interface, and the different scenarios in which we should use one or the other.

Questions

1. Which of the following statements is correct with regard to C, C++, and C#?
    - C is an object-oriented language.
    - C++ applications are independent of the underlying system.
    - C# applications are independent of the underlying system.
    - C implements all the functionality and features of C++ and C#.

2. An assembly consists of related namespaces and classes that interact with each other to provide a certain functionality.
    - True
    - False

3. For a console project, we can set any function as the starting point of execution for the application.
    - True
    - False

Answers

1. **C is not an object-oriented language**. C and C++ are not independent of the underlying platform, unlike C#, which implements the feature using Common language runtime. C is a subset of the functionality and features provided by C# and C++.

2. **True**. An assembly consists of a number of related namespaces and classes grouped together.

3. **False**. For a console application, the point of entry is always the *main* program.

2
Understanding Classes, Structures, and Interfaces

In `Chapter 1`, *Learning the Basics of C#*, we looked at an overview of the very basic components of a C# application. All classes in a C# application are composed of attributes and methods. Using namespaces and assemblies, we can bundle related classes together.

To maintain structure and to reduce complexity, it's essential that only the required classes/functionality are exposed outside the scope of a class. In a C# program, this is achieved via access modifiers. While defining the attributes present in a class, we also need to be clear about the different data types of variables available in C#.

Using a code implementation of struct and class, we will look at how data and reference type variables differ in implementation and behavior during program execution. We will also be looking at some good practices that we can follow to choose the right data type for our variables.

We will then look at interfaces and inheritance and how they are implemented in a C# application. Using examples, we will look at the different scenarios in which we should use each of them.

The following topics will be covered in this chapter:

- Different types of access modifiers in C#
- Different types of data types in C#
- Understanding the difference between a class and a struct
- Understanding inheritance
- Understanding interfaces and how they are different from inheritance

Technical requirements

As in the previous chapters of this book, the programs explained in this chapter will be developed in Visual Studio 2017.

Sample code for this chapter can be found on GitHub at `https://github.com/PacktPublishing/Programming-in-C-Exam-70-483-MCSD-Guide/tree/master/Book70483Samples`.

Access modifiers

All classes, along with their respective attributes and functions, have an access modifier associated with them. An access modifier basically indicates how the respective element will be accessed in the application, both in its own assembly as well as in other assemblies. Collectively, attributes and functions in an application are referred to as class members.

In C#, a class and its class members can acquire the following access modifiers:

- **Public**: A class or a class member declared as *public* can be accessed by all classes in the same assembly as well as by classes in different assemblies present in the application.
- **Private**: A class member declared as *private* can be accessed only in the same class but not outside it.
- **Protected**: A class or a class member declared as *protected* can be accessed inside the class or by classes that inherit from the respective class.
- **Internal**: A class or a class member declared as *internal* can only be accessed by classes in the same assembly but not by outside assemblies.
- **Protected internal**: A class or a class member declared as *protected internal* can only be accessed by classes in the same assembly or by classes present in the outside assembly that inherit from the respective class.
- **Private protected**: A class or a class member declared as *private protected* can only be accessed in the same class or in classes present in the same assembly that inherit from the respective class.

Let's look at the following image to summarize this knowledge about access modifiers. In the following example, we have **Assembly A** and **Assembly B** in the application. **Assembly A** has **Class A**, which has different functions, each with a separate access modifier. Please refer to the comments against each of the functions to understand which classes under which assemblies can access the respective functions:

Based upon the accessibility level and the security that we wish to embed in the different class members, we can choose either of the previously mentioned access modifiers. To keep some structure and avoid introducing undue complexity, it's advisable to only expose class members to classes that require some information to be shared with the respective class.

In the next section, we will look at the different data types that a class member can acquire.

Data types in C#

In C#, a variable can acquire one of the following types:

- A value type
- A reference type

C# differentiates between these two types in terms of how these values are saved and maintained in the **Global Assembly Cache** (**GAC**) during the program execution. Value type variables are saved in the stack, while reference type variables are saved in a managed heap data structure.

There are other **pointer types** that allow us to access value in the memory location of a variable. In Chapter 8, *Creating and Using of Types in C#*, we will explore those data types in detail. For now, let's look at these two data types and explore them in detail.

Value type variables

In value types, the variables contain the data or the contents of the variable. This implies that if any change is made to a value type variable in a different scope of the program, the change will not be reflected back once the control shifts to the calling function.

The following are the different types of value types in C#.

Simple types

Following is the list of simple types:

- `Int`: For example 1, 2, 4, and -100. They can be both signed and unsigned. A signed `int` type can be both positive and negative. An unsigned `int` type cannot be negative; its minimum value is `0`.
- `Float`: For example, 3.14.
- `Long`: Unlike `Int`, which is 32-bit, `Long` is a 64-bit integer value. It can also be both signed and unsigned.
- `Decimal`: Like `Float`, decimal data types also represent decimal digit numbers with the main difference being in terms of precision. For `Float` data members, the precision is 7; however, in the case of decimal data types, the precision is 28 digits.
- `Char`: Represents a single character sequence. It can acquire values such as `C`, `c`, or white-space, any special characters – such as % and # – and even a digit such as 1.
- `bool`: It can be used to represent variables that acquire a digital value such as true or false.

Enum types

Enum types are used to indicate an attribute that can acquire a constant set of values, for example, `enum Day {Sat, Sun, Mon, Tues, Wed, Thurs, Fri}`.

By default, the value of the first enumerator in the declaration starts from 0. It then increments the value of the subsequent enumerators by 1. For the preceding example, the following would be the value of the enumerators:

- `Sat` – 0
- `Sun` – 1
- `Mon` – 2
- `Tues` – 3
- `Wed` – 4
- `Thurs` – 5
- `Fri` - 6

We can also override the default values of the enumerators by explicitly defining the values in the declaration itself. For example, in the preceding example, if we do not want the enumerators to start from 0, we can use the following declaration:

```
enum Day {Sat = 1, Sun, Mon, Tues, Wed, Thurs, Fri}
```

For the preceding declaration, the enumerators will acquire the following values:

- `Sat` – 1
- `Sun` – 2
- `Mon` – 3
- `Tues` – 4
- `Wed` – 5
- `Thurs` – 6
- `Fri` – 7

Each Enumerator attribute also has an underlying data type that, by default, is of type `Int`. If required, we can also change the type of the enumerated values to long or short. However, it cannot take `char` as an underlying data type. Refer to the following `enum` declaration, in which we are setting the type of Enumerator value to `short`:

```
enum Day : short {Sat = 1, Sun, Mon, Tues, Wed, Thurs, Fri}
```

Struct types

Just like classes, structs in C# can be used to group together related data. Like classes, they can have constructors, fields, and methods. However, there are some differences between the implementation of structs and classes. The following are some of the key differences:

Feature	Struct	Class
Type	Structs are managed as value type variables. This implies that the value assigned in their objects is not persisted in different scopes of the program.	Classes are managed as reference type variables. This implies that the value assigned in their objects is persisted across different scopes of the program.
Constructor	Unlike classes, no default constructor is managed by C#. When we go through `Chapter 8`, *Creating and Using of Types in C#*, we will explore default constructors in detail.	When declaring a class, if no constructor is specified for the class, C# automatically creates a default constructor for the class.
Inheritance	A struct cannot inherit from another struct. This implies that code reuse could become a challenge if we use structs.	A class can inherit from other classes.

 Being value type variables, when a struct object is created, the entire object – inclusive of attributes, methods, and so on – is saved in a stack. Therefore, from a performance perspective, it's essential that structs should only be used for creating lightweight objects with only a few members.

In the coming section, we will go through a code example to show how struct implementation is different from a similar implementation in classes.

Reference type variables

In reference type variables, the data member contains the exact address of the variable in memory. As the variable just contains a reference to the memory address, two separate reference type variables can point to the same memory address. Therefore, if a change is made to a reference type variable, the change is directly done at the memory location of the variable. Due to the change being directly made at the memory location of the variable, both variables will reflect the updated value.

The following are the reference types available in C#:

- **Class**: As discussed in `Chapter 1`, *Learning the Basics of C#*, a class represents a collection of related properties and methods.
- **Interface**: An interface in C# represents a collection of related properties, events, and methods, with just a declaration and no definition. In this chapter, in upcoming sections, we will deep dive into interfaces and see how they are implemented in C#.
- **Dynamic**: A dynamic type variable avoids compile-time type checking. For example, if we declare a dynamics variable type and assign a variable to it, its type is defined at runtime when a value is assigned to it.

For example, in the following code snippet, we are creating a dynamics type variable, assigning different variables to it and evaluating its type at runtime:

```
dynamic typeVariable = 100;
Console.WriteLine(typeVariable + " " +
typeVariable.GetType().ToString());// Output 100 System.Int32
typeVariable = "Hello";
Console.WriteLine(typeVariable + " " +
typeVariable.GetType().ToString());// Output Hello System.String
typeVariable = true;
Console.WriteLine(typeVariable + " " +
typeVariable.GetType().ToString());// Output True System.Boolean
Console.ReadLine();
```

- **Object**: When a new instance of a class is created using the `new` keyword, an object for the class is created in the memory.
- **String**: A `string` object is a sequence of `Char` objects whose value is immutable or read-only. This basically implies that, when we modify a variable of type `String`, it creates a new object in memory.

In the next section, we will go through a code example to show how a reference type variable such as `Class` and a value type variable such as struct are implemented in C# and how their behavior differs.

Structs versus classes

In the first chapter, we created a basic `Hello World` program. In this topic, we will extend that program and use it to implement a struct and a class. While doing so, we will analyze the difference between the implementation and use of reference and value type variables. As you are already aware by now, a struct is a value type variable and a class is a reference type variable:

1. Open the `Console` project created in `Chapter 1`, *Learning the Basic Structure of C#*, and declare a `CoordinatePoint` class with just two member attributes of `x` and `y` coordinates. Also create two constructors – one without any parameters and one with two parameters. Please refer to the following code implementation for this:

```
class CoordinatePoint
{
    public float xCoordinate;
    public float yCoordinate;
    public CoordinatePoint()
    {
    }
    public CoordinatePoint(float x, float y)
    {
        this.xCoordinate = x;
        this.yCoordinate = y;
    }
}
```

 Please note that, in the preceding code, the use of the `this` variable is optional. It is used to refer to the current instance of the class and can be used to differentiate between class members and method parameters if they have the same name.

2. Declare a similar structure. Notice that the compiler gives an error for the default constructor:

```
struct CoordinatePointStruct
{
    public float xCoordinate;
    public float yCoordinate;
    public CoordinatePointStruct()
    {
        // This default constructor will give an error.
    }
    public CoordinatePointStruct(float x, float y)
```

```
        {
            this.xCoordinate = x;
            this.yCoordinate = y;
        }
    }
```

As indicated in the preceding code, we will see a red label on the `struct` constructor. This is because, unlike classes, a struct cannot have an implementation of a default constructor. To remove the error, we need to remove the default constructor. On doing this, we will see that the compiler error goes away. The following would be the correct implementation of the struct:

```
struct CoordinatePointStruct
{
    public float xCoordinate;
    public float yCoordinate;
    public CoordinatePointStruct(float x, float y)
    {
        this.xCoordinate = x;
        this.yCoordinate = y;
    }
}
```

3. In the `Main` class, we will now declare two functions, one for each class and struct, respectively. In both functions, we will be passing a parameter by the name of `obj`, which is an object of type class and struct, respectively. In the same function, we will change the values of the x and y coordinate variables in both the struct and the class to a default value of `0.5F`. The following is the code implementation for this:

```
static void ChangeValuesClass(CoordinatePoint obj)
{
    obj.xCoordinate = .5F;
    obj.yCoordinate = .5F;
}
static void ChangeValuesStruct(CoordinatePointStruct obj)
{
    obj.xCoordinate = .5F;
    obj.yCoordinate = .5F;
}
```

4. Now, in the main function, declare the objects of both the class and the structure. Notice that, during the declaration of the respective objects, we are specifying the same values in the xCoordinate and yCoordinate member attributes.

For the sake of explanation, we will write syntax that will output the values in the respective member attributes to the console. The following is the code implementation for this:

```
Console.WriteLine("Hello World");
CoordinatePoint classCoordinate = new CoordinatePoint(.82F, .34F);
CoordinatePointStruct structCoordinate = new
CoordinatePointStruct(.82F, .34F);
Console.WriteLine("Initial Coordinates for Class are :" +
classCoordinate.xCoordinate.ToString() + " " +
classCoordinate.yCoordinate.ToString());
Console.WriteLine("Initial Coordinates for Struct are :" +
structCoordinate.xCoordinate.ToString() + " " +
structCoordinate.yCoordinate.ToString());
```

5. Now write syntax to call the respective ChangeValues function for each of structure and class. After the call to the function, have another statement to print the current values in the attributes of the struct and class objects.

Refer to the following code implementation for this:

```
ChangeValuesClass(classCoordinate);
ChangeValuesStruct(structCoordinate);
Console.WriteLine("Initial Coordinates for Class are :" +
classCoordinate.xCoordinate.ToString() + " " +
classCoordinate.yCoordinate.ToString());
Console.WriteLine("Initial Coordinates for Struct are :" +
structCoordinate.xCoordinate.ToString() + " " +
structCoordinate.yCoordinate.ToString());
```

6. Click on **Build | Build Solution** and ensure that there are no compile-time errors.
7. Click on **Debug | Start Debugging**. Alternatively, the user can also click on the *F5* key or the triangular icon next to **Start** to launch the debugger. Please refer to the following screenshots:

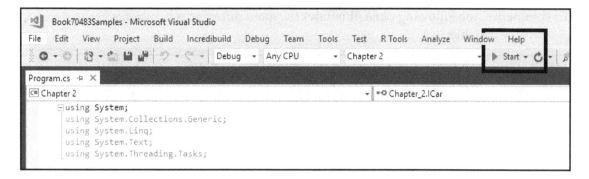

Notice that the console shows the following output:

```
C:\Users\sbhalla1\source\repos\SampleConsoleApplication\ConsoleApp1\bin\Debug\ConsoleApp1.exe    —    □    ×
Hello World
Initial Coordinates for Class are :0.82 0.34
Initial Coordinates for Struct are :0.82 0.34
Initial Coordinates for Class are :0.5 0.5
Initial Coordinates for Struct are :0.82 0.34
```

Notice that, after calling the change function, the value of the `class` object gets modified. However, there is no change to the values in the struct.

This is due to the fact that `struct` is a value type variable. Therefore, any change in the object, outside the scope of the function, has no impact as the change happens at an entirely different object in memory.

On the other hand, `class` being a reference type variable is affected by changes happening outside the scope of the function as well. For this reason, changes are propagated back to the main object as well.

To summarize, the following table illustrates the main differences between a `struct` and a `class` type variable:

Feature	Class	Struct
Default Constructor	If a class does not have a constructor, then whenever an object is created for the class, the default constructor triggers and sets default values against the member variables present in the class. The default values are set in accordance with the default values of the type of those member variables.	In contrast to a class, a struct cannot have any default constructors. This means that the application doesn't assign a default value to the member variables of the struct.
Memory Implementation	As illustrated in the previous code example, a class is implemented as a reference type. This means that the value of an object of class is persisted across different scopes of the program execution.	As illustrated in the previous code example, a struct is implemented as a value type. This means that its value is not persisted across different scopes of the program.
Inheritance	We will be exploring inheritance in detail both in this chapter as well as in the next chapter. However, a class in C# can inherit from other classes.	In contrast to a class, a struct cannot inherit from other structs or classes. This implies that code reuse is slightly difficult in structs compared to in classes.

Based upon the preceding differences, depending upon the requirements, a developer can choose the right data type between a struct and a class.

In the next section, we will look at how an interface is implemented in a C# application.

Interfaces and inheritance

An interface is a collection of properties, methods, and events with just a declaration and no definition. We use them in programming to group together a set of functionalities that must be implemented in classes that, theoretically, are of the same basic type.

Let's look at an example of a car. In a real-world scenario, any implementation of the `Car` class must implement certain common basic features such as driving, stopping, and accelerating. Along with those, any object that is classified as a car will also have certain features specific to the make of the car, such as Honda or Nissan.

In the preceding example, an interface could help to promote code reuse and maintain structure across all types of `Car`. What we can do in this case is to declare `Car` as an interface that all car derivatives, such as Nissan or Honda must implement.

Similar to an interface, we can also implement *inheritance* in a C# application. In inheritance, we can define classes with certain methods and properties, which can then be inherited in a child class. In the next subsections, we will look at how interfaces and inheritance are implemented in a C# application.

 Inheritance is one of the main pillars of OOP programming. In Chapter 3, *Understanding Object-Oriented Programming*, we will look into more advanced features related to inheritance and understand how it works.

Inheritance

Inheritance is one of the main principles of any object-oriented programming. With inheritance, we can define attributes and functions that can be reused in child classes. In short, it helps us to reuse code written in the application across multiple modules. Let's go through an example to understand how inheritance helps us.

Let's consider two cars, CarA and CarB. From a very high-level perspective, we can think that both these classes will have similar features such as:

- A brake function
- An accelerator function
- A car type; that is, diesel/petrol and so on
- Color
- Gear type

If we need to implement this in a C# application, one way would be to define them as two separate classes: CarA and CarB . However, the main concern with this approach is that both of these classes will need to have their own implementation of the shared features listed. Please refer the following code for how a possible implementation of CarA would look in C#:

```
public class CarA
{
    public DateTime manufacturingDate;
    public string bodyType;
    public float fuelCapacity;
    public void ImplementBrake()
    {
        Console.WriteLine("Inside Base Class Implement Brake");
    }
    public void ImplementAccelerator()
```

```
    {
        Console.WriteLine("Inside Base Class Implement Accelerator");
    }
    public void FoldableSeat()
    {
        Console.WriteLine("Inside Base Class Implement Accelerator");
    }
}
```

Similarly, please refer to the following code for what a possible implementation of CarB would look like in C#:

```
public class CarB
{
    public DateTime manufacturingDate;
    public string bodyType;
    public float fuelCapacity;
    public void ImplementBrake()
    {
        Console.WriteLine("Inside Base Class Implement Brake");
    }
    public void ImplementAccelerator()
    {
        Console.WriteLine("Inside Base Class Implement Accelerator");
    }
    public void RoofTopExtendable()
    {
        Console.WriteLine("Inside Car B Foldable Seat");
    }
}
```

This kind of implementation could have the following repercussions:

- **No code reuse**: As you will understand from the preceding example, there are features that both CarA and CarB have in common. However, instead of maintaining common features separately, we are duplicating the code, which could cause maintenance issues as well.

- **Scalability**: From a business/implementation perspective, there could be millions of different types of cars. Thus, for every new Car or a new common feature added to the Car implementation, we may face some scalability challenges in the application.

As clearly illustrated, change management in such applications would be a nightmare and would be very difficult to carry out.

Now we will use the concept of inheritance and see how the preceding scenario could be implemented in a better way. From an implementation perspective, we will be creating a base class, `Car`, which will have all of the common member variables across different implementations of `Car`. We will then define individual types of `Car`, which will inherit from the base class, `Car`. Let's look at the following code example to understand this better:

1. Create a base class, `Car`. The class will have all the member attributes that are common across `CarA` and `CarB`:

```
public class Car
{
    public DateTime manufacturingDate;
    public string bodyType;
    public float fuelCapacity;
    public void ImplementBrake()
    {
        Console.WriteLine("Inside Base Class Implement Brake");
    }
    public void ImplementAccelerator()
    {
        Console.WriteLine("Inside Base Class Implement
Accelerator");
    }
}
```

2. Create a class, `CarA`, which will inherit the base class. In C#, we use the : syntax to define inheritance:

```
public class CarA : Car
{
    public CarA()
    {
        this.bodyType = string.Empty;
        this.manufacturingDate = DateTime.MinValue;
        this.fuelCapacity = 0.0F;
    }
    public CarA(DateTime manufacturingDate, string bodyType, float
fuelCapacity)
    {
        this.bodyType = bodyType;
        this.manufacturingDate = manufacturingDate;
        this.fuelCapacity = fuelCapacity;
        Console.WriteLine("Inside Car A Constructor");
    }
```

```
public void FoldableSeat()
{
    Console.WriteLine("Inside Car A Foldable Seat");
}
}
```

As indicated earlier, the attributes declared inside the parent class are automatically available in the derived class.

Please note that the attributes from the base class that will be available in the child class depend upon the access modifiers used against the corresponding attributes in the base class.

In our example, we have used `public` access modified in the base class. If it had been `private` or `protected internal`, its accessibility would have differed in the child class.

Let's consider a scenario wherein, for some reason, we also need to declare an attribute by the same name, `bodyType`, in `CarA`. In C#, we can differentiate between the attributes present in the base class and in the derived class by using the `base` keyword. Refer to the following code for this:

```
public class CarA : Car
{
    string bodyType;
    public CarA()
    {
        this.bodyType = string.Empty;
        base.bodyType = string.Empty;
        this.manufacturingDate = DateTime.MinValue;
        this.fuelCapacity = 0.0F;
    }
}
```

If `base` is used, it refers to the attribute in the parent class and, if `this` is used, it refers to the attribute in the child class.

3. Similarly, declare a class for `CarB`:

```
class CarB : Car
{
    public CarB()
    {
        this.bodyType = string.Empty;
        this.manufacturingDate = DateTime.MinValue;
        this.fuelCapacity = 0.0F;
    }
    public CarB(DateTime manufacturingDate, string bodyType, float
fuelCapacity)
    {
        this.bodyType = bodyType;
        this.manufacturingDate = manufacturingDate;
        this.fuelCapacity = fuelCapacity;
        Console.WriteLine("Inside Car B Constructor");
    }
    public void RoofTopExtendable()
    {
        Console.WriteLine("Inside Car B Foldable Seat");
    }
}
```

Please note that, in derived classes, we can also create member variables independent of the base classes. As indicated in the preceding screenshots, the `CarA` class has an implementation of `FoldableSeat`, which is not present in the base class.

Similarly, the `CarB` class has an implementation of `RoofTopExtendable`, which is not present in the base class.

4. In the main method, declare the `CarA` and `CarB` objects and call the respective methods:

```
CarA carA = new CarA();
carA.ImplementAccelerator();
carA.ImplementBrake();
carA.FoldableSeat();

CarB carB = new CarB();
carB.ImplementAccelerator();
carB.ImplementBrake();
carB.RoofTopExtendable();
Console.ReadLine();
```

5. Click on **Build | Build Solution**. Notice that there are no compile-time errors. Now click on **Debug | Start Debugging**. Notice that the following output comes up in the console window:

The following provides a brief analysis of each of the output line items:

- The first method we call is `ImplementAccelerator`, which is present in the base class. As expected, it executes the method in the base class.
- Similarly, the next method we call is `ImplementBrake`, which is also present in the base class. In this case also, the method in the base class is executed.
- In the next call, we execute a method just present in `CarA`. In this case, the control executes the code present in that function.
- The same thing applies to B as well.

Thus, using inheritance, we can promote a greater degree of code reuse, along with making the maintenance activity quite scalable.

Once we move on to `Chapter 3`, *Understanding Object-Oriented Programming*, we will cover more features in regard to inheritance, such as overriding sealed, abstract classes and so on. However, for now, we will go over how an interface helps us in C# code development.

Interfaces in C#

In the preceding example, we illustrated how we can declare a base class with some member variables and have them inherited in a derived class. However, there could be some scenarios when we need to have a class inherited from two different classes. Moreover, if we are using a struct, we will not be able to inherit from another struct or class.

Unfortunately, using inheritance, we will not be able to achieve this in a C# application due to the following reasons:

- Multiple inheritance is not allowed in C#.
- A struct data type in C# cannot inherit from other structs or class types.

In such scenarios, interfaces come in handy. An interface defines a set of related methods, attributes which each class implementing the interface must implement. Please note that an interface must have just declarations.

 In reference to interfaces, a declaration refers to the specification of the methods along with their signatures – that is, input and output parameters – while a definition refers to the actual implementation of the logic in the method body. While discussing the following code example, we will look further into this.

Let's look at the example we used for inheritance and see how we can use an interface in it:

- In the preceding example, wherein we created `CarA` and `CarB`, we can deduce that it is bound to have several other properties as well, such as color, weight, height, brand, logo, manufacturer, and so on.
- From a data model perspective, we can classify them as attributes common to any *utility or product* rather than just a car.
- So, when we are choosing a product, we can say that there are certain actions, such as `ImplementBrand`, `ImplementColor`, and so on that will be common across all the product implementations and not just for `CarA` and `CarB`.
- Therefore, it means that the two classes must inherit from both `Car` and `Product` to function correctly.

Let's try and create another base class of `Product` and try to implement multiple inheritance for `CarA`. Here's the following code implementation for the `Product` class:

```
public class Product
{
    public void ImplementBrand()
    {
        Console.WriteLine("Inside Base Class Implement Brake");
    }
    public void ImplementColor()
    {
        Console.WriteLine("Inside Base Class Implement Accelerator");
    }
}
```

However, when we try to implement multiple inheritance for the `CarA` class, the compiler gives us an error. The following screenshot shows the error we get from the compiler:

```
public class CarA : Car, Product
{
    public CarA()
    {
        this.bodyType = string.Empty;
        this.manufacturingDate = DateTime.MinValue;
        this.fuelCapacity = 0.0F;
    }

    public CarA(DateTime manufacturingDate, string bodyType, float fuelCapacity)
    {
        this.bodyType = bodyType;
        this.manufacturingDate = manufacturingDate;
        this.fuelCapacity = fuelCapacity;
        Console.WriteLine("Inside Car A Constructor");
    }

    public void FoldableSeat()
    {
        Console.WriteLine("Inside Car A Foldable Seat");
    }
}
```

00 % ▼					
List					
Entire Solution ▼	❌ 1 Error	⚠ 0 Warnings	ⓘ 0 Messages	ᵡ࢟	Build + IntelliSense ▼
	Code	Description			
❌	CS1721	Class 'CarA' cannot have multiple base classes: 'Car' and 'Product'			

A solution would be to merge the implementations of `Car` and `Product` together; however, it's clear that from a data model perspective, these two entities are not related to each other.

To overcome the preceding dilemma, we will use an interface. When declaring an interface, we need to adhere to the following conventions:

- To declare an interface, we need to use the `interface` keyword.
- An interface cannot have an access modifier for any function declaration.
- An interface must also just have function declarations and no definitions.

The following is the code syntax of the `ICar` interface, wherein we are declaring the methods that should be in the interface:

```
public interface ICar
{
    void ImplementBrake();
    void ImplementAccelerator();
    void ImplementBrand();
    void ImplementColor();
}
```

Please note that, in the preceding example, we have only specified the signature that the methods present in the interface should acquire. This is referred to as a declaration. The class implementing this interface – in our case, `Car`, will be responsible for providing complete implementation for the methods presents in the interface.

To implement an interface, we can use syntax similar to inheritance. The following is the screenshot for this:

```
public class Car : ICar
{
    public DateTime manufacturingDate;
    public string bodyType;
    public float fuelCapacity;
    public void ImplementBrake()
    {
        Console.WriteLine("Inside Base Class Implement Brake");
    }

    public void ImplementAccelerator()
    {
        Console.WriteLine("Inside Base Class Implement Accelerator");
    }
}

public class CarA : Car
{
    public CarA()
    {
        this.bodyType = string.Empty;
        this.manufacturingDate = DateTime.MinValue;
```

```
100 % ▾ ◂
```

```
Error List

Entire Solution          ▾    ⊗ 2 Errors    ⚠ 0 Warnings    ❶ 0 Messages    ✖▾    Build + IntelliSense    ▾

     ⌐ Code    Description
     ⊗ CS0535   'Car' does not implement interface member 'ICar.ImplementBrand()'
     ⊗ CS0535   'Car' does not implement interface member 'ICar.ImplementColor()'
```

Review the compile-time error. The error indicates that the `Car` class must implement all the functions declared in the interface. To overcome the preceding error, we must define all the functions in the interface. Similar to `ICar`, we can also create an interface for `IProduct`, which each of the `CarA` and `CarB` classes can then implement.

While inheritance and interfaces can be used in similar scenarios, some of the differences between them are as follows:

Feature	Inheritance	Interface
Multiple derivations	A class can only inherit from one class.	A class can implement multiple interfaces.
Data types	A class can inherit from another class. However, a struct cannot inherit from another class or struct.	Both classes and structs can implement interfaces.
Method definitions	In inheritance, a base class can define methods.	An interface cannot have any definitions against methods.
Access modifiers	A base class and its member attributes can assume different access modifiers, such as `public`, `private`, `protected`, `protected internal`, and `private protected`.	The access modifier of an interface is always public.

Based on these differences, a programmer can decide the right approach for their application and choose between creating an interface or managing through inheritance.

Summary

The topics covered in this chapter are the basics of programming in the C# language. Using access modifiers, we can control access to different properties and methods in different modules of an application. While writing the code, a very common mistake that people make is to declare all the properties and methods as public. This is not the recommended way of programming in C#. We must logically evaluate the need for different access modifiers for each of the properties and methods present in a class.

Similarly, we should analyze the data types that we need to associate with each property used in the class. We must also analyze if we need a reference data type variable, or whether we are fine with a value type variable as they have a different implementation in the compiler memory and functionality. We should also utilize inheritance as it helps us to reuse code and structure our programs in a very precise manner.

In the next chapter , we will go through OOP concepts, which are the main building blocks of any high-level programming language like C#. We will go over polymorphism, abstraction, encapsulation, and inheritance and understand each of these concepts in detail, and will also go over some code examples to see their implementation.

Questions

1. Which of the following attributes declared in the `Car` class is not a *value type* variable?
   1. `public Decimal fuelCapacity;`
   2. `public Enum carColor;`
   3. `public String registrationNumber;`
   4. `public Int numberOfSeats`

2. Which of the following is not a reference type variable?
   1. Class
   2. String
   3. Struct
   4. Interface

3. In C#, a child class can inherit from multiple parent classes. Is this statement correct?
   1. Yes
   2. No

4. Which of the following statements about interfaces and classes is not correct?
   1. A class can implement multiple interfaces.
   2. An interface can have both function declarations and definitions.
   3. A struct data variable cannot inherit from another struct.
   4. In inheritance, if both the base class and the derived class have a function with the same name, we can use the *base* keyword to implicitly call the function of the base class.

5. Which of the following statements about access modifiers is not correct?
   1. If a member variable is declared as `public`, it can be accessed across the entire application.
   2. If a member variable is declared as `private`, it can only be accessed in the same class.
   3. If a member variable is declared as `protected`, it can be accessed throughout the namespace.
   4. If a member variable is declared as `protected internal`, it can be accessed by classes in the name namespace and the classes that derive from it.

Answers

1. `public String registrationNumber;`. String is a reference type variable. All others are value type variables.
2. **Struct** is a value type variable unlike all others which are reference type variables.
3. **No**, in C# we cannot have multiple inheritance. A class can only inherit from one base class.
4. In C#, an interface must only have function declarations and not definitions. All other statements are correct.
5. If a member variable is declared as `protected`, it can only be accessed in the classes that inherit from its base parent class.

Understanding Object-Oriented Programming

3

When we are writing any program, apart from making sure that it serves the required purpose, we must make sure that we also take the following aspects into consideration:

- **Code reuse**: We must try to implement the program flow in such a way that common functionalities can be used across multiple modules.
- **Code maintenance**: We must accept that any program code that's written is bound to have a few bugs. However, we must ensure that the code that's written is clear and structured enough that it's understandable and easy to maintain.
- **Design patterns**: Design patterns allow us to write programs in such a manner that there is a common template/structure/functionality that can be used across multiple modules. This ensures that the performance of the application is not compromised, which is a key aspect of any program application.

All of these aspects are difficult to achieve in a procedural language. However, using object-oriented programming, which is the main essence of any high-level programming language, we can achieve the aforementioned objectives.

In this chapter, we will cover the following topics:

- Understanding object-oriented programming
- Understanding encapsulation
- Understanding abstraction
- Understanding inheritance
- Understanding polymorphism

We will also go through code examples to understand how these features are implemented in a C# application.

Technical requirements

Like in the previous chapters in this book, the programs that we will cover will be developed in Visual Studio 2017.

The sample code for this chapter can be found in this book's GitHub repository at `https://github.com/PacktPublishing/Programming-in-C-Exam-70-483-MCSD-Guide/tree/master/Book70483Samples`.

Understanding object-oriented programming

Object-oriented programming is a programming concept that is based on objects. An object is a collection of related data such as fields and procedures, that is, methods. For example, an object could be anything right from a very simple object such as a pencil to a very complex type such as a car. Each object will have its own set of attributes, that is, properties and functions or the methods that are implemented in that object. For example, for a car object, the possible attributes could be color, registration number, model, and so on. The possible functions could be start, stop, and accelerate.

Before object-oriented programming came into the picture, we did our programming under the principles of procedural programming. In a procedural language, an application was divided into a set of functions. The data that was used in the program was stored in a bunch of local variables that were used by the functions. It formed the basis of legacy programming languages such as COBOL and BASIC.

The main disadvantages of this programming concept were as follows:

- **No code reuse**: As the entire application was divided into a set of sequential functions, there was no code reuse in this programming concept.
- **Maintenance and scalability**: The following diagram is just an indicative flow of how a typical program written in a procedural language will run. In the program, the blocks indicate the different code functions, which are interlinked and interacting with each other to complete a task:

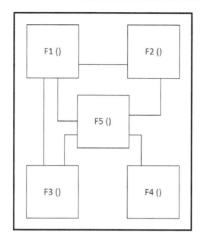

Here, as in any typical program written on procedural language, there would be a bunch of functions, passing around parameters and executing them in a conceptual manner. So, any change or upgrade that's made to any one of these functions will have a good chance of causing issues in the execution of another function. Therefore, from both the standpoint of maintenance and scalability, an application that's written in a procedural language will have its challenges.

In object-oriented programming, each application can be divided into a bunch of objects that have their own properties and procedures. For example, let's consider the same car scenario we explored in the previous chapter. A car can have the following properties and methods:

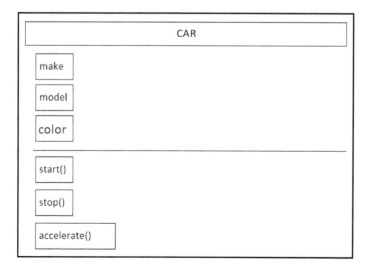

Now, what we can do in an object-oriented programming language is directly declare a `car` object, set the values related to the properties, and call the corresponding properties, such as start.

Since the object is grouped with the corresponding properties, we don't need to pass any data for the respective properties. Instead, while executing the respective functions such as `start`, `stop`, or `accelerate`, we can then pass data against these properties as a function parameter list.

Thus, in this case, if, in the future, we change the `start()` function of the `car` class, we won't need to bother all the other places that it's getting called from.

This is a major upgrade in terms of the maintainability and scalability of the application compared to the standard way of doing things in a procedural language.

Now, let's deep dive into each of the four pillars of an object-oriented language and understand how we can use them in our C# applications.

Understanding encapsulation

Encapsulation basically involves grouping all the related properties and methods that access them in an object. Whenever an application is being designed, we need to decide how many objects should be defined in it, along with the associated attributes and methods available in it.

For instance, in the car example, we have the following associated attributes and methods:

- `car` is an object.
- The `make`, `model`, and `color` are the different attributes that are present in the object.
- `start`, `stop`, and `accelerate` are the different methods that are present in the object.

Encapsulation allows us to achieve the following functionality in any application:

- **Security**: Using encapsulation, we can define our attributes in such a way that not all of the attributes of an object are exposed to the entire application. In Chapter 2, *Understanding Classes, Structures, and Interfaces,* we used access modifiers to control the security access of any property/method in the class/in the namespace/in the assembly, as well as in the entire application.
- **Code maintenance**: From a maintenance perspective of a function, it's always desirable that the function has as few attributes as possible.

Using encapsulation, we can organize the required parameters of a function as an attribute of the class and thus we are not passing them explicitly in every call.

In the following code example, we will go through a code sample in C# and understand how this can be achieved.

Code example

Let's consider an example of a banking application. In this banking application, we need to implement a scenario related to opening an account.

From a class implementation perspective, the following are the possible attributes that should be in the Account class. Please also note that there will be an additional class, Customer, to signify the person who is opening the account:

- openingDate
- customer
- float currentBalance

The following are some of the methods that could be present in the Account class:

- bool OpenAccount();
- bool depositMoney(float deposit);
- bool withdrawMoney(float withdrawalAmt);

In regard to the Customer class, we will just go simple now and define the following attributes:

- string name
- string customerId

Please refer to the following code for the declaration of the `Customer` class in a C# program. Here, we have created a `Customer` class and defined two attributes in it, that is, the name of the customer and a field of `CustomerID`, which will be a unique field for that customer.

In the following code, we will declare two variables and use them to showcase examples for the operators we mentioned previously:

```csharp
using System;
using System.Collections.Generic;
using System.Linq;
using System.Text;
using System.Threading.Tasks;

namespace ConsoleApp1
{
    public class Customer
    {
        public string name;
        public string customerId;
    }
}
```

Please refer to the following code for the declaration of the `Account` class in a C# program:

```csharp
public class Account
{
  public DateTime openingDate;
  public Customer customer;
  private float currentBalance;
  public bool OpenAccount(Customer customer)
  {
      this.openingDate = DateTime.Now.Date;
      this.currentBalance = 0.0f;
      this.customer = customer;
      return true;
  }
  public bool DepositMoney(float deposit)
  {
      if(deposit > 0.0f)
      {
          this.currentBalance = this.currentBalance + deposit;
          return true;
      }
      else
      {
          return false;
```

```
        }
    }
    public bool WithdrawMoney(float withdraw)
    {
        if(this.currentBalance >= withdraw)
        {
            this.currentBalance = this.currentBalance - withdraw;
            return true;
        }
        else
        {
            return false;
        }
    }
  }
}
```

The following are some of the key items in the implementation:

- In the Account class, note that currentBalance is marked as private, as a customer may not want their balance to be exposed to the entire application.
- In the Account class, in the methods of OpenAccount, DepositMoney, and WithdrawMoney, we are not passing all of the attributes related to the customer, current balance, or opening date. This is because the required attributes are already grouped together in the Account class.

Now, let's look at how we will invoke these classes:

```
Customer customer = new Customer();
customer.name = "Sample Customer";
customer.customerId = "12345";

Account newAccount = new Account();
newAccount.OpenAccount(customer);
newAccount.DepositMoney(1000);
newAccount.WithdrawMoney(400);
```

If you look at the function calling part, you will understand that because the properties are linked to the Account class, we are not passing them explicitly to the functions. Therefore, if the implementation of the functions is changed, from a maintenance perspective, there will be minimal impact.

Therefore, it's always beneficial to use the principles of encapsulation and divide the application into chunks of classes with the related information.

Understanding abstraction

Abstraction is also a concept in object-oriented programming and implies that, when we write code, we should hide the complexity and details of the implementation from the outside world.

In other words, when we write a program that, on receiving an input, does a bunch of complex operations and returns an output, we should hide the inner complexity of the operations that are done inside the program so that the outer applications can just focus on the input they are sending to the application and the output that they are getting from it.

For example, let's consider the same example of `Account` that we worked on in the previous example. If we consider the example of the `OpenAccount` function, you will understand that opening an account for the customer will not be that simple. There will be several subtasks that need to be executed before we can finally open the account for the customer. For example, some of the steps could be as follows:

- Verifying the identification documents of the customer
- Linking and opening different bank accounts, which could be `Salary`, `Current`, and `Savings`
- Fetching, that is, counting the initial amount deposit of the customer

Basically, in real life, the function that we have written above will look more similar to the following code snippet. In `OpenAccount`, we are passing a `Customer` object. Before creating the bank account of the customer, we are doing three distinct tasks:

1. `VerifyCustomerIdentity()`: In this function, the idea is to verify the identity of the customer, which is a common practice before an account is opened.
2. `OpenAndLinkRelatedAccounts()`: In this function, the idea is to open different accounts for the same customer, that is, `Savings`, `Current`, and `Salaried`.
3. `RetrieveAndCountDeposit()`: In this function, the idea is to retrieve the money the customer intends to save, count it, and finally deposit it in the customer's account:

```
public bool OpenAccount(Customer customer)
{
    this.openingDate = DateTime.Now.Date;
    this.currentBalance = 0.0f;
    this.customer = customer;
    if(VerifiyCustomerIdentity() && OpenAndLinkRelatedAccounts() &&
RetrieveAndCountDeposit())
    {
        return true;
```

```
        }
        else
        {
            return false;
        }
    }
    private bool VerifiyCustomerIdentity()
    {
        //This function will verify the customer documents.
        return true;
    }
    private bool OpenAndLinkRelatedAccounts()
    {
        //This function will open the related accounts of savings ,
    current and salary and link them together.
        return true;
    }
    private bool RetrieveAndCountDeposit()
    {
        //This function will fetch the deposit, count and verify the
    amount.
        return true;
    }
    public bool DepositMoney(float deposit)
    {
        this.currentBalance = this.currentBalance + deposit;
        return true;
    }
```

Please note the following:

- The three functions, that is, `VerifyCustomerIdentity()`, `OpenAndLinkRelatedAccounts()`, and `RetrieveAndCountDeposit()`, all of which have `Private` as the access modifier. This will ensure that the complexities in these three functions are not exposed to the outside.
- These three functions are being internally called in the `OpenAccount` function, so the calling application doesn't need to worry about calling these functions explicitly.
- Let's say we discover some issues in the internal private function. In this case, we can easily make changes in these internal functions without needing to worry about the external implementation.

Understanding inheritance

If you went through `Chapter 2`, *Understanding Classes, Structures, and Interfaces*, you will already know how inheritance helps us in code reuse and reduced maintenance, and that it gives us more control of the entire application.

We also looked at a few code examples and saw how inheritance works and how it's implemented in C#. Now, we will look at some advanced features in inheritance, their use, and how they are implemented in C#.

Method overriding

Method overriding is a technique in C# that we can use to invoke the methods that are defined in the base class from the classes that are deriving from that base class. In method overriding, a derived class implements a function that's declared in the base class with the same signature:

- The same name as the function that's declared in the base class
- The same number and type of parameters in the function
- The same return type as the function declared in the base class

In C#, method overriding is implemented using the following two methods:

- **Virtual methods**: A virtual method is a method in the base class that can also be defined or overridden in the derived class as well. Please note that, when a method is declared as virtual, it's optional to define the implementation of the method in the base class. In case it's defined, it becomes even more optional for the derived class to override it further. A method is declared as virtual using the *virtual* keyword.
- **Override**: Once a method has been declared as `virtual` or `abstract` in the base class, then by using the *override* keyword, the derived class can redefine the implementation of the method for its own use. In this section, we will be looking at *virtual methods*. In the next section, *Abstract and sealed classes*, we will do a deep dive into `abstract` methods.

Let's look at a code example to understand how method overriding is implemented in C#. Let's assume that we have a base class, Car, and two classes, `Ferrari` and `Suzuki`, that are inheriting from the Car class. For the sake of explanation, we will keep things simple by just specifying a default constructor and a common `Accelerate` method across the three classes. The following would be the code implementation for the same:

```
public class Car
{
    public Car()
    {
        Console.WriteLine("Inside Car");
    }
    public void Accelerate()
    {
        Console.WriteLine("Inside Acceleration of Car");
    }
}
public class Ferrari : Car
{
    public Ferrari()
    {
        Console.WriteLine("Inside Ferrari");
    }
    public void Accelerate()
    {
        Console.WriteLine("Inside Acceleration of Ferrari");
    }
}
public class Suzuki : Car
{
    public Suzuki()
    {
        Console.WriteLine("Inside Suzuki");
    }
    public void Accelerate()
    {
        Console.WriteLine("Inside Acceleration of Suzuki");
    }
}
```

Now, let's create some objects for these classes by using the following code:

```
Car ferrari = new Ferrari();
ferrari.Accelerate();
Console.WriteLine("End of Ferrari Implementation");
Car suzuki = new Suzuki();
suzuki.Accelerate();
Console.WriteLine("End of Suzuki Implementation");
```

Note that in the preceding code, we have created a new object of the Ferrari class and have assigned it to a variable, ferrari, which is of the Car type. Similarly, we have also created a new object of the Suzuki class and have assigned it to a variable, suzuki, which is also of the Car type.

When we execute the code, we get the following output:

```
C:\Users\sbhalla1\source\repos\ConsoleApp3\ConsoleApp3\bin\Debug\ConsoleApp3.exe
Inside Car
Inside Ferrari
Inside Acceleration of Car
End of Ferrari Implementation
Inside Car
Inside Suzuki
Inside Acceleration of Car
End of Suzuki Implementation
```

Note that, even though we have the `Accelerate` method in both the parent `Car` class and the derived `Ferrari` and `Suzuki` classes, when we are calling the `Accelerate` method from the `ferrari` object, it's calling the `Accelerate` method that's present in the parent `Car` class. This is due to the fact that the type of the variable is `Car` and that, even though it's instantiated with the objects of the `Ferrari` and `Suzuki` child classes, the method in the base class has not been overridden.

Now let's make a slight change to the implementation and declare the method in the base class as `virtual` and the methods in the classes deriving from this class as `override`:

```csharp
public class Car
{
    public Car()
    {
        Console.WriteLine("Inside Car");
    }
    public virtual void Accelerate()
    {
        Console.WriteLine("Inside Acceleration of Car");
    }
}
public class Ferrari : Car
{
    public Ferrari()
    {
        Console.WriteLine("Inside Ferrari");
    }
    public override void Accelerate()
    {
        Console.WriteLine("Inside Acceleration of Ferrari");
    }
}
public class Suzuki : Car
{
    public Suzuki()
```

```
    {
        Console.WriteLine("Inside Suzuki");
    }
    public override void Accelerate()
    {
        Console.WriteLine("Inside Acceleration of Suzuki");
    }
}
```

Now, execute the same code again and review that we receive the following output:

Note that now, the `Accelerate` method executes the code mentioned in the derived classes of `Ferrari` and `Suzuki` and not the code specified in the parent class of `Car`.

Later in this chapter, we will also do a deep dive into polymorphism. There are two types of polymorphism: runtime polymorphism and compile-time polymorphism. Runtime polymorphism is implemented using method overriding.

In the next section, we will look at `abstract` classes and also explore the use of `virtual` methods in `abstract` classes.

Abstract classes

An `abstract` class in C# is a class that cannot be instantiated, that is, the program execution cannot create an object of this class. Instead, these classes can only act as base classes from which other classes can inherit.

We use the `abstract` class in scenarios where we specifically want all the deriving classes to implement the specific implementation of a particular function that's declared in the base class. The following are some of the properties of an `abstract` class:

* Just like all the other classes, an `abstract` class can have both functions and properties.
* An `abstract` class can have both abstract and non-abstract functions.

Let's take a look at a program to analyze how abstract classes work. We will define an Animal class using the abstract keyword. Now, let's assume that each animal type, such as dog, speaks differently, so they must implement the function in their own way. To implement this, we will declare our base Animal class as abstract and have an abstract method Speak in it. Review that if we try to implement the Speak method, the compiler throws an error:

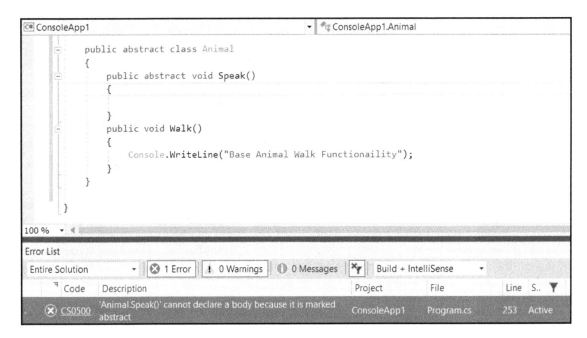

To remove this error, we can simply remove the declaration of the abstract method:

```
public abstract class Animal
{
    public abstract void Speak();
    public void Walk()
    {
        Console.WriteLine("Base Animal Walk Functionality");
    }
}
```

Now, let's create a `Dog` class that inherits from this base class of `Animal`. Note that the compiler will throw an error if the `Speak` method is not implemented:

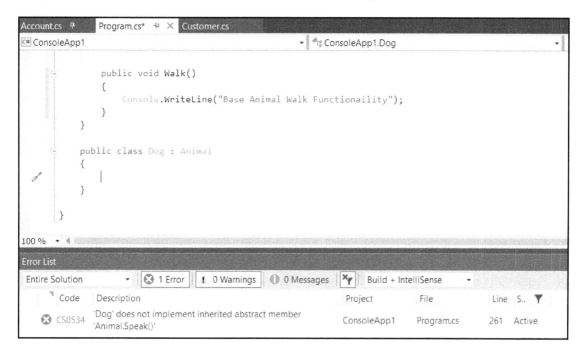

We can get over this error by creating an implementation of the `Speak` function:

```
public class Dog : Animal
{
    public override void Speak()
    {
        Console.WriteLine("A dog will bark");
    }
}
```

Please note that we use the `override` keyword to let the compiler know that we are overriding the implementation of the `abstract` function called `Speak` in the derived class.

In the next section, we will look at the same example and understand how `abstract` methods differ from `virtual` methods.

Abstract versus virtual methods

In the preceding example, we declared the `Speak` method as `abstract`. This forced our `Dog` class to provide an implementation of the method because, otherwise, we would get a compile-time error. Now, what if we don't want to have that particular restriction in our code?

We can do this by replacing the `abstract` method with the `virtual` method. The following is the changed implementation of the preceding code:

```
public abstract class Animal
{
    public virtual void Speak()
    {
    }
}
```

Note that when you compile the code, there are no errors. Also, just for the sake of experimenting, comment out the `Speak` method in the `Dog` class.

Now, compile the program. Note that, unlike the previous case, when we use `abstract` methods, no compile-time errors occur:

In the next section, we will look at `sealed` classes and how they are implemented in C# applications.

Sealed classes

A `sealed` class in C# is a class that we do not want to be inherited by any derived class. Once we insert the keyword `sealed`, a compiler will give a compile-time error if a derived class tries to inherit from the `sealed` class. The following is the screenshot of the same. For explanation purposes, we will use the same two classes we used in the preceding example:

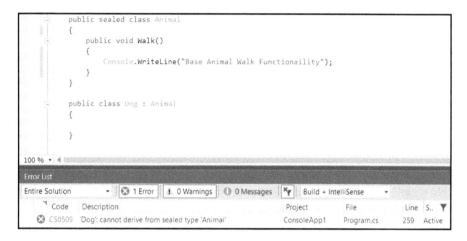

Note that `abstract` and `sealed` do not go hand in hand. `abstract` means that the class must never be instantiated, whereas the `sealed` class indicates that the class must never be inherited. Therefore, in hindsight, if we declare a `sealed` class as `abstract`, this will not make any sense. Thus, if we do try to declare an `abstract` class as `sealed`, we will get a compile-time error, as follows:

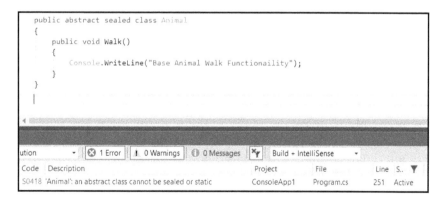

In the next section, we will look at another pillar of OOP programming, that is, *polymorphism*.

Understanding polymorphism

Polymorphism is a Greek word whose literal translation to English is *many-shaped*. In programming terms, it's referred to as one interface with multiple functions. Let's try to understand polymorphism by looking at the following diagram:

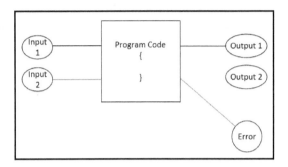

In the preceding diagram, we have some program code that runs on **Input 1** and gives **Output 1**. Now, let's say we make a mistake and send an incorrect input of **Input 2** instead. In this case, unfortunately, the program code may error out and send an error message. In such a scenario, we can use polymorphism. With polymorphism, the same example will be represented as follows:

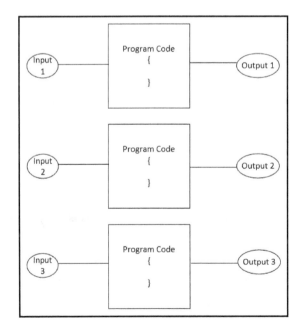

As we can see, by using polymorphism, we will maintain three copies of the code in memory and depending on the type of input received, the appropriate copy of the program code will be loaded and executed.

There are two types of polymorphism possible in C#:

- Static/compile-time polymorphism, that is, method overloading or function overloading
- Execution time polymorphism, that is, method overriding or virtual functions

Let's go through each of these types and use code examples to understand how they work.

Static/compile-time polymorphism

Static polymorphism, also known as function overloading, involves creating functions with the same name but with different numbers or types of parameters.

The compiler loads the appropriate function based on the input that's passed. Let's go through the following code example to see how it works. Here, we will create two copies of a function called ADD that will differ in terms of the number of parameters accepted by the function:

```
static int AddNumber (int a, int b)
{
    Console.WriteLine("Accepting two inputs");
    return a + b;
}
static int AddNumber(int a, int b, int c)
{
    Console.WriteLine("Accepting three inputs");
    return a + b + c;
}
```

Now, when the call is made to the function, based on the number of parameters passed, the respective function will be loaded:

```
int result = AddNumber(1, 2);
Console.WriteLine(result);
int result2 = AddNumber(1, 2, 3);
Console.WriteLine(result2);
Console.ReadLine();
```

After the program is executed, we will get the following output:

```
Accepting two inputs
3
Accepting three inputs
6
```

Now, let's consider another example. In the preceding example, we implemented polymorphism based on the number of parameters. In this example, we will implement polymorphism based on the type of parameter:

1. Create two classes, one each for Dog and Cat:

```
public class Dog
{
}
public class Cat
{
}
```

2. Create two functions with the same name but one accepting the input of a Dog object and another accepting the input of a Cat object:

```
static void AnimalImplementation(Dog dog)
{
    Console.WriteLine("The implementation is for a dog.");
}
static void AnimalImplementation(Cat cat)
{
    Console.WriteLine("The implementation is for a cat.");
}
```

Now, when a call is made to the function, based on the type of parameter, the appropriate function will be loaded:

```
Cat cat = new Cat();
Dog dog = new Dog();
AnimalImplementation(cat);
AnimalImplementation(dog);
Console.ReadLine();
```

When the program is executed, it will show the following output:

```
The implementation is for a cat.
The implementation is for a dog.
```

Runtime polymorphism

Runtime polymorphism in C# is executed via virtual methods. In this type of polymorphism, the compiler executes the code by identifying its form at runtime.

In the *Method overriding* section, we learned about virtual methods and saw how they allow the derived class to override the implementation of a function in the base class. In runtime polymorphism, the object of the base class holds the reference to objects of the base and derived classes. Now, based on the object that the base object is pointing to, the appropriate function will be loaded.

To recap our understanding of this, let's go through another code example. In this example, we will create a base class called `Animal` that will be inherited by two classes, `Man` and `Dog`.

The following is the implementation in the `Animal` class:

```
public class Animal
{
    public int numOfHands;
    public int numOfLegs;
    public virtual void Speak()
    {
        Console.WriteLine("This is a base implementation in the base
animal class");
    }
}
```

In the `Animal` class, we have declared two attributes to represent `numOfHands` and `numOfLegs` of the `Animal`. We have also declared a function called `Speak` and have marked it as `Virtual` so that any class that inherits from this class can give its own implementation of the `Speak` functionality.

> We have declared the `Speak` function as virtual, which means that this function can be overridden in the derived class.

The following is the implementation in the `Dog` class:

```
public class Dog : Animal
{
    public string breed;
    public Dog(string breed, int hands, int legs)
    {
```

```
        this.breed = breed;
        base.numOfHands = hands;
        base.numOfLegs = legs;
    }

    public override void Speak()
    {
        Console.WriteLine("A dog will bark , its breed is " + this.breed +
" and number of legs and hands        are " + this.numOfLegs + " " +
this.numOfHands);
    }
}
```

In this implementation, we have created a `Dog` class that is inheriting from the `Animal` class. The `Dog` class has an attribute called `Breed` and a constructor that takes three parameters of `breed`, `hands`, and `legs`, respectively. We also have a `Speak` function to provide an impression of how a dog object will implement the `Speak` functionality.

The following code is for another class, `Human`, which will also inherit from the base class of `Animal`:

```
public class Human : Animal
{
    public string countryOfCitizenship;
    public Human(string citizenship, int hands, int legs)
    {
        this.countryOfCitizenship = citizenship;
        base.numOfHands = hands;
        base.numOfLegs = legs;
    }
    public override void Speak()
    {
        Console.WriteLine("A man can speak multiple languages, its
citizenship is " +                           this.countryOfCitizenship +
" and number of legs and hands are " + this.numOfLegs + " " +
this.numOfHands);
    }
}
```

In the preceding code, we are doing the following:

- We are inheriting the `Dog` class from the base class of `Animal`.
- We are overriding the `Speak` function in the derived class.
- We are also using the attributes that were declared in the base class.

Now, let's see how runtime polymorphism works. In the following code, we are declaring an object of the base `Animal` class and pointing it to an object of the derived class:

```
Animal animal = new Animal();
animal.numOfHands = 2;
animal.numOfLegs = 4;
animal.Speak();

animal = new Dog("Labrador", 0, 4);
animal.Speak();

animal = new Human("India", 2, 2);
animal.Speak();
Console.ReadLine();
```

Once we execute this code, we will notice that, based on the class object reference that the base object `animal` is pointing to, the appropriate implementation of the `Speak` method will be loaded. This loading is decided at runtime, which is why this is called **runtime polymorphism**:

```
This is a base implementation in the base animal class
A dog will bark , its breed is Labrador and number of legs and hands are 4 0
A man can speak multiple languages, its citizenship is India and number of legs and hands are 2 2
```

Summary

In this chapter, we learned about object-oriented programming, which is the main essence of any high-level programming language, including C#. We learned about the four pillars of OOP, that is, encapsulation, abstraction, polymorphism, and inheritance, and understood how they help us write applications that are easy to maintain, are scalable, and have a good amount of reuse.

We learned how encapsulation helps us in keeping our code structured by grouping together all the related properties and methods in one class. Then, we learned how abstraction helps us reduce the complexity of a module that is exposed to the entire application. Using abstraction, we can make sure that all the complexities of a class are not exposed to outside classes, which also helps us maintain the application better. We also learned how we can use both runtime and static polymorphism to implement similar functionalities that can be reused across different inputs, thus helping us reuse our code throughout the application. Finally, we learned how inheritance helps us have more control over the application's implementation. Using inheritance, we can make sure that similar classes implement a set of properties and methods that are common across them.

While writing any program in C#, it's highly important that we keep these principles in mind. The biggest mistake that some C# programmers make these days is they don't utilize these core principles of OOP programming and, instead, the program that's written resembles more of a procedural language program. From a maintenance perspective, it helps us a lot as, to some extent, it ensures that the bug fixes in one module do not impact the complete application.

In the next chapter, we will look at the different operators that are used across C# programming. We will look at how we can manage program flow using operators and different conditional selection statements. We will also look at different iteration statements such as for and while loop, which help us control the program's flow.

Questions

1. Which of the following best describes a program in which we have multiple functions with the same name but they differ in terms of the number of parameters and types of parameters accepted by them?

    a. Method overloading

    b. Method overriding

    c. Encapsulation

    d. Abstraction

2. Which keyword must be used when a derived class is defining the implementation of a function that's present in the base class?

    a. New

    b. Abstract

    c. Virtual

    d. Override

3. Which keyword can we use to prevent the inheritance of a particular class?
     a. Abstract

     b. Private

     c. Sealed

     d. Protected

Answers

1. Method overloading or function overloading is the concept in which different implementations of a function with same name is made. Depending upon the number of arguments or type of argument, appropriate implementation of the function is loaded.
2. The override keyword allows a derived class to implement the abstract method declared in the base class.
3. Sealed. If a class is declared as sealed, it will prevent the inheritance of the base class throughout the application.

4
Implementing Program Flow

This chapter focuses on how we can manage program flow in C#. In other words, this chapter will help you understand how the program controls and validates input and output arguments and makes decisions using statements that are available in C#. We will cover various Boolean expressions, such as If/Else and Switch, which control the flow of code based on certain conditions. We will also evaluate various operators, such as the conditional operator and the equality operator (<, >, ==), both of which govern the flow of code. We will focus on how we can iterate across collections (with `for` loops, `while` loops, and so on) and explicit jump statements.

The following topics will be covered in this chapter.

- Understanding operators
- Understanding conditional/selection statements
- Iteration statements

Technical requirements

The exercises in this chapter can be practiced using Visual Studio 2012 or above with .NET Framework version 2.0 or above. However, any new C# features from version 7.0 and above require you to have Visual Studio 2017.

If you don't have a license for any of these products, you can download the community version of Visual Studio 2017 from `https://visualstudio.microsoft.com/downloads/`.

The sample code for this chapter can be found in this book's GitHub repository at `https://github.com/PacktPublishing/Programming-in-C-sharp-Exam-70-483-MCSD-Guide/tree/master/Chapter04`.

Understanding operators

Before we dive into this topic, let's understand what operators and operands are. These are two important terms we will use in this section of this book:

- An operator is a programming element that is applied to one or more operands in an expression or statement.
- An operand is an object that can be manipulated.

C# offers different types of operators, such as the Unary operator ([increment operator] ++, new) which takes one operand, Binary operators of the arithmetic type (+, – , *, /), relational types (> ,<, <=, >=), equality types (=, !=), and shift types (>>, <<), all of which are used between two operands. C# also offers a ternary operator that takes three operands (? :).

Unary operators

An operator that requires only one operand is called a **Unary operator**. They can perform operations such as increment, decrement, negation and so on. They can also be applied before (prefix) or after (postfix) the operand.

The following table lists a few Unary operators. x, in the left-hand column, is an operand where we apply the operators:

Expression	Description
+x	**Identity**: This operator can be used as a Unary or Binary operator. If it's used on numeric values, it returns the value. If it's applied on two numeric operands, it returns the sum of operands. On strings, it concatenates both operands.
–x	**Negation**: This operator can be used as a Unary or Binary operator. Applying this operator on numeric types results in the numeric negation of the operand.
!x	**Logical negation**: This operator negates the operand. It is applied for bool operands and returns if the operand is false.
~x	**Bitwise negation**: This produces a complement of its operand by reversing each bit.
++x	**Pre-increment**: This is an increment operator and can appear before or after the operand. When prefixed, the result is placed after the increment. If postfixed, the result is placed before the increment.
--x	**Pre-decrement**: This is a decrement operator and can appear before or after the operand. When prefixed, the result is placed after decrement. If postfixed, the result is placed before the decrement.

In the following code, we will declare a few variables and use them to showcase examples of the preceding operators:

```
int firstvalue = 5;
int secondvalue = 6;
string firststring = "Hello ";
string secondstring = "World";
```

+ and – can be used with a single operand or multiple operands. When used with multiple operands of the integer type, they either sum the operands or get the difference. The + operator can be used with string type operands as well. In this case, it will concatenate both the strings. A string and an operator is always a Binary operator:

```
//'+' operator
Console.WriteLine(+firstvalue); // output: 5
Console.WriteLine(firstvalue + secondvalue); // output: 11
Console.WriteLine(firststring + secondstring); // output: Hello World
//'-' operator
Console.WriteLine(-firstvalue); // output: -5
Console.WriteLine(firstvalue - secondvalue); // output = -1
```

The ! operator works well with Boolean operands where it produces logical negation; that is, true becomes false, whereas the ~ operator works with bitwise operands. In the following example, a Binary digit representation and its bitwise negation are displayed. We are taking an integer value and converting it into a Binary value and then negating it using the ~ operator and displaying it in base 2 format:

```
//'!' operator
Console.WriteLine(!true);

//output : false

//'~' operator
Console.WriteLine("'~' operator");
int digit = 60;
Console.WriteLine("Number is : {0} and binary form is {1}:", digit,
IntToBinaryString(digit));
int digit1 = ~digit;
Console.WriteLine("Number is : {0} and binary form is {1}:", digit1,
Convert.ToString(digit1, 2));

//Output:
Number is : 60 and binary form is 111100:
Number is : -61 and binary form is 11111111111111111111111111000011
```

The ++ and -- operators, when applied on integer operands, perform increments or decrements on the operands, respectively. These can be applied pre or post an operand. The following example shows both the post and pre increment and decrement operators. Pre produces results before displaying and post produces results after displaying:

```
// '++' Operator
Console.WriteLine(++firstvalue); // output: 6
// '--' Operator
Console.WriteLine(--firstvalue); // output: 5
// '++' Operator
Console.WriteLine(firstvalue++); // output: 5
Console.WriteLine(firstvalue--); // output: 6
```

Relational operators

As the name suggests, relational operators test or define the relationship between two operands, for example, if the first operand is less than the second one, or greater than or equal to it. These operators are applied to numeric operands.

The following table lists a few Binary operators:

Expression	Description
<	Defined as less than the operator. Used as X < Y. Returns true if the first operand is less than the second operand.
>	Defined as greater than an operator. Used as X > Y. Returns true if the first operand is greater than the second operand.
<=	Less than Or Equal To operator. Used as X <= Y.
>=	Greater than Or Equal To operator. Used as X >= Y.

We will use the same variables we defined in the preceding example to understand these relational operators. Here, we are trying to find out whether firstvalue is less than secondvalue or whether firstvalue is greater than secondvalue:

```
// '<' Operator
Console.WriteLine(firstvalue < secondvalue);
// output = true

// '>' Operator
Console.WriteLine(firstvalue > secondvalue);
// output = false

// '>=' Operator
Console.WriteLine(secondvalue >= firstvalue);
// output = true
```

```
// '<=' Operator
Console.WriteLine(firstvalue <= secondvalue);
// output = true
```

Equality operators

Equality operators are a type of Binary operator, where 2 operands are required. Because they check for the equality of the operands, these can be termed under relational operators as well.

The following table lists the available equality operators:

Expression	Description
==	This works for predefined value types. Defined as the equality operator. Used as X == Y. Returns true if the first operand is equal to the second operand.
!=	Defined as the inequality operator. Used as X! = Y. Returns true if the operands are not equal.

We will use the same variables we created in the preceding examples to try and understand the equality operators. Here, we are trying to check if firstvalue is equal or not equal to secondvalue:

```
//using variables created earlier.
// '==' Operator
Console.WriteLine(secondvalue == firstvalue); // output = false
// '!=' Operator
Console.WriteLine(firstvalue != secondvalue); // output = true
```

Shift operators

Shift operators are another type of Binary operator. They take two integer operands and left shift or right shift the bits by the number specified.

The following table lists the available shift operators:

Expression	Description
<<	This is an example of a Binary operator that allows you to shift the first operand left by the number of bits specified in the second operand. The second operator must be a type of Int.
>>	This is an example of a Binary operator that allows you to shift the first operand right by the number of bits specified in the second operand. The second operator must be a type of Int.

In the following example, the program accepts an integer operand and shifts left or right by 1 bit. Shift works on Binary operators, so, for our understanding, I wrote a method that will convert an integer into Binary format and display it. When we pass an integer number of 9 to the program, i, and use the >> operator, its Binary string is shifted by 1 and the result is displayed. When 1001 is right-shifted, it becomes 100:

```
public static string IntToBinaryString(int number)
{
    const int mask = 1;
    var binary = string.Empty;
    while (number > 0)
    {
        // Logical AND the number and prepend it to the result string
        binary = (number & mask) + binary;
        number = number >> 1;
    }
    return binary;
}

// '>>' Operator
Console.WriteLine("'>>' operator");
int number = 9;
Console.WriteLine("Number is : {0} and binary form is {1}:", number,
IntToBinaryString(number));
number = number >> 1;
Console.WriteLine("Number is : {0} and binary form is {1}:", number,
IntToBinaryString(number));

//Output:
//Number is : 9 and binary form is 1001
//Number is : 4 and binary form is 100

// '<<' Operator
Console.WriteLine("'<<' operator");
Console.WriteLine("Number is : {0} and binary form is {1}:", number,
IntToBinaryString(number));
number = number << 1;
Console.WriteLine("Number is : {0} and binary form is {1}:", number,
IntToBinaryString(number));

//Output:
//Number is : 4 and binary form is 100
//Number is : 8 and binary form is 1000
```

Logical, conditional, and null operators

C# allows you to combine the aforementioned operators with OR (| |), AND (& &), or XOR (^). These are applied to both operands in an expression.

The following table lists the logical, conditional, and null operators:

Expression	Description and example
Logical OR (	)	This operator computes both operands and returns false if both are false.
Logical AND (&)	This operator can be used in two forms: Unary address operator or Binary logical operator. When used as a Unary address operator, it returns the address of the operand. If used as a Binary, it evaluates both operands and returns true if both operands are true; otherwise, it will return false.
Conditional AND (& &)	This conditional operator is used when two bool operands need to be evaluated. When applied, both operands are computed and returns true if both operands are true. If the first operand returns false, the conditional operator doesn't evaluate the other operator. This is also known as the *short-circuiting* logical AND operator.
Conditional OR (| |)	This is also known as the *short-circuiting* logical OR operator. The conditional OR operator evaluates both bool operands and returns true if either of them is true. If the first operand returns true, it won't evaluate the second operator.
Logical XOR (^)	This operator is evaluated as a bitwise exclusive OR for integral types and logical exclusive and OR for bool types. When applied, it computes both operands and returns true if one of the operands is true; otherwise, it returns false.
Null coalescing (? ?)	The null coalescing operator computes both operands and returns the operand that is not null. It's used like so: int y = x ?? 1;. In this scenario, if x is null, y is assigned a value of 1; otherwise, y is assigned a value of x.
Ternary operator (? :)	The conditional operator is also known as the Ternary operator and evaluates a Boolean expression. The condition is ? true value : false value. If the condition is true, the operator returns true value, but if the condition is false, the operator returns false value. Ternary operators support nested expressions or operators, which is also known as being *right-associative*.

The following code will allow us to understand each of these statements in detail. Initially, we will define the required variables and methods and then proceed with each statement. The following code is available on GitHub. The link is provided in the *Technical requirements* section:

```
int firstvalue = 5;
int secondvalue = 6;
int? nullvalue = null;
private bool SecondOperand(bool result)
{
    Console.WriteLine("SecondOperand computed");
```

```
        return result;
    }
    private bool FirstOperand(bool result)
    {
        Console.WriteLine("FirstOperand computed");
        return result;
    }
```

In the following code block, logical OR (|) shows usage of the | operator. We have two Boolean expressions in the following code block that are evaluated at runtime and return either true or false. This operator always returns true except when both operands return false:

```
//LOGICAL OR (|)
Console.WriteLine((firstvalue > secondvalue) | (firstvalue < secondvalue));
// output : true
Console.WriteLine((firstvalue < secondvalue) | (firstvalue < secondvalue));
// output : true
Console.WriteLine((firstvalue < secondvalue) | (firstvalue > secondvalue));
// output : true
Console.WriteLine((firstvalue > secondvalue) | (firstvalue > secondvalue));
// output : false
```

In the following code block, logical AND shows how the & operator can be used. Logical AND evaluates both operands and returns true if both operands are evaluated as true; otherwise, it returns false:

```
//LOGICAL AND (&)
Console.WriteLine(FirstOperand(true) & SecondOperand(true));
// output : FirstOperand computed, SecondOperand computed, true
Console.WriteLine(FirstOperand(false) & SecondOperand(true));
// output : FirstOperand computed, SecondOperand computed, false
Console.WriteLine(FirstOperand(true) & SecondOperand(false));
// output : FirstOperand computed, SecondOperand computed, false
Console.WriteLine(FirstOperand(false) & SecondOperand(false));
// output : FirstOperand computed, SecondOperand computed, false
```

In the following code clock, the conditional AND (&&) illustrates the && operator. This operator evaluates the first operator and, if it is true, it evaluates the second operator. Otherwise, it returns false:

```
//CONDITIONAL AND (&&)
Console.WriteLine(FirstOperand(true) && SecondOperand(true));
// output = FirstOperand computed, SecondOperand computed, true
Console.WriteLine(FirstOperand(false) && SecondOperand(true));
// output = FirstOperand computed, false
Console.WriteLine(FirstOperand(true) && SecondOperand(false));
```

```
// output = FirstOperand computed, false
Console.WriteLine(FirstOperand(false) && SecondOperand(false));
// output = FirstOperand computed, false
```

In the following code block, the conditional OR (||) illustrates the || operator. This operator returns true if any of the operands is true; otherwise, it returns false:

```
//CONDITIONAL OR (||)
Console.WriteLine(FirstOperand(true) || SecondOperand(true));
// output = FirstOperand computed, true
Console.WriteLine(FirstOperand(false) || SecondOperand(true));
// output = FirstOperand computed, SecondOperand computed, true
Console.WriteLine(FirstOperand(true) || SecondOperand(false));
// output = FirstOperand computed, true
Console.WriteLine(FirstOperand(false) || SecondOperand(false));
// output = FirstOperand computed, SecondOperand computed, false
```

In the following code, the logical XOR (^) explains the ^ operator on bool operands. This returns true if one of the operands is true. This is similar to the logical OR operator:

```
//LOGICAL XOR (^)
Console.WriteLine(FirstOperand(true) ^ SecondOperand(true));
// output = FirstOperand computed, SecondOperand computed, false
Console.WriteLine(FirstOperand(false) ^ SecondOperand(true));
// output = FirstOperand computed, SecondOperand computed,true
Console.WriteLine(FirstOperand(true) ^ SecondOperand(false));
// output = FirstOperand computed, SecondOperand computed,true
Console.WriteLine(FirstOperand(false) ^ SecondOperand(false));
// output = FirstOperand computed, SecondOperand computed,false
```

Here, we will look at null coalescing and the ternary operator. The null coalescing operator, ??, is used to check if an operand is null before returning its value. It returns the value if the first operand is not null; otherwise, it returns the second operand. This can be used in a nested form as well.

The ternary operator, (? :), is used to evaluate an expression. If it is true, then it returns true-value; otherwise, it returns false-value:

```
//Null Coalescing (??)
Console.WriteLine(nullvalue ?? firstvalue);// output : 5

//Ternary Operator (? :)
Console.WriteLine((firstvalue > secondvalue) ? firstvalue : secondvalue);//
output : 6
Console.WriteLine((firstvalue < secondvalue) ? firstvalue : secondvalue);//
output : 5
```

Understanding conditional/selection statements

C# offers multiple conditional/selection statements to help us make decisions throughout our programming. We can use all of the operators we learned about in the previous sections alongside these statements. These statements help the program take on a specific flow based on whether the expression is evaluated as `true` or `false`. These statements are the most widely used ones in C#.

The following table lists the available conditional/selection statements:

Expression	Description
`If..else`	If statements evaluate the expression that's provided. If it is `true`, then the statements are executed. If it is `false`, then else statements are executed.
`Switch..case..default`	Switch statements evaluate a specific expression and execute the switch section if the pattern matches the match expression.
`break`	`break` allows us to terminate a control flow and move on to the next statement.
`goto`	`goto` is used to transfer control to a specific label when the expression evaluates to `true`.

In the following subsections, we will cover each of these statements in detail.

if...else

Using the `if` statement is simple and easy in a scenario where the user wants to execute a specific code block when a condition is met. C# provides us with widely used if statements that allow us to achieve the desired functionality.

`If (true)` **then-statements** `Else (false)` else-statements. The following is the general syntax of the `If / Else` statement:

```
If(Boolean expression)
{
    Then statements;  //these are executed when Boolean expression is true
}
Else
{
    Else statements; //these are executed when Boolean expression is false
}
```

When the Boolean expression evaluates to true, `then-statements` are executed, and when the Boolean expression evaluates to false, `else-statements` are executed. When the Boolean expression evaluates to either true or false, the program allows you to execute single or multiple statements. However, multiple statements need to be enclosed in curly braces, `{ }`. This will ensure that all the statements are executed in one context and in sequence. This is also called a **code block**. For single statements, these braces are optional, but they are recommended from a code readability point of view. Also, we need to understand that the scope of the variables is limited to the code block they were defined in.

The else statement is optional. If this is not provided, the program evaluates the Boolean expression and executes the `then-statement`. At any given time, either the `then-statements` or the `else-statements` of an `if-else` statement will be executed.

Let's look at a few examples. In the following code block, we have already set the condition variable to `true`, so when the Boolean expression in the if statement is evaluated, it returns `true` and the code block (`then-statement`) is executed. `Else-statement` is ignored:

```
bool condition = true;
if (condition)
{
    Console.WriteLine("Then-Statement executed");
}
else
{
    Console.WriteLine("Else-Statement executed");
}
//output: Then-Statement executed
```

In the following scenario, if the statement doesn't include the else part, when the Boolean expression is evaluated to `true`, `then-statements` is executed by default:

```
if (condition)
{
    Console.WriteLine("Then-Statement without an Else executed");
}
//output: Then-Statement without an Else executed
```

C# also allows nested `if` and nested `else` statements. In the following code, we will see how nested if statements can be used in a program.

When condition 1 is evaluated to `true`, by default, the then-statements of condition 1 are executed. Similarly, when condition 2 is evaluated to `true`, the then-statements of condition 2 are executed:

```
int variable1 = 15;
int variable2 = 10;


if (variable1 > 10)//Condition 1
{
    Console.WriteLine("Then-Statement of condition 1 executed");
    if (variable2 < 15) //Condition 2
    {
        Console.WriteLine("Then-Statement of condition 2 executed");
    }
    else
    {
        Console.WriteLine("Else-Statement of condition 2 executed");
    }
}
else
{
    Console.WriteLine("Then-Statement condition 1 executed");
}
//Output:
Then-Statement of condition 1 executed
Then-Statement of condition 2 executed
```

We can also define a nested if in an `Else` statement. For example, the user wants to find out whether the character that was entered was a vowel and, if so, to print it. The following code block illustrates how multiple if statements can be used. The program checks if the entered character is a vowel or not and prints the results:

```
Console.Write("Enter a character: ");
char ch = (char)Console.Read();
if (ch.Equals('a'))
{
    Console.WriteLine("The character entered is a vowel and it is 'a'.");
}
else if (ch.Equals('e'))
{
    Console.WriteLine("The character entered is a vowel and it is 'e'.");
}
else if (ch.Equals('i'))
{
    Console.WriteLine("The character entered is a vowel and it is 'i'.");
}
```

```
else if (ch.Equals('o'))
{
    Console.WriteLine("The character entered is a vowel and it is 'o'.");
}
else if (ch.Equals('u'))
{
    Console.WriteLine("The character entered is a vowel and it is 'u'.");
}
else
{
    Console.WriteLine("The character entered is not vowel. It is:" + ch );
}
```

switch..case..default

The switch statement evaluates an expression against a condition or multiple conditions and executes a labeled code block. These labeled code blocks are called switch labels. Each switch label is followed by a break statement which helps the program come out of the loop and move on to the next statement. In the preceding example, where we checked for vowels using the if...else statement, we used if...else for each vowel and a default value for any other character. This can be further simplified using a switch...case...default statement.

All we want is to have a condition expression check the character. If it matches any of the matching expressions, that is, a vowel, it prints the vowel; otherwise, it prints that it is not a vowel:

```
Console.Write("Enter a character: ");
char ch1 = (char)Console.Read();
switch (ch1)
{
    case 'a' :
    case 'e':
    case 'i' :
    case 'o' :
    case 'u':
     Console.WriteLine("The character entered is a vowel and it is: " +
ch1);
        break;
    default:
        Console.WriteLine("The character entered is not vowel and it is: "
+ ch1);
        break;
}
```

break

In C#, the `break;` statement allows us to break a loop or a block of statements where it is enclosed. For example, in a recursive function, you might need to break after n number of iterations. Alternatively, in an example where you want to print the first 5 numbers in a loop of 10 iterations, you will want to use the break statement:

```
for (int i = 1; i <= 10; i++)
{
    if (i == 5)
    {
        break;
    }
    Console.WriteLine(i);
}

//output:
1
2
3
4
```

goto

`Goto` statements allow the program to transfer control to a specific section or code block. This is also called a labeled statement. The classic example is the `Switch..case` statement, which we discussed in the previous section. When an expression matches a case, the labeled criteria statements in that code block are executed:

```
for (int i = 1; i <= 10; i++)
{
    if (i == 5)
    {
        goto   number5;
    }
    Console.WriteLine(i);
}
number5:
    Console.WriteLine("You are here because of Goto Label");
//Output
1
2
3
4
You are here because of Goto Label
```

continue

The `continue;` statement allows the program to skip the execution of statements until the end of that code block and continues with the next iteration. For example, in a `for` loop of `1..10`, if the continue statement is placed within an expression, that is, `i <= 5`, it looks at all 10 numbers, but the action will only be performed on 6, 7, 8, 9, and 10:

```
for (int i = 1; i <= 10; i++)
{
    if (i <= 5)
    {
        continue;
    }
    Console.WriteLine(i);
}
//output
6
7
8
9
10
```

Iteration statements

Iteration statements help execute a loop for a specific number of times or while a conditional expression is met. All of the statements in a code block are executed in sequence when a loop initiates. If the program encounters a `jump statement` or `continue statement`, the execution flow is altered for that scenario. In the case of `go-to`, control moves to the labeled code block and, in the case of `continue statement`, the loop ignores all of the statements after `continue`.

The following are the keywords that are used in C# when an iteration or a loop is required:

- `do`
- `for`
- `foreach...in`
- `while`

do...while

A do statement is always used along with a `while` statement. The do statement executes a code block and evaluates the `while` expression. If the `while` statement evaluates to `true`, the code block is executed again. This continues as long as `while` evaluates to `true`. Because the condition expression is evaluated after the code block is executed, `do...while` always executes the code block at least once.

`break;`, `continue;`, `return`, or `throw` can be used to come out of this loop any time during execution:

```
int intvariable = 0;
do
{
    Console.WriteLine("Number is :" + intvariable);
    intvariable++;

} while (intvariable < 5);

//Output
Number is :0
Number is :1
Number is :2
Number is :3
Number is :4
```

for

Unlike `do..while`, `for` evaluates the condition expression first and if `true`, executes the code block. The code block will not be executed once unless the condition is true. Similar to `do..while`, we can come out of the loop using the `return`, `throw`, `goto`, or `continue` statements.

Take a look at the following `for` statement's structure:

```
for (initializer; condition; iterator)
{
    body
}
```

The initializer, condition, and iterator are all optional. The body can be one statement or an entire code block:

```
for (int i = 0; i <= 5; i++)
{
    Console.WriteLine("Number is :" + i);
}

//output
Number is :0
Number is :1
Number is :2
Number is :3
Number is :4
Number is :5
```

Initializer section

This section is executed only once. When the program's control encounters a `for` loop, the initialization section is triggered. # allows one or more of the following statements in the initializer section of the `for` loop, separated by a comma:

- Declaration of the local loop variable. This is not available outside of the loop.
- An assignment statement.
- Method invocation.
- Pre/post increment or decrement.
- New object creation.
- Await expression. We will look at this in more detail in the upcoming chapters.

Condition section

As we mentioned earlier, this is an optional section. If it's not provided, by default, it is evaluated as `true`. If it is provided, the condition expression is evaluated before executing every iteration. If the condition evaluates to `false`, the loop is terminated.

Iteration section

The iteration section defines what happens to the body of the loop. As detailed in the *Initializer section* section, it can contain one or more of the aforementioned statements.

Examples of rare usage for statements

Here is an example for your reference:

```
int k;
int j = 10;
for (k = 0, Console.WriteLine("Start: j={j}"); k < j; k++, j--,
Console.WriteLine("Step: k={k}, j={j}"))
{
    // Body of the loop.
}
for (; ; )
{
    // Body of the loop.
}
```

foreach...in

Foreach is applicable to instances of the IEnumerable type or Generic collections. This works similar to the for loop. Foreach is not just limited to these types; it can also be applied to any instance that implements the GetEnumerator method without parameters and returns a class, struct, or interface type. Foreach can also be applied to types that are returned by the Current property of GetEnumerator and parameter less MoveNext methods, which return a bool value.

> From C# 7.3 onward, the Current property returns a reference to the return value (ref T), where T is of the collection element type.

In the following example, we declare the list of strings and would like to iterate through the list and display every item on the screen:

```
List<string> stringlist = new List<string>() { "One", "Two", "Three" };
foreach (string str in stringlist)
{
    Console.WriteLine("Element #"+ str);
}

//Output:
Element #One
Element #Two
Element #Three
```

IEnumerator has a property called Current and a method called MoveNext. As the foreach loop works to iterate the throw collections that implement these two, it keeps track of which item in the collection is currently being evaluated and processed. This makes sure that control is not passed through the end of the collection. Also, the foreach loop doesn't allow the user to make changes to the initialized loop variable but does allow them to modify the value in the object that's referred to in the variable.

while

Similar to the for loop, a condition is evaluated before we execute the code block. This means that the code block is either executed more than once or not executed at all. Just like any other loop, you can come out of the loop using the break, continue, return, or throw statements:

```
int n = 0;
while (n < 5)
{
    Console.WriteLine(n);
    n++;
}
//output
0
1
2
3
4
```

Summary

In this chapter, we looked at Unary operators, relational operators, shift operators, and equality, conditional, and logical operators, which can be used with one or two operands and evaluated as boolean expressions using logical and conditional operators.

We looked at conditional statements and selective statements, which help us make decisions. Some examples of these are the if condition, then statements, and else statements. Switch...case...default helps match multiple expressions and execute multiple switch labels.

We also looked at iteration statements, which allow users to loop through a collection. When they're used with jump statements such as goto, continue, and so on, they can exit from the loop.

In the next chapter, we will look into delegates and events in detail. Delegates and events play a major role in C# programming. Being able to call back delegates for the base for events allows us to decouple our program. We will also understand Lambda expressions, which can be used to create delegates. These are also called **anonymous** methods.

Questions

1. You have a scenario where you are evaluating a lot of conditions. In one particular scenario, you want both operands to be evaluated and, if true, execute the code block. Which one of the following statements would you use?
   a. `&&`
   b. `||`
   c. `&`
   d. `^`

2. You are using a `for` loop in your code and want to execute a specific code block if a condition is met. Which one of the following statements would you use?
   a. `break;`
   b. `continue;`
   c. `throw;`
   d. `goto;`

3. In your program, there is a code block that you want to execute at least once and execute until the condition evaluates to true. Which of the following statements would you use?
   a. `While;`
   b. `Do...while;`
   c. `For;`
   d. `foreach;`

Answers

1. **c**
2. **d**
3. **b**

Further reading

More information on statements, expressions, and operators can be found at `https://docs.microsoft.com/en-us/dotnet/csharp/programming-guide/statements-expressions-operators/`.

There is a video available on the Packt Publishing site that's helpful as well. It's called *Programming in C# .NET* (`https://search.packtpub.com/?query=70-483&refinementList%5Breleased%5D%5B0%5D=Available`).

5
Creating and Implementing Events and Callbacks

This chapter focuses on events and callbacks in C#. They are important to understand since they give us more control over programs. An event is a message or notification from an object when either its property has been changed or a button has been clicked. A callback, also known as a delegate, holds a reference to a function. C# comes with Lambda expressions, which can be used to create delegates. These are also called anonymous methods.

We will also spend some time looking at a new operator, known as a Lambda operator. These are used in Lambda expressions. They were introduced in version 3.0 of C# so that developers could instantiate delegates. Lambda expressions replaced the anonymous methods that were introduced in C# 2.0 and are now widely used.

In this chapter, we will be covering the following topics:

- Understanding delegates
- Handling and raising events

By the end of this chapter, you will know what delegates are and how you can use them in events and callbacks.

Technical requirements

The exercises in this chapter can be practiced using Visual Studio 2012 or above with .NET Framework 2.0 or above. However, any new C# features from 7.0 onward require that you have Visual Studio 2017 installed.

If you don't have a license for any of the aforementioned products, you can download the community version of Visual Studio 2017 from `https://visualstudio.microsoft.com/downloads/`.

The sample code for this chapter can be found on GitHub at `https://github.com/PacktPublishing/Programming-in-C-Sharp-Exam-70-483-MCSD-Guide`.

Understanding delegates

A **delegate** is nothing but a reference to a method, along with some parameters and a return type. When a delegate is defined, it can be associated with any instance that provides a compatible signature and a return type of the method. In other terms, delegates can be defined as function pointers in C and C++. However, delegates are type-safe, secure, and object-oriented.

A delegate model follows the observer pattern, which allows the subscriber to register with and receive notifications from the provider. To get a better understanding of the observer pattern, take a look at the references provided at the end of this chapter, in the *Further reading* section.

A classic example of a delegate is event handlers in a Windows application, which are methods that are invoked by delegates. In the context of events, a delegate is an intermediary between the event source and the code that handles the event.

Delegates are ideal for callbacks because of their ability to pass methods as parameters. Delegates are derived from the `System.Delegate` class.

The general syntax of `delegate` is as follows:

```
delegate <return type> <delegate name> <parameter list>
```

An example of a delegate declaration is as follows:

```
public delegate string delegateexample (string strVariable);
```

In the preceding example, the delegate that's been defined can be referenced by any method that has a single string parameter and returns a string variable.

Instantiating a delegate

The named method can be used to a when we're using versions of C# prior to 2.0. Version 2.0 introduced a new way to instantiate delegates. We will try to understand these methods in the upcoming sections. Version 3.0 of C# replaces anonymous methods with Lambda expressions, which are now widely used.

Initiating delegates using NamedMethod

Let's look at an example of `NamedMethod` so that we can understand how to initiate a delegate. This is the method that was used prior to C# 2.0:

```
delegate void MathDelegate(int i, double j);
public class Chapter5Samples
{
  // Declare a delegate
  public void NamedMethod()
  {
    Chapter5Samples m = new Chapter5Samples();
    // Delegate instantiation using "Multiply"
    MathDelegate d = m.Multiply;
    // Invoke the delegate object.
    Console.WriteLine("Invoking the delegate using 'Multiply':");
    for (int i = 1; i <= 5; i++)
    {
      d(i, 5);
    }
    Console.WriteLine("");

  }
  // Declare the associated method.
  void Multiply(int m, double n)
  {
    System.Console.Write(m * n + " ");
  }
}
//Output:
Invoking the delegate using 'Multiply':
5 10 15 20 25
```

In the preceding code, first, we defined a delegate called `MathDelegate`, which accepts 2 parameters, 1 integer and another double type. Then, we defined a class where we wanted to invoke `MathDelegate` using a named method known as `Multiply`.

The `MathDelegate d = m.Multiply;` line is where we assigned a named method to a delegate.

Named method delegates can encapsulate a static or instance method with any accessible class or structure that matches the type of delegate. This allows the developer to extend these methods.

In the following example, we will see how a delegate can be mapped to static and instance methods. Add the following method to the `Chapter5Samples` class we created previously:

```
public void InvokeDelegate()
{
  HelperClass helper = new HelperClass();

  // Instance method mapped to delegate:
  SampleDelegate d = helper.InstanceMethod;
  d();

  // Map to the static method:
  d = HelperClass.StaticMethod;
  d();
}

//Create a new Helper class to hold two methods
// Delegate declaration
delegate void SampleDelegate();

internal class HelperClass
{
  public void InstanceMethod()
  {
    System.Console.WriteLine("Instance Method Invoked.");
  }

  static public void StaticMethod()
  {
    System.Console.WriteLine("Invoked function Static Method.");
  }
}

//Output:
Invoked function Instance Method.
Invoked function Static Method.
```

In the preceding code, we defined two methods: the first one is a normal method, while the second one is a static method. In the case of invoking delegates using a named method, we can either use the first normal method or the second static method:

- `SampleDelegate d = helper.InstanceMethod;`: This is a normal method.
- `d = HelperClass.StaticMethod;`: This is a static method.

Initiating a delegate using anonymous functions

In a situation where creating new methods can be classed as overhead, C# allows us to initiate a delegate and specify a code block. The delegate will process this code block when it is invoked. This is the method that's used in C# 2.0 to invoke delegates. They are also known as anonymous methods.

An expression or a statement that's defined inline instead of a delegate type is known as an anonymous function.

There are two types of anonymous function:

- Lambda expressions
- Anonymous methods

We will look at these two types of functions in the upcoming subsections. However, before we move on, we should also understand one new operator, called the **Lambda operator**. This is used to represent Lambda expressions.

Lambda expressions

With C# 3.0, Lambda expressions were introduced and are widely used in invoking delegates. Lambda expressions are created using Lambda operators. On the left-hand side of the operator, we specify the input parameters, while on the left-hand side, we specify the expression or code block. When a Lambda operator is used in an expression body, it separates the member's name from the member's implementation.

The Lambda operator is represented as a => token. This operator is right-associative and has the same precedence as an assignment operator. An assignment operator assigns a right-hand operand value to a left-hand operand.

In the following code, we are using a Lambda operator to compare a specific word in a string array and return it. Here, we are applying a Lambda expression to each element of the `words` array:

```
words.Where(w => w.Equals("apple")).FirstOrDefault();
```

This example also shows how we can use a LINQ query to get the same output.

We are trying to find "apple" from an array of words using a LINQ query. Any enumerable collection allows us to query using LINQ and returns the desired output:

```
public void LambdaOperatorExample()
{
    string[] words = { "bottle", "jar", "drum" };
    // apply Lambda expression to each element in the array
    string searchedWord = words.Where(w =>
                            w.Equals("drum")).FirstOrDefault();
    Console.WriteLine(searchedWord);
    // Get the length of each word in the array.
    var query = from w in words
                where w.Equals("drum")
                select w;
    string search2 = query.FirstOrDefault();
    Console.WriteLine(search2);
}

//Output:
drum
drum
```

A Lambda expression is the right-hand side operator of a Lambda operator and is widely used in expression trees.

 More information on expression trees can be on the Microsoft documentation website.

This Lambda expression must be a valid expression. If the member type is void, it's classed as a statement expression.

From C# 6 onward, these expressions support method and property get statements, while from C# 7 onward, these expressions support constructors, finalizers, property set statements, and indexers.

In the following code, we are using an expression to write the first name and last name of the variable and we have also used the `Trim()` function:

```
public override string ToString() => $"{fname} {lname}".Trim();
```

With this basic understanding of Lambda expressions and the Lambda operator, we can move on and look at how we can use Lambda expressions to invoke a delegate.

Recall that a Lambda expression can be represented like so:

```
Input-Parameters => Expression
```

In the following example, two extra lines have been added to the existing method to invoke the delegate using a Lambda expression. X is the input parameter, where the type of X is identified by the compiler:

```
delegate void StringDelegate(string strVariable);
public void InvokeDelegatebyAnonymousFunction()
{
  //Named Method
  StringDelegate StringDel = HelperClass.StringMethod;
  StringDel("Chapter 5 - Named Method");

  //Anonymous method
  StringDelegate StringDelB = delegate (string s) { Console.WriteLine(s);
};
  StringDelB("Chapter 5- Anonymous method invocation");

  //LambdaExpression
  StringDelegate StringDelC = (X)=> { Console.WriteLine(X); };
  StringDelB("Chapter 5- Lambda Expression invocation");

}

//Output:
Chapter 5 - Named Method
Chapter 5- Anonymous method invocation
Chapter 5- Lambda Expression invocation
```

Anonymous methods

C# 2.0 introduced anonymous methods, while C# 3.0 introduced Lambda expressions, which were later replaced with anonymous methods.

One case where anonymous methods provide functionality that isn't possible when using a Lambda expression is that they allow us to avoid parameters. These allow anonymous methods to be converted into delegates with a number of different signatures.

Let's look at an example of how to use anonymous methods to initiate a delegate:

```
public void InvokeDelegatebyAnonymousFunction()
{
  //Named Method
  StringDelegate StringDel = HelperClass.StringMethod;
  StringDel("Chapter 5");

  //Anonymous method
  StringDelegate StringDelB = delegate (string s) { Console.WriteLine(s);
};
  StringDelB("Chapter 5- Anonymous method invocation");

}
internal class HelperClass
{
  public void InstanceMethod()
  {
    System.Console.WriteLine("Instance method Invoked.");
  }

  public static void StaticMethod()
  {
    System.Console.WriteLine("Invoked function Static Method.");
  }

  public static void StringMethod(string s)
  {
    Console.WriteLine(s);
  }
}

//Output:
Chapter 5
Chapter 5- Anonymous method invocation
```

In the preceding code, we defined a string delegate and wrote some inline code to invoke it. The following is the code where we defined the inline delegate, also known as an anonymous method:

```
StringDelegate StringDelB = delegate (string s) { Console.WriteLine(s); };
```

The following code shows how we can create an anonymous method:

```
// Creating a handler for a click event.
sampleButton.Click += delegate(System.Object o, System.EventArgs e)
                  { System.Windows.Forms.MessageBox.Show(
                    "Sample Button Clicked!"); };
```

Here, we created a code block and passed it as a `delegate` parameter.

An anonymous method will throw an error if the runtime encounters any jump statements, such as `goto`, `break`, or `continue`, inside the code block and the target is outside the code block. Also, in a scenario where a jump statement is outside the code block and the target is in it, with the `int` anonymous method, an exception will be thrown.

Any local variables that are created outside of the delegate's scope and contained in an anonymous method declaration are called *outer* variables of the anonymous method. For example, in the following code segment, `n` is an outer variable:

```
int n = 0;
Del d = delegate() { System.Console.WriteLine("Copy #:{0}", ++n); };
```

Anonymous methods are not allowed on the left-hand side of the is operator. No unsafe code can be accessed or used in an anonymous method, including the `in`, `ref`, or `out` parameters of an outer scope.

Variance in delegates

C# supports variance in delegate types with matching method signatures. This feature was introduced in .NET Framework 3.5. This means delegates can now be assigned with matching signatures but also that methods can return derived types.

If a method has a return type derived from the one defined in a delegate, it is defined as covariance in delegates. Similarly, if a method has fewer derived parameter types than those defined in a delegate, it is defined as contravariance.

Let's look at an example to understand covariance. For the purpose of this example, we will create a few classes.

Here, we will create the `ParentReturnClass`, `Child1ReturnClass`, and `Child2Return` classes. Each of these has a string type property. Both child classes are inherited from `ParentReturnClass`:

```
internal class ParentReturnClass
{
  public string Message { get; set; }
}

internal class Child1ReturnClass : ParentReturnClass
{
  public string ChildMessage1 { get; set; }
}
internal class Child2ReturnClass : ParentReturnClass
{
  public string ChildMessage2 { get; set; }
}
```

Now, let's add two new methods to the previously defined helper class, each returning the respective child classes we defined earlier:

```
public Child1ReturnClass ChildMehod1()
{
    return new Child1ReturnClass
    {
        ChildMessage1 = "ChildMessage1"
    };
}
public Child2ReturnClass ChildMehod2()
{
    return new Child2ReturnClass
    {
        ChildMessage2 = "ChildMessage2"
    };
}
```

Now, we will define a delegate that returns `ParentReturnClass`. We'll also define a new method that will initiate this delegate for each of the child methods. One important point to observe in the following code is that we have used explicit typecast to convert `ParentReturnClass` into `ChildReturnClass1` and `ChildReturnClass2`:

```
delegate ParentReturnClass covrianceDelegate();
public void CoVarianceSample()
{
  covrianceDelegate cdel;
  cdel = new HelperClass().ChildMehod1;
  Child1ReturnClass CR1 = (Child1ReturnClass)cdel();
```

```
    Console.WriteLine(CR1.ChildMessage1);
    cdel = new HelperClass().ChildMehod2;
 Child2ReturnClass CR2 = (Child2ReturnClass)cdel();
Console.WriteLine(CR2.ChildMessage2);
}
```

```
//Output:
ChildMessage1
ChildMessage2
```

In the preceding example, the delegate is returning `ParentReturnClass`. However, both `ChildMethod1` and `ChildMethod2` are returning child classes that were inherited from `ParentReturnClass`. This means that methods that return more derived types than those defined in the delegate are permitted. This is called covariance.

Now, let's look at another example to understand contravariance. Extend the previously created helper class by adding a new method that accepts `ParentReturnClass` as a parameter and returns void:

```
public void Method1(ParentReturnClass parentVariable1)
{
    Console.WriteLine(((Child1ReturnClass)parentVariable1).ChildMessage1);
}
```

Define a delegate that accepts `Child1ReturnClass` as a parameter:

```
delegate void contravrianceDelegate(Child1ReturnClass variable1);
```

Now, create a method to initiate the delegate:

```
public void ContraVarianceSample()
{
  Child1ReturnClass CR1 = new Child1ReturnClass() { ChildMessage1 =
"ChildMessage1" };
  contravrianceDelegate cdel = new HelperClass().Method1;
  cdel(CR1);
}
```

```
//Output:
ChildMessage1
```

Because method one works with the parent class, it will definitely work with the class that is inherited from the parent class. C# permits fewer derived types as parameters than those defined in the delegate.

Built-in delegates

So far, we have seen how we can create custom delegates and use them in our program. C# comes with a couple of built-in delegates, which developers can use instead of having to create custom delegates. They are as follows:

- Func
- Action

Func takes zero or more parameters and returns one value as an out parameter, whereas Action accepts zero or more parameters but returns nothing.

There is no requirement to declare an explicit delegate when working with Func or Action:

```
public delegate TResult Func<out TResult>();
```

Action can be defined as follows:

```
public delegate void Action();
```

As we mentioned earlier, both take zero or more parameters. C# supports 16 different forms of both delegates, all of which can be used in our program.

The general form of Func with two or more parameters is as follows. It takes comma-separated in and out parameters, where the last parameter is always an out parameter called TResult:

```
public delegate TResult Func<in T1,in T2,in T3,in T4,out TResult>(T1 arg1,
T2 arg2, T3 arg3, T4 arg4);
```

Similar to Func, here is the general form for Action with two or more parameters:

```
public delegate void Action<in T1,in T2,in T3,in T4>(T1 arg1, T2 arg2, T3
arg3, T4 arg4);
```

Multicast delegates

Invoking more than one method through a delegate is called multicasting. You can use +, - , +=, or -+ to add or remove methods from the list of invoking methods. This list is called the invocation list. It's used in event handling.

The following example shows how we can invoke multiple methods by invoking a delegate. We have two methods, both of which accept a string parameter and display it on the screen. In the multicast delegate method, we are associating two methods with `stringdelegate`:

```
delegate void StringDelegate( string strVariable);
public void MulticastDelegate()
{
  StringDelegate StringDel = HelperClass.StringMethod;
  StringDel += HelperClass.StringMethod2;
  StringDel("Chapter 5 - Multicast delegate Method1");
}

//Helper Class Methods
public static void StringMethod(string s)
{
  Console.WriteLine(s);
}

public static void StringMethod2(string s)
{
  Console.WriteLine("Method2 :" + s);
}


/Output:
Chapter 5 - Multicast delegate Method1
Method2 :Chapter 5 - Multicast delegate Method1
```

Handling and raising events

As we mentioned in the introduction of this chapter, events are any actions, such as a keypress, mouse movement, or I/O operation, performed by the user. Sometimes, events can be raised by system-generated operations such as creating/updating a record in a table.

.NET Framework events are based on the delegate model, which follows the observer pattern. The observer pattern allows a subscriber to register for notifications and a publisher to register for push notifications. It's like late binding and is a way for an object to broadcast that something has happened.

A design pattern that allows you to subscribe/unsubscribe to a stream of events coming from a publisher is called an observer pattern.

For example, in the previous chapter, we worked on a code snippet where the program finds whether the character that was entered by the user is a vowel or not. Here, the user pressing a key on the keyboard is the publisher, which notifies the program regarding which key was pressed. Now, our program, which is a subscriber to the provider, responds to it by checking whether the character that was entered was a vowel or not and displays it on the screen.

A message that's sent by an object to notify it that an action has occurred is called an event. The object that raises this event is called an event sender or publisher. An object that receives and responds to an event is called a subscriber.

A publisher event can have multiple subscribers, while a subscriber can handle publishing events. Remember that multicast delegates, which we discussed in the previous sections, are extensively used in events (publish-subscribe pattern).

By default, if a publisher has multiple subscribers, all are invoked synchronously. C# supports calling these event methods asynchronously. We will understand this in more detail in the upcoming chapters.

Before we dive into an example, let's try to understand a few of the terms we are going to use:

event	This is a keyword that's used to define an event in the `publisher` class in C#.
EventHandler	This method is used to handle an event. This may or may not have event data.
EventArgs	It represents a base class for the class that contains event data.

Event handlers support two variations: one with no event data and another with event data. The following code represents a method that handles an event with no event data:

```
public delegate void EventHandler(object sender, EventArgs e);
```

The following code represents a method that handles an event with event data:

```
public delegate void EventHandler<TEventArgs>(object sender, TEventArgs e);
```

Let's look at an example and try to understand how we can raise events and handle them.

 In this scenario, we are going to have a banking application where customers make transactions such as creating new accounts, looking at their credit and debit amounts, and making requests for their total balance. We will raise events whenever such a transaction is made and notify the customer.

We will start with an `Account` class (`publisher` class), along with all the supporting methods, such as `credit()`, `debit()`, `showbalance()`, and `initialdeposit()`. These are the types of transactions a customer can operate their account with. Because the customer needs to be notified whenever such a transaction happens, we will define an event and an event handler with event data to handle the event:

```
public delegate void BankTransHandler(object sender,
BankTransEventArgs e); // Delegate Definition
    class Account
    {
        // Event Definition
        public event BankTransHandler ProcessTransaction;
        public int BALAmount;
        public void SetInitialDeposit(int amount)
        {
            this.BALAmount = amount;
            BankTransEventArgs e = new BankTransEventArgs(amount,
                            "InitialBalance");
            // InitialBalance transaction made
            OnProcessTransaction(e);
        }
        public void Debit(int debitAmount)
        {
            if (debitAmount < BALAmount)
            {
                BALAmount = BALAmount - debitAmount;
                BankTransEventArgs e = new BankTransEventArgs(
                                    debitAmount, "Debited");
                OnProcessTransaction(e); // Debit transaction made
            }
        }
        public void Credit(int creditAmount)
        {
            BALAmount = BALAmount + creditAmount;
            BankTransEventArgs e = new BankTransEventArgs(
                                creditAmount, "Credited");
            OnProcessTransaction(e); // Credit transaction made
        }
        public void ShowBalance()
        {
            BankTransEventArgs e = new BankTransEventArgs(
                                BALAmount, "Total Balance");
            OnProcessTransaction(e); // Credit transaction made
        }
        protected virtual void OnProcessTransaction(
                                BankTransEventArgs e)
        {
```

```
                    ProcessTransaction?.Invoke(this, e);
        }
    }
```

You may have observed the new class that we used in the previous example, that is, TrasactionEventArgs. This class carries event data. We are going to define this class now, which inherits from the EventArgs base class. We are going to define two variables, amt and type, to carry variables to the event handler:

```
public class BankTransEventArgs : EventArgs
    {
        private int _transactionAmount;
        private string _transactionType;
        public BankTransEventArgs(int amt, string type)
        {
            this._transactionAmount = amt;
            this._transactionType = type;
        }
        public int TransactionAmount
        {
            get
            {
                return _transactionAmount;
            }
        }
        public string TranactionType
        {
            get
            {
                return _transactionType;
            }
        }
    }
```

Now, let's define a subscriber class to test how our event and event handler work. Here, we will define an AlertCustomer method whose signature matches the delegate that was declared in the publisher class. Pass a reference of this method to the delegate so that it reacts to the event:

```
public class EventSamples
{
 private void AlertCustomer(object sender, BankTransEventArgs e)
 {
  Console.WriteLine("Your Account is {0} for Rs.{1} ",
                    e.TranactionType, e.TransactionAmount);
 }
 public void Run()
```

```
  {
  Account bankAccount = new Account();
  bankAccount.ProcessTransaction += new
      BankTransHandler(AlertCustomer);
  bankAccount.SetInitialDeposit(5000);
  bankAccount.ShowBalance();
  bankAccount.Credit(500);
  bankAccount.ShowBalance();
  bankAccount.Debit(500);
  bankAccount.ShowBalance();
  }
}
```

When you execute the preceding program, for each transaction made, a transaction handler event is raised that invokes the notify-customer method and displays what type of transactions took place on the screen, as follows:

```
//Output:
Your Account is InitialBalance for Rs.5000
Your Account is Total Balance for Rs.5000
Your Account is Credited for Rs.500
Your Account is Total Balance for Rs.5500
Your Account is Debited for Rs.500
Your Account is Total Balance for Rs.5000
```

Summary

In this chapter, we learned about delegates and how we can define, initiate, and use them in our program. We understood variance in delegates, built-in delegates, and multicast delegates. Finally, we looked at how delegates form the base for events before understanding events, event handlers, and `EventArgs`.

Now, we can say that events encapsulate delegates and that delegates encapsulate methods.

In the next chapter, we will learn about multithreading and asynchronous processing in C#. We will understand and use threads in our program, and understand tasks, parallel classes, async, await, and much more.

Questions

1. Delegates are ideal for ___ because of their ability to pass a method as a parameter.
    1. Multicast delegates
    2. Built-in delegates
    3. Callbacks
    4. Events

2. What are the different ways to initiate delegates? Choose all that apply.
    1. Anonymous methods
    2. Lambda expressions
    3. Named methods
    4. All of the above

3. Which method can have a derived return type than the one defined in the delegate.
    1. Anonymous method
    2. Covariance
    3. Anonymous function
    4. Lambda expression

4. Which built-in delegate accepts zero or more parameters and returns void?
    1. `Action`
    2. `Func`
    3. `event`
    4. `delegate`

5. Which of the following is used in the declaration of a C# event?
    1. `event`
    2. `delegate`
    3. `EventHandler`
    4. `class`

6. A subscriber can notify the publisher about a change that happened to an object.
    1. True
    2. False

Answers

1. **Callbacks**
2. **All of the above**
3. **Covariance**
4. **Action**
5. **event**
6. **False**

Further reading

To get a better understanding of the observer pattern, please take a look at `https://docs.microsoft.com/en-us/dotnet/standard/events/observer-design-pattern`.

The following is a good article that talks about declaring, initiating, and using delegates. Samples can also be found there: `https://docs.microsoft.com/en-us/dotnet/csharp/programming-guide/delegates/how-to-declare-instantiate-and-use-a-delegate`.

6
Managing and Implementing Multithreading

What happens when a long-running program starts executing on a client's computer? How do operating systems handle such long-running processes? Does the operating system notify the user about their progress? How does the operating system let the user know when it has finished with these processes? Threading is the way in which the operating system handles the responsiveness of your program while managing other system resources. This is achieved using multiple threads of execution, which is one of the most powerful ways to keep your application responsive while using the processor for other events.

An operating system organizes each running application as a process. Each process may contain one or more threads. A thread allows the operating system to allocate processor time as required. Each thread holds scheduling priority and a set of structures that are used by the system to pause or execute the thread. This is called **thread context**. In other words, the thread context holds all the information that's required by the system to seamlessly resume execution. As we've already mentioned, a process can contain multiple threads, all of which share the same virtual address space of the process.

In this chapter, we will focus on creating and managing threads, synchronizing data across threads, and multithreading. We'll also look at how the operating system uses this concept to keep the responsiveness of the application.

In this chapter, we will cover the following topics:

- Understanding threads and the threading process
- Synchronizing data in multithreading
- Multithreading

Technical requirements

The exercises in this chapter can be practiced using Visual Studio 2012 or above with .NET Framework 2.0 or above. However, any new C# features from C# 7.0 and above require that you have Visual Studio 2017 installed.

If you don't have a license for any of the aforementioned products, you can download the community version of Visual Studio 2017 from `https://visualstudio.microsoft.com/downloads/`.

The sample code for this chapter can be found on GitHub at `https://github.com/PacktPublishing/Programming-in-C-sharp-Exam-70-483-MCSD-Guide/tree/master/Chapter06`.

Understanding threads and the threading process

A primary thread is started whenever a .NET program is started. Additional threads are created by this primary thread to execute the application login either concurrently or in parallel. These threads are called **worker threads**. These threads can execute any part of the program code, which may include parts that are executed by another thread. As these threads are free to cross application boundaries, .NET Framework provides a way to isolate these threads within a process using application domains (not available in .NET Core).

If our program can perform multiple operations in parallel, it will drastically decrease the total execution time. This can be achieved by utilizing multiple threads with multiprocessors or the multicore environment. The Windows operating system, when used alongside .NET Framework, ensures that these threads complete their respective tasks. Managing these tasks does have overhead, however. The OS allocates each thread a certain period of CPU time so that they can execute. After this period, a thread switch happens, which is called context switching. This context is saved and restored for each switch. To do this, Windows uses CPU registers and state data.

In an environment where multiple processors and multicore systems are available, we can take advantage of these resources and increase the throughput of the application. Consider a Windows application in which one thread (the primary thread) is handling the user interface by responding to user actions and other threads (worker threads) perform operations that require more time and processing. If the primary thread completes all of these operations, the user interfaces won't be responsive.

Because of this overhead, we need to carefully determine when to use multithreading.

In the upcoming sections, we will focus on how we can create and manage threads, understand different thread properties, how we can create and pass parameters to threads, the difference between foreground and background threads, how to destroy threads, and more.

Managing threads

Threads can be created by creating a new instance of the `System.Threading` thread class and providing the name of the method that you want to execute on a new thread to the constructor. Using this class gives us more control and configuration of the program; for example, you can set the priority of the thread and whether it is a long-running thread, abort it, put it to sleep, and implement advanced configuration options.
The `Thread.Start` method is used to create a thread call, while
the `Thread.Abort` method is used to terminate the execution of a thread. The abort method raises `ThreadAbortException` when invoked. `Thread.Sleep` can be used to pause the execution of the thread for a certain amount of time. Finally, the `Thread.Interrupt` method is used to interrupt a blocked thread.

Let's understand these concepts by looking at a few examples.

In the following code, `ThreadSample` is the primary thread, which starts the worker thread. The worker thread loops 10 times and writes to the console, letting the process know it has completed. After starting the worker thread, the primary thread loops four times. Note that the output depends on the environment you are running this program on. Try to change the seconds in the `thread.sleep` statement and observe the output:

```
internal class ThreadingSamples
    {
        public static void ThreadSample()
        {
            Console.WriteLine("Primary thread: Starting a new worker
thread.");
            Thread t = new Thread(new ThreadStart(ThreadOne));
            t.Start();
            //Thread.Sleep(1);
            for (int i = 0; i < 4; i++)
            {
                Console.WriteLine("Primary thread: Do something().");
                Thread.Sleep(1);

            }
```

```
            Console.WriteLine("Primary thread: Call Join(), to wait until
ThreadOne ends.");
            t.Join();
            Console.WriteLine("Primary thread: ThreadOne.Join has
returned.");
        }

        public static void ThreadOne()
        {
            for (int i = 0; i < 10; i++)
            {
                Console.WriteLine("ThreadOne running: {0}", i);
                Thread.Sleep(0);
            }
        }
    }
```

Let's check the output of our program. `ThreadOne` starts its execution first and initiates 10 different worker threads and then the primary thread is executed. If you delay the execution of `ThreadOne` by using sleep, you will see the primary thread wait until `ThreadOne` returns:

```
Primary thread: Starting a new worker thread.
Primary thread: Do something().
ThreadOne running: 0
ThreadOne running: 1
ThreadOne running: 2
ThreadOne running: 3
ThreadOne running: 4
ThreadOne running: 5
ThreadOne running: 6
ThreadOne running: 7
ThreadOne running: 8
ThreadOne running: 9
Primary thread: Do something().
Primary thread: Do something().
Primary thread: Do something().
Primary thread: Call Join(), to wait until ThreadOne ends.
Primary thread: ThreadOne.Join has returned.
Press any key to exit.
```

When the program is executed, a foreground thread is created automatically to execute the code. This primary thread then creates worker threads as required to execute the sections of the code from the same process. As you can see, the thread takes a delegate in its constructor.

In the preceding program, we used `thread.join`, which lets the primary thread wait until all the worker threads have completed their execution. Also, `Thread.Sleep(0)` tells Windows that the current thread has finished its execution so that a context switch can happen instead of Windows having to wait for the allocated time.

Thread properties

Each thread carries certain properties. The following table details each of them:

`IsAlive`	Returns `true` if the thread is in a started state.
`IsBackground`	Gets or sets this property to let the system know how to execute the thread.
`Name`	Name of the thread.
`Priority`	Gets or sets thread priority. The default is `Normal`.
`ThreadState`	Gets the thread's current state.

In the following code sample, we will call a method that will display information about some thread properties. We will also understand how we can pause a thread and terminate it:

```
public static void ThreadProperties()
{
    var th = new Thread(ThreadTwo);
    th.Start();
    Thread.Sleep(1000);
    Console.WriteLine("Primary thread ({0})
exiting...",Thread.CurrentThread.ManagedThreadId);
}

private static void ThreadTwo()
{
    var sw = Stopwatch.StartNew();
    Console.WriteLine("ThreadTwo Id: {0} Threadtwo state: {1}, Threadtwo
Priority: {2}",
                            Thread.CurrentThread.ManagedThreadId,
                            Thread.CurrentThread.ThreadState,
                            Thread.CurrentThread.Priority);
    do
    {
        Console.WriteLine("Threadtwo Id: {0}, Threadtwo elapsed time {1:N2}
seconds",
                            Thread.CurrentThread.ManagedThreadId,
                            sw.ElapsedMilliseconds / 1000.0);
        Thread.Sleep(500);
    } while (sw.ElapsedMilliseconds <= 3000);
```

```
        sw.Stop();
    }
```

When you execute the program, you will see the properties of each thread. You will also observe that although the primary thread has completed, the worker threads are still executing:

```
ThreadTwo Id: 3 Threadtwo state: Running, Threadtwo Priority: Normal
Threadtwo Id: 3, Threadtwo elapsed time 0.00 seconds
Threadtwo Id: 3, Threadtwo elapsed time 0.51 seconds
Primary thread (1) exiting...
Press any key to exit.
Threadtwo Id: 3, Threadtwo elapsed time 1.01 seconds
Threadtwo Id: 3, Threadtwo elapsed time 1.52 seconds
Threadtwo Id: 3, Threadtwo elapsed time 2.02 seconds
Threadtwo Id: 3, Threadtwo elapsed time 2.52 seconds
```

You might have observed that only one thread is writing to the console at a time. This is known as **synchronization**. In this case, it is handled by the console class for us. Synchronization allows no two threads to execute the same code block at the same time.

Parameterized threads

Here, we will look at how we can pass arguments to the `ThreadStart` method. To achieve this, we will be using the `ParameterizedThreadStart` delegate on the constructor. The signature of this delegate is as follows:

```
public delegate void ParameterizedThreadStart(object obj)
```

When you pass a parameter as an object to the `ThreadStart` method, it will cast the parameter to the appropriate type. The following sample program uses the same logic that we used previously, except that we pass the interval as an argument via the `ThreadStart` method:

```
public static void ParameterizedThread()
{
    var th = new Thread(ThreadThree);
    th.Start(3000);
    Thread.Sleep(1000);
    Console.WriteLine("Primary thread ({0}) exiting...",
Thread.CurrentThread.ManagedThreadId);
}

private static void ThreadThree(object obj)
```

```
{
    int interval = Convert.ToInt32(obj);
    var sw = Stopwatch.StartNew();
    Console.WriteLine("ThreadTwo Id: {0} ThreadThree state: {1},
ThreadThree Priority: {2}",
            Thread.CurrentThread.ManagedThreadId,
            Thread.CurrentThread.ThreadState,
            Thread.CurrentThread.Priority);
    do
    {
        Console.WriteLine("ThreadThree Id: {0}, ThreadThree elapsed time
{1:N2} seconds",
            Thread.CurrentThread.ManagedThreadId,
            sw.ElapsedMilliseconds / 1000.0);
        Thread.Sleep(500);
    } while (sw.ElapsedMilliseconds <= interval);
    sw.Stop();
}
```

The following screenshot shows the output of the preceding code:

```
ThreadTwo Id: 3 ThreadThree state: Running, ThreadThree Priority: Normal
ThreadThree Id: 3, ThreadThree elapsed time 0.00 seconds
ThreadThree Id: 3, ThreadThree elapsed time 0.51 seconds
Primary thread (1) exiting...
Press any key to exit.
ThreadThree Id: 3, ThreadThree elapsed time 1.01 seconds
ThreadThree Id: 3, ThreadThree elapsed time 1.51 seconds
ThreadThree Id: 3, ThreadThree elapsed time 2.01 seconds
ThreadThree Id: 3, ThreadThree elapsed time 2.51 seconds
```

Now, let's look at foreground and background threads.

Foreground and background threads

By default, when a thread is created, it is created as a foreground thread. You can use the IsBackground property to make a thread a background thread. The main difference between foreground and background threads is that a background thread does not run if all the foreground threads are terminated. The runtime aborts all the background threads when foreground threads are stopped. If a thread is created using a thread pool, then these threads are executed as background threads. Note that when an unmanaged thread enters the managed execution environment, it is executed as a background thread.

Let's jump into an example to understand the difference between foreground and background threads:

```
public static void BackgroundThread()
{
    Console.WriteLine("Thread Id: {0}" + Environment.NewLine + "Thread
State: {1}" + Environment.NewLine + "Priority {2}" + Environment.NewLine +
"IsBackground: {3}",
                            Thread.CurrentThread.ManagedThreadId,
                            Thread.CurrentThread.ThreadState,
                            Thread.CurrentThread.Priority,
                            Thread.CurrentThread.IsBackground);
    var th = new Thread(ExecuteBackgroundThread);
    th.IsBackground = true;
    th.Start();
    Thread.Sleep(500);
    Console.WriteLine("Main thread ({0})
exiting...",Thread.CurrentThread.ManagedThreadId);
}
private static void ExecuteBackgroundThread()
{
    var sw = Stopwatch.StartNew();
    Console.WriteLine("Thread Id: {0}" + Environment.NewLine + "Thread
State: {1}" +          Environment.NewLine + "Priority {2}" +
Environment.NewLine + "IsBackground {3}",
                            Thread.CurrentThread.ManagedThreadId,
                            Thread.CurrentThread.ThreadState,
                            Thread.CurrentThread.Priority,
                            Thread.CurrentThread.IsBackground);
    do
    {
        Console.WriteLine("Thread {0}: Elapsed {1:N2} seconds",
                            Thread.CurrentThread.ManagedThreadId,
                            sw.ElapsedMilliseconds / 1000.0);
        Thread.Sleep(2000);
    } while (sw.ElapsedMilliseconds <= 5000);
    sw.Stop();
}
```

The following screenshot shows the output of the preceding code:

```
Thread Id: 1
Thread State: Running
Priority Normal
IsBackground: False
Thread Id: 3
Thread State: Background
Priority Normal
IsBackground True
Thread 3: Elapsed 0.00 seconds
Main thread (1) exiting...
Press any key to exit.
Thread 3: Elapsed 2.01 seconds
Thread 3: Elapsed 4.02 seconds
```

As you can see, the primary thread was created as a foreground thread while the worker thread was created as a background thread. When we stopped the primary thread, it stopped the background thread. This is why the elapsed time statement was not displayed through the loop, which is running for 5 seconds (`while(sw.ElapsedMilliseconds <=5000)`).

Thread states

When a thread is created, it will be in an **Unstarted** state until the **Start** method is invoked. A thread is always in at least one state and sometimes it may be in multiple states at the same time. In the following diagram, each oval represents a state. The text on each line represents the action that is performed:

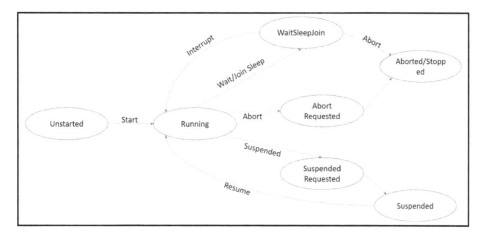

A thread can be in two different states at the same time. For example, if a thread is in a waiting state and another thread aborts, it can be in both the **Wait/Join Sleep** and **Abort Requested** states. When the thread returns to the wait call, it will receive a `ThreadAbortException`.

Destroying threads

The `Thread.Abort` method is used to stop a thread. Once aborted, it cannot be restarted. However, when you invoke `Thread.Abort`, it doesn't terminate the thread immediately since the `Thread.Abort` statement throws a `ThreadAbortException`, which needs to be caught. Then, the cleanup code should be executed. If you call the `Thread.Join` method, this will make sure the thread waits until the other thread's execution is completed. The `join` method depends on the timeout interval, so if it's not specified, then the wait is not guaranteed.

When your own code aborts a thread and you don't want to rethrow it, use the `ResetAbort` method. You will learn more about how to rethrow exceptions in Chapter 7, *Implementing Exception Handling*.

Thread pools

A thread pool provides a pool of threads that can be used as worker threads and are managed by the system. This allows us to focus on application logic instead of managing threads. This is an easy way for us to use multiple threads. From .NET Framework 4 onward, it became easy to use thread pools as they allowed us to create tasks and perform asynchronous tasks. The **Task Parallel Library** (**TPL**) and asynchronous method calls are mainly dependent on the thread pool.

Threads that are created from a thread pool are background threads. Each thread uses default properties. When a thread completes its task, it is returned to a queue of waiting threads so that they can be reused. In turn, this reduces the cost of creating new threads for every task. You can have one thread pool per process.

.NET Framework allows us to set and get `MaxThread` for a thread pool, though the number of threads that can be queued is limited by available memory. Once the thread pool threads are busy, other tasks are queued until the threads are available.

It is important to understand that any unhandled exception in a thread pool will terminate this process. More information on thread pools can be found at https://docs.microsoft.com/en-us/dotnet/standard/ threading/the-managed-thread-pool.

The following example shows how we can create multiple threads using a thread pool:

```
public static void PoolOfThreads()
{
    Console.WriteLine("Primary Thread Id: {0}" + Environment.NewLine +
"Thread State: {1}" + Environment.NewLine + "Priority {2}" ,
                        Thread.CurrentThread.ManagedThreadId,
                        Thread.CurrentThread.ThreadState,
                        Thread.CurrentThread.Priority);
    PoolProcessmethod();
    //Thread.CurrentThread.Join();
}
private static void PoolProcessmethod()
{
    for (int i = 0; i < 5; i++)
    {
        ThreadPool.QueueUserWorkItem(new WaitCallback(PoolMethod));
    }
}
private static void PoolMethod(object callback)
{
    Thread.Sleep(1000);
    Console.WriteLine("ThreadPool Thread Id: {0}" + Environment.NewLine +
"Thread State: {1}" + Environment.NewLine + "Priority {2}" +
Environment.NewLine + "IsBackground: {3}" +Environment.NewLine +
"IsThreadPoolThread: {4}",
                        Thread.CurrentThread.ManagedThreadId,
                        Thread.CurrentThread.ThreadState,
                        Thread.CurrentThread.Priority,
                        Thread.CurrentThread.IsBackground,
                        Thread.CurrentThread.IsThreadPoolThread);

}
```

The following screenshot shows the output of running the preceding code:

```
Primary Thread Id: 1
Thread State: Running
Priority Normal
Press any key to exit.
ThreadPool Thread Id: 3
Thread State: Background
Priority Normal
IsBackground: True
IsThreadPoolThread: True
ThreadPool Thread Id: 6
Thread State: Background
Priority Normal
IsBackground: True
IsThreadPoolThread: True
ThreadPool Thread Id: 4
Thread State: Background
Priority Normal
IsBackground: True
IsThreadPoolThread: True
ThreadPool Thread Id: 10
Thread State: Background
Priority Normal
IsBackground: True
IsThreadPoolThread: True
ThreadPool Thread Id: 8
Thread State: Background
Priority Normal
IsBackground: True
IsThreadPoolThread: True
```

Her, we created five worked threads using the thread pool. If you uncomment `Thread.CurrentThread.Join` in the preceding code, the primary thread won't exit until all of the threads have been processed.

Thread storage

Thread-relative static fields and data slots are the two ways in which we can store data that is unique to the thread and application domain. Thread-relative static fields are defined at compile time and provide the best performance. Another benefit is that they do compile-time type checking. These fields are used when the requirement about what kind of data to be stored is clear beforehand.

Thread-relative static fields can be created using `ThreadStaticAttribute`.

There are scenarios where these storage requirements may arise at runtime. In such scenarios, we can opt for data slots. These are a bit slower than static fields. Since these are created at runtime, they store information as an object type. It is important for us to convert these objects into their respective types before using them.

.NET Framework allows us to create two types of data slots: named data slots and unnamed data slots. Named data slots use the `GetNamedDataSlot` method so that we can retrieve it as and when required. However, one disadvantage of `NamedDataslot` is when two threads from the same application domain use the same data slot in two different components of code and execute them at the same time. When this happens, they can corrupt each other's data.

`ThreadLocal<T>` can be used to create local data storage.

These two ways of storing data can be referred to as **thread-local storage** (**TLS**). A couple of the benefits of managed TLS are as follows:

- Within an application domain, one thread cannot modify data from another thread, even when both threads use the same field or slot
- When a thread accesses the same field or slot from multiple application domains, a separate value is maintained in each application domain

Now, we will jump into an example and look at how the `ThreadStatic` attribute can be used. In the following example, a static variable is being defined and decorated with the `ThreadStatic` attribute. This ensures that each thread has its own copy of the variable. When you execute the following program, you will observe that `_intvariable` goes up to 6 for each thread:

```
[ThreadStatic]
public static int _intvariable;
public static void ThreadStaticSample()
{
    //Start three threads
    new Thread(() =>
    {
        for (int i = 0; i <= 5; i++)
        {
            _intvariable++;
            Console.WriteLine($"Thread
Id:{Thread.CurrentThread.ManagedThreadId}, Int field
Value:{_intvariable}");
        }
    }).Start();
```

```
    new Thread(() =>
    {
        for (int i = 0; i <= 5; i++)
        {
            _intvariable++;
            Console.WriteLine($"Thread
Id:{Thread.CurrentThread.ManagedThreadId}, Int field
Value:{_intvariable}");
        }
    }).Start();

    new Thread(() =>
    {
        for (int i = 0; i <= 5; i++)
        {
            _intvariable++;
            Console.WriteLine($"Thread
Id:{Thread.CurrentThread.ManagedThreadId}, Int field
Value:{_intvariable}");
        }
    }).Start();
}
```

The following screenshot shows the output of running the preceding program. Comment
the ThreadStatic attribute and run the program again—you will find that
the _intvariable value goes up to 18 as each thread updates its value:

```
Press any key to exit.
Thread Id:4, Int field Value:1
Thread Id:4, Int field Value:2
Thread Id:4, Int field Value:3
Thread Id:4, Int field Value:4
Thread Id:4, Int field Value:5
Thread Id:4, Int field Value:6
Thread Id:3, Int field Value:1
Thread Id:5, Int field Value:1
Thread Id:5, Int field Value:2
Thread Id:5, Int field Value:3
Thread Id:5, Int field Value:4
Thread Id:5, Int field Value:5
Thread Id:5, Int field Value:6
Thread Id:3, Int field Value:2
Thread Id:3, Int field Value:3
Thread Id:3, Int field Value:4
Thread Id:3, Int field Value:5
Thread Id:3, Int field Value:6
```

Let's see how we can use `ThreadLocal<T>` to create local storage:

```
  public static ThreadLocal<string> _threadstring = new
ThreadLocal<string>(() => {
    return "Thread " + Thread.CurrentThread.ManagedThreadId; });
public static void ThreadLocalSample()
{
    //Start three threads
    new Thread(() =>
    {
        for (int i = 0; i <= 5; i++)
        {
            Console.WriteLine($"First Thread string :{_threadstring}");
        }
    }).Start();

    new Thread(() =>
    {
        for (int i = 0; i <= 5; i++)
        {
            Console.WriteLine($"Second Thread string :{_threadstring}");
        }
    }).Start();

    new Thread(() =>
    {
        for (int i = 0; i <= 5; i++)
        {
            Console.WriteLine($"Third Thread string :{_threadstring}");
        }
    }).Start();

}
```

The output of the preceding code is as follows:

```
Press any key to exit.
First Thread string :Thread 3
First Thread string :Thread 3
First Thread string :Thread 3
First Thread string :Thread 3
First Thread string :Thread 3
First Thread string :Thread 3
Second Thread string :Thread 4
Third Thread string :Thread 5
Third Thread string :Thread 5
Third Thread string :Thread 5
Third Thread string :Thread 5
Third Thread string :Thread 5
Third Thread string :Thread 5
Second Thread string :Thread 4
Second Thread string :Thread 4
Second Thread string :Thread 4
Second Thread string :Thread 4
Second Thread string :Thread 4
```

Now that we've understood how to manage threads, let's look at how to synchronize data in multithreading.

Synchronizing data in multithreading

Multiple threads can invoke the methods or properties of an object, which can make the state of an object invalid. It is possible to make conflicting changes regarding two or more threads on the same object. This makes it important to synchronize these calls, which will allow us to avoid such issues. When the members of a class are protected from conflicting changes, they are known to be **thread-safe**.

The CLR provides multiple ways in which we can synchronize access to the object instance and static members:

- Synchronize code regions
- Manual synchronization
- Synchronize context
- Thread-safe collection

By default, there is no synchronization for objects, which means any thread can access methods and properties at any time.

Synchronizing code regions allows us to synchronize blocks of code, methods, and static methods. However, synchronizing static fields is not supported. Synchronizing is possible if we use a `Monitor` class or a keyword. C# supports the `lock` keyword, which can be used to mark blocks of code for synchronization.

When applied, the threads attempt to acquire the lock while executing the code. If another thread has already been acquired by the lock on this block, then the thread blocks until the lock is available. The lock is released when the thread has executed the code block or exits in any other way.

`MethodImplAttribute` and `MethodImplOptions.Synchronized` give us the same results as using `Monitor` or keywords to lock the code block.

Let's look at an example to understand lock statements with tasks. We will learn more about tasks in the upcoming sections.

For the purpose of this example, we created an `Account` class that synchronizes its private field balance amount by locking it to an instance. This ensures that no two threads update this field at the same time:

```
internal class BankAcc
    {
        private readonly object AcountBalLock = new object();
        private decimal balanceamount;
        public BankAcc(decimal iBal)
        {
            balanceamount = iBal;
        }
        public decimal Debit(decimal amt)
        {
            lock (AcountBalLock)
            {
                if (balanceamount >= amt)
                {
                    Console.WriteLine($"Balance before debit
:{balanceamount,5}");
                    Console.WriteLine($"Amount to debit    :{amt,5}");
                    balanceamount = balanceamount - amt;
                    Console.WriteLine($"Balance after debit
:{balanceamount,5}");
                    return amt;
                }
                else
                {
                    return 0;
                }
```

```
                }
        }
        public void Credit(decimal amt)
        {
            lock (AcountBalLock)
            {
                Console.WriteLine($"Balance before
credit:{balanceamount,5}");
                Console.WriteLine($"Amount to credit          :{amt,5}");
                balanceamount = balanceamount + amt;
                Console.WriteLine($"Balance after credit
:{balanceamount,5}");
            }
        }
    }
```

The `TestLockStatements()` method looks as follows:

```
//Create methods to test this Account class
public static void TestLockStatements()
{
    var account = new BankAcc(1000);
    var tasks = new Task[2];
    for (int i = 0; i < tasks.Length; i++)
    {
        tasks[i] = Task.Run(() => UpdateAccount(account));
    }
    Task.WaitAll(tasks);
}
private static void UpdateAccount(BankAcc account)
{
    var rnd = new Random();
    for (int i = 0; i < 10; i++)
    {
        var amount = rnd.Next(1, 1000);
        bool doCredit = rnd.NextDouble() < 0.5;
        if (doCredit)
        {
            account.Credit(amount);
        }
        else
        {
            account.Debit(amount);
        }
    }
}
```

We are creating two tasks, and each task invokes `UpdateMethod`. This method loops 10 times and updates the account balance using either credit or debit methods. Because we are using the `lock(obj)` field at the instance level, the balance amount field won't be updated at the same time.

The following code shows the desired output:

```
Balance before debit : 1000
Amount to debit : 972
Balance after debit : 28
Balance before credit: 28
Amount to credit : 922
Balance after credit : 950
Balance before credit: 950
Amount to credit : 99
Balance after credit : 1049
Balance before debit : 1049
Amount to debit : 719
Balance after debit : 330
Balance before credit: 330
Amount to credit : 865
Balance after credit : 1195
Balance before debit : 1195
Amount to debit : 962
Balance after debit : 233
Balance before credit: 233
Amount to credit : 882
Balance after credit : 1115
Balance before credit: 1115
Amount to credit : 649
Balance after credit : 1764
Balance before credit: 1764
Amount to credit : 594
Balance after credit : 2358
Balance before debit : 2358
Amount to debit : 696
Balance after debit : 1662
Balance before credit: 1662
Amount to credit : 922
Balance after credit : 2584
Balance before credit: 2584
Amount to credit : 99
Balance after credit : 2683
Balance before debit : 2683
Amount to debit : 719
Balance after debit : 1964
Balance before credit: 1964
```

```
Amount to credit : 865
Balance after credit : 2829
Balance before debit : 2829
Amount to debit : 962
Balance after debit : 1867
Balance before credit: 1867
Amount to credit : 882
Balance after credit : 2749
Balance before credit: 2749
Amount to credit : 649
Balance after credit : 3398
Balance before credit: 3398
Amount to credit : 594
Balance after credit : 3992
Balance before debit : 3992
Amount to debit : 696
Balance after debit : 3296
Press any key to exit.
```

Accessing shared variables across multiple threads may cause data integrity issues. Such issues can be addressed by using a synchronization primitive. These are derived by the `System.Threading.WaitHandle` class. While performing manual synchronization, a primitive can protect access to shared resources. Different synchronization primitive instances are used to protect access to a resource or some parts of code access, which allows multiple threads to access a resource concurrently.

 You can read more about synchronization primitives at `https://docs.` `microsoft.com/en-us/dotnet/standard/threading/overview-of-` `synchronization-primitives`.

The `System.Collections.Concurrent` namespace was introduced by .NET Framework and can be used without additional synchronization in the user code. This namespace includes several collection classes that are both thread-safe and scalable. This allows multiple threads to add or remove items from these collections.

More information on these thread-safe collections can be found at `https:/` `/docs.microsoft.com/en-us/dotnet/standard/collections/thread-` `safe/index.`

Multithreading

Developers are allowed to create multiple threads within a process and manage them throughout the program's execution. This allows us to focus on the application logic instead of managing threads. However, starting with .NET Framework 4, we can create multithreaded programs using the following methods:

- TPL
- **Parallel Language-Integrated Query(PLINQ)**

To understand both of these features, we need to talk about parallel programming.

Parallel programming

Parallel programming helps the developer take advantage of the hardware on workstations where multiple CPU cores are available. They allow multiple threads to be executed in parallel.

In previous versions, parallelization required low-level manipulation of threads and locks. From .NET Framework 4 onward, enhanced support for parallel programming was provided in the form of the runtime, class library types, and diagnostic tools.

The following diagram shows the high-level architecture of parallel programming:

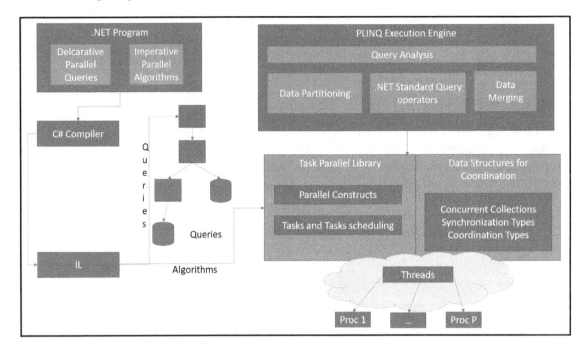

In the upcoming sections, we will talk about some of the components listed in the preceding architecture diagram.

TPL

TPL makes developers more productive by creating parallel and concurrent applications. These are available as public types in the System.Threading and System.Threading.Tasks namespaces. TPL allows us to maximize code performance while focusing on program work. TPL is based on tasks, which represent a thread or thread pool. When one or more tasks are run concurrently, this is known as task parallelism. A task has a couple of benefits: being scalable and efficient, and having more programmatic control than threads.

Because TPL handles the partitioning of the work, scheduling, cancellation, state, and other low-level details, it can scale the degree of concurrency dynamically and use the system resources or processors that are available.

It is important to be aware of when to apply parallel programming, otherwise the overhead of parallelization decreases the speed of code execution. A basic understanding of threading concepts such as locks and deadlocks is important so that we can use TPL effectively.

Data parallelism

When an operation can be performed concurrently on source collection elements, it is referred to as data parallelism. In this process, the source collection is partitioned into multiple threads and executed in parallel. .NET Framework supports data parallelism via the `System.Threading.Tasks.Parallel` class. Methods such as `Parallel.For` and `Parallel.ForEach` are defined in this class. When you use these methods, the framework manages all the low-level work for us.

A task represents an asynchronous operation and does not return a value. These are defined in the `System.Threading.Tasks` class.

Using tasks

A task represents an operation that may or may not return a value and executes asynchronously. Since they are executed asynchronously, they are executed as worker threads from the thread pool rather than the primary thread. This allows us to use the `isCanceled` and `IsCompleted` properties to understand the state of the task. You can also make a task run synchronously, which will be executed on the main or primary thread.

A task can implement the `IAsyncResult` and `IDisposable` interfaces like so:

```
public class Task : IAsyncResult, IDisposable
```

Let's look at an example so that we can understand how we can create and initiate a task in different ways. In this example, we will use an action delegate that takes an argument of the `object` type:

```
public static void Run()
{
    Action<object> action = (object obj) =>
    {
        Console.WriteLine("Task={0}, Milliseconds to sleep={1},
Thread={2}",Task.CurrentId, obj,
        Thread.CurrentThread.ManagedThreadId);
        int value = Convert.ToInt32(obj);
        Thread.Sleep(value);
    };
```

```
    Task t1 = new Task(action, 1000);
    Task t2 = Task.Factory.StartNew(action, 5000);
    t2.Wait();
    t1.Start();
    Console.WriteLine("t1 has been started. (Main Thread={0})",
                    Thread.CurrentThread.ManagedThreadId);
    t1.Wait();

    int taskData = 4000;
    Task t3 = Task.Run(() => {
        Console.WriteLine("Task={0}, Milliseconds to sleep={1},
Thread={2}",
                        Task.CurrentId, taskData,
                        Thread.CurrentThread.ManagedThreadId);
    });
    t3.Wait();

    Task t4 = new Task(action, 3000);
    t4.RunSynchronously();
    t4.Wait();
}
```

Here, we create four different tasks. For the first task, we used start methods, while for the second task, we used a task `factory.startnew` method. The third task was started using the `run(Action)` method, while the fourth task was executed synchronously on the main thread using the run synchronously method. Here, tasks 1, 2, and 3 are worker threads that are using a thread pool, while task 4 is executing on the primary thread.

The following screenshot shows the output of running the preceding code:

```
Task=1, Milliseconds to sleep=5000, Thread=3
t1 has been started. (Main Thread=1)
Task=2, Milliseconds to sleep=1000, Thread=4
Task=3, Milliseconds to sleep=4000, Thread=4
Task=4, Milliseconds to sleep=3000, Thread=1
```

The `Wait` method is similar to `Thread.Join`, which waits until the task completes. This is useful when synchronizing the execution of calling threads and asynchronous tasks since we can wait for one or more threads to complete. The `Wait` method also accepts certain parameters that allow us to conditionally wait for a task to complete.

The following table shows the different options that are available for a thread when it comes to waiting:

`Wait`	Waits for the task's execution to complete.
`Wait(int32)`	Makes the tasks wait for a specified number of milliseconds before executing.
`Wait(Timespan)`	Waits for the task's execution to complete within a specified time interval.
`Wait(CancellationToken)`	Waits for the task's execution to complete. The wait is terminated if `cancellationToken` is issued before the task's execution is completed.
`Wait(Int32, CancellationToken)`	Waits for the task's execution to complete. The wait terminates on timeout or when a cancellation token is issued before the task completes.
`WaitAll`	Waits for all the provided tasks to complete their execution. Similar to the `Wait` method, `WaitAll` tasks multiple parameters and performs them accordingly.
`WaitAny`	Waits for the provided task to complete its execution. Similar to the `Wait` method, `WaitAll` tasks multiple parameters and performs them accordingly.

Tasks support two other methods: `WhenAll` and `WhenAny`. Now, `WhenAll` is used to create a task that will complete its execution when all the provided tasks have been completed. Similarly, `WhenAny` creates tasks and completes when the provided task completes its execution.

A task can also return a value. However, reading the result of a task means waiting until its execution has completed. Without completing its execution, it isn't possible to use the result object. The following is an example of this:

```
public static void TaskReturnSample()
{
    Task<int> t = Task.Run(() => { return 30 + 40; });
    Console.WriteLine($"Result of 30+40: {t.Result}");
}
```

By executing the preceding code, you will see that the main thread waits until the task returns a value. Then, it displays a `Press any key to exit` message:

```
Result of 30+40: 70
Press any key to exit.
```

It's also possible to add a continuation task. .NET Framework provides a keyword called ContinueWith, which allows you to create a new task and execute it once the previous tasks have finished executing. In the following code, we are instructing the task to continue with the result from the parent task:

```
public static void TaskContinueWithSample()
{
    Task<int> t = Task.Run(() =>
        {
            return 30 + 40;
        }
    ).ContinueWith((t1) =>
    {
        return t1.Result * 10;
    });
    Console.WriteLine($"Result of two tasks: {t.Result}");
}
```

When task t has completed its execution, the result is used in the second task, t1, and the final result is displayed:

```
Result of two tasks: 700
Press any key to exit.
```

ContinueWith has a couple of overload methods that allow us to configure when the continuation task should execute, such as when a task is canceled or completed successfully. To make this configuration work, we will use TaskContinuationOptions. You can find more of the options that are available at https://docs.microsoft.com/en-us/dotnet/api/system.threading.tasks.taskcontinuationoptions?view=netframework-4.7.2.

The following code block shows how we can use continuationOptions:

```
Task<int> t = Task.Run(() =>
{
    return 30 + 40;
}
).ContinueWith((t1) =>
{
    return t1.Result * 10;
}, TaskContinuationOptions.OnlyOnRanToCompletion);
```

`TaskFactory` supports creating and scheduling tasks. It also allows us to do the following:

- Create a task and start it immediately using the `StartNew` method
- Create a task that starts when any one of the tasks in an array has completed by calling the `ContinueWhenAny` method
- Create a task that starts when all the tasks in an array have completed by calling the `ContinueWhenAll` method

 Further reading on `TaskFactory` can be found at `https://docs.microsoft.com/en-us/dotnet/api/system.threading.tasks.taskfactory?view=netframework-4.7.2`.

Using the Parallel class

The `System.Threading` class has another class named `Parallel`. This class provides parallel implementations for `For` and `ForEach` loops. Their implementation is similar to the sequential loop. When you use `ParallelFor` or `ParallelForEach`, the system automatically splits the process into multiple tasks and acquires locks if required. All of this low-level work is handled by TPL.

A sequential loop may look as follows:

```
foreach (var item in sourceCollection)
{
    Process(item);
}
```

The same loop can be represented using `Parallel` as follows:

```
Parallel.ForEach(sourceCollection, item => Process(item));
```

TPL manages the data source and creates partitions so that the loop can operate on multiple parts in parallel. Each task will be partitioned by the task scheduler as per system resources and workload. Then, if the workload becomes unbalanced, the work will be redistributed into multiple threads and processes by the task scheduler.

Parallel programming can increase performance when you have a lot of work to be done in parallel. If this isn't the case, it can become a costly affair.

It is important to understand how parallelism works in a scenario given. In the following example, we'll look at how we can use `Parallel.For` and make a time comparison between sequential and parallel loops.

Here, we are defining an array of integers and calculating the sum and product of each element of the array. In the main program, we invoke this method using sequential and parallel loops and calculate how much time each loop takes to complete the process:

```
static int[] _values = Enumerable.Range(0, 1000).ToArray();

private static void SumAndProduct(int x)
{
    int sum = 0;
    int product = 1;
    foreach (var element in _values)
    {
        sum += element;
        product *= element;
    }
}

public static void CallSumAndProduct()
{
    const int max = 10;
    const int inner = 100000;
    var s1 = Stopwatch.StartNew();
    for (int i = 0; i < max; i++)
    {
        Parallel.For(0, inner, SumAndProduct);
    }
    s1.Stop();

    Console.WriteLine("Elapsed time in seconds for ParallelLoop: " +
s1.Elapsed.Seconds);

    var s2 = Stopwatch.StartNew();
    for (int i = 0; i < max; i++)
    {
        for (int z = 0; z < inner; z++)
        {
            SumAndProduct(z);
        }
    }
    s2.Stop();
    Console.WriteLine("Elapsed time in seconds for Sequential Loop: " +
s2.Elapsed.Seconds );
}
```

In the preceding code, we executed two loops: one using a parallel loop and the other using a sequential loop. The results show the time each operation took:

```
Elapsed time in seconds for ParallelLoop: 1
Elapsed time in seconds for Sequential Loop: 6
Press any key to exit.
```

`System.Threading.Tasks.Parallel` comes with multiple helper classes, such as `ParallelLoopResult`, `ParallelLoopState`, and `ParallelOptions`.

`ParallelLoopResult` provides the completion status of the parallel loop, as shown here:

```
ParallelLoopResult result = Parallel.For(int i, ParallelLoopState
loopstate) =>{});
```

`ParallelLoopState` allows iterations of parallel loops to interact with other iterations. Finally, `LoopState` allows you to identify any exceptions in iterations, break from an iteration, stop an iteration, identify if any iteration has invoked break or stop, and break long-running iterations.

PLINQ

Language-Integrated Query (LINQ) was introduced in .NET Framework 3.5. It allows us to query in-memory collections such as `List<T>`. You will learn more about LINQ in `Chapter 15`, *Using LINQ Queries*. However, if you want to find out more sooner, more information can be found at `https://docs.microsoft.com/en-us/dotnet/csharp/programming-guide/concepts/linq/index`.

PLINQ is the parallel implementation of the LINQ pattern. They resemble LINQ queries and operate on any in-memory collections but differ in terms of execution. PLINQ uses all the available processors in the system. However, the processors are limited to 64 bits. This is achieved by partitioning the data source into smaller tasks and executing each task on separate worker threads on multiple processors.

Most of the standard query operators are implemented in the `System.Linq.ParallelEnumerable` class. The following table lists the various parallel execution-specific methods:

AsParallel	When you want a system to perform parallel execution on an enumerable collection, the `AsParallel` instruction can be provided to the system.
AsSequential	Instructing the system to run sequentially can be achieved by using `AsSequential`.
AsOrdered	To maintain the order on the result set, use `AsOrdered`.
AsUnordered	To not maintain the order on the result set, use `AsUnordered`.

WithCancellation	A cancellation token carries the user's request to cancel the execution. This has to be monitored so that execution can be canceled at any time.
WithDegreeofParallelism	Controls the number of processors to be used in a parallel query.
WithMergeOptions	Provides options so that we can merge results to the parent task/thread/result set.
WithExecutionMode	Forces the runtime to use either parallel or sequential modes.
ForAll	Allows results to be processed in parallel by not merging to the parent thread.
Aggregate	A unique PLINQ overload to enable intermediate aggregation over thread-local partitions. Also allows us to merge the final aggregation to combine the results of all partitions.

Let's try to use some of these methods so that we can understand them in more detail. The `AsParallel` extension method binds query operators such as `where` and `select` to the `parallelEnumerable` implementation. By simply specifying `AsParallel`, we tell the compiler to execute the query in parallel:

```
public static void PrintEvenNumbers()
{
    var numbers = Enumerable.Range(1, 20);
    var pResult = numbers.AsParallel().Where(i => i % 2 == 0).ToArray();

    foreach (int e in pResult)
    {
        Console.WriteLine(e);
    }

}
```

When executed, the preceding code block identifies all even numbers and prints them on the screen:

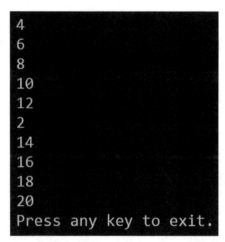

As you can see, the even numbers weren't printed in order. One thing to remember regarding parallel processing is that it does not guarantee any particular order. Try executing the code block multiple times and observe the output. It will differ each time since it is based on the number of processors that are available at the time of execution.

By using the `AsOrdered` operator, the code block accepts a range of numbers between 1 and 20. However, using `AsOrdered` will order the numbers:

```
public static void PrintEvenNumbersOrdered()
{
    var numbers = Enumerable.Range(1, 20);
    var pResult = numbers.AsParallel().AsOrdered()
        .Where(i => i % 2 == 0).ToArray();

    foreach (int e in pResult)
    {
        Console.WriteLine(e);
    }

}
```

This example shows how we can maintain the order of the result set when using `Parallel`:

```
2
4
6
8
10
12
14
16
18
20
Press any key to exit.
```

When you execute a code block using PLINQ, the runtime analyzes whether it is safe to parallelize the query. If it is, it partitions the query into tasks and then runs them concurrently. If it isn't safe to parallelize the query, it executes the query in a sequential pattern. In terms of performance, using a sequential algorithm is better than using a parallel algorithm, so by default, PLINQ selects the sequential algorithm. Using `ExecutionMode` will allow us to instruct PLINQ to select the parallel algorithm.

The following code block shows how we can use `ExecutionMode`:

```
public static void PrintEvenNumbersExecutionMode()
{
    var numbers = Enumerable.Range(1, 20);
```

```
        var pResult =
numbers.AsParallel().WithExecutionMode(ParallelExecutionMode.ForceParalleli
sm)
            .Where(i => i % 2 == 0).ToArray();

        foreach (int e in pResult)
        {
            Console.WriteLine(e);
        }
    }
```

As we mentioned previously, PLINQ uses all the processors by default. However, by using the `WihtDegreeofParallelism` method, we can control the number of processors to be used:

```
    public static void PrintEvenNumbersDegreeOfParallel()
    {
        var numbers = Enumerable.Range(1, 20);
        var pResult = numbers.AsParallel().WithDegreeOfParallelism(3)
            .Where(i => i % 2 == 0).ToArray();

        foreach (int e in pResult)
        {
            Console.WriteLine(e);
        }


    }
```

Execute the preceding code block by changing the number of processors and observe the output. In the first scenario, we left the system to use the available cores/processors, but in the second one, we instructed the system to use three cores. You will see that the difference in performance is based on your system's configuration.

PLINQ also comes with a method called `AsSequential`. This is used to instruct PLINQ to execute queries sequentially until `AsParallel` is called.

`forEach` can be used to iterate through all the results of a PLINQ query and merges the output from each task to the parent thread. In the preceding examples, we used `forEach` to display even numbers.

`forEach` can be used to preserve the order of the PLINQ query results. So, when order preservation is not required and we want to achieve faster query execution, we can use the `ForAll` method. `ForAll` does not perform the final merge step; instead, it parallelizes the processing of results. The following code block is using `ForAll` to print output to the screen:

```
public static void PrintEvenNumbersForAll()
{
    var numbers = Enumerable.Range(1, 20);
    var pResult = numbers.AsParallel().Where(i => i % 2 == 0);

    pResult.ForAll(e => Console.WriteLine(e));
}
```

In this scenario, the I/O is being used by multiple tasks, so the numbers will appear in a random order:

When PLINQ executes in multiple threads, as the code runs, the application logic may fail in one or more threads. PLINQ uses the `Aggregate` exception to encapsulate all the exceptions that are thrown by a query and sends them back to the calling thread. When doing this, you need to have one `try..catch` block on the calling thread. When you get the results from the query, the developer can traverse through all the exceptions encapsulated in `AggregatedException`:

```
public static void PrintEvenNumbersExceptions()
{
    var numbers = Enumerable.Range(1, 20);
    try
    {
        var pResult = numbers.AsParallel().Where(i => IsDivisibleBy2(i));

        pResult.ForAll(e => Console.WriteLine(e));
    }
    catch (AggregateException ex)
    {
        Console.WriteLine("There were {0} exceptions",
ex.InnerExceptions.Count);
        foreach (Exception e in ex.InnerExceptions)
        {
            Console.WriteLine("Exception Type: {0} and Exception Message:
```

```
{1}", e.GetType().Name,e.Message);
        }
     }
}

private static bool IsDivisibleBy2(int num)
{
    if (num % 3 == 0) throw new ArgumentException(string.Format("The number
{0} is divisible by 3", num));
    return num % 2 == 0;
}
```

The preceding code block is writing all the details from an exception that was thrown in a PLINQ. Here, we are traversing and showcasing all six exceptions:

```
2
8
4
14
16
20
10
There were 6 exeptions
Exception Type: ArgumentException and Exception Message: The number 9 is divisible by 3
Exception Type: ArgumentException and Exception Message: The number 12 is divisible by 3
Exception Type: ArgumentException and Exception Message: The number 6 is divisible by 3
Exception Type: ArgumentException and Exception Message: The number 3 is divisible by 3
Exception Type: ArgumentException and Exception Message: The number 15 is divisible by 3
Exception Type: ArgumentException and Exception Message: The number 18 is divisible by 3
Press any key to exit.
```

You can loop through the `InnerExceptions` property and take necessary actions. We will look at inner exceptions in more detail in `Chapter` 7, *Implementing Exception Handling*. However, in this case, when a PLINQ is executed, instead of terminating the execution on an exception, it will run through all the iterations and provide the final results.

Asynchronous programming with async and await

Asynchronous programming can help you enhance the responsiveness and performance of an application. In a traditional approach, it is difficult to write and maintain asynchronous code. However, C# 5 introduced two new keywords that simplify asynchronous programming: `async` and `await`. When encountered, the C# compiler does all the difficult work for you. It resembles synchronous code. `Task` and `Task<T>` are at the core of asynchronous programming.

Any I/O-bound or CPU-bound code can utilize asynchronous programming. In the case of IO-bound code, when you want to return a task from an `async` method, we use the `await` operation, whereas in CPU-bound code we wait for the operation that started a background thread using `Task.Run`.

When the `await` keyword is used, it returns control to the calling methods, thus allowing the UI to be responsive.

Internally, when the compiler encounters the `async` keyword, it splits the method into tasks, and each task is marked with the `await` keyword. The `await` keyword generates code that will check whether the asynchronous operation has already completed; that is, the C# compiler transforms the code into a state machine that keeps track of the metadata related to each task/thread so that it can resume execution when the background task has finished executing:

```
private readonly HttpClient _httpClient = new HttpClient();

public async Task<int> GetDotNetCountAsync()
{
    var html = await
_httpClient.GetStringAsync("https://dotnetfoundation.org");
    return Regex.Matches(html, @"\.NET").Count;
}

public void TestAsyncMethods()
{
    Console.WriteLine("Invoking GetDotNetCountAsync method");
    int count = GetDotNetCountAsync().Result;
    Console.WriteLine($"Number of times .NET keyword displayed is
{count}");
}
```

In the preceding code block, we are trying to find how many times a specific word has been used on a website. The output of the previous code is as follows:

```
Invoking GetDotNetCountAsync method
Number of times .NET keyword displayed is 22
Press any key to exit.
```

Here, we used the `async` keyword on the `GetDotnetCountAsync` method. Although the method is executed synchronously, the `await` keyword allows us to return to the calling method and wait until the `async` method has finished executing, which is when it returns the result.

 It is important to understand that an `async` method body should always have an `await`, otherwise this method will never yield. No error is raised by the compiler either.

When writing asynchronous methods, you should always use `async` as the suffix. Note that `async` must be used for event handlers. This is the only method that allows `async` events handlers to work as events do not have return types.

You can read more about the **Task-Based Asynchronous Pattern (TAP)** from MSDN at https://docs.microsoft.com/en-us/dotnet/standard/asynchronous-programming-patterns/task-based-asynchronous-pattern-tap.

Summary

In this chapter, we looked at threads, their properties, how we can use parameterized threads, and the difference between foreground and background threads with detailed examples. We also learned about thread states and how threads store and share data across multiple threads. This is where we discussed different synchronization methods. We focused on parallel programming, tasks and asynchronous programming using tasks, how to use parallel classes, and PLINQ.

In the next chapter, we will explore exception handling in C#. Exception handling helps us deal with any unexpected or exceptional situations that occur during program execution. Exception handling uses the `try`, `catch`, and `finally` blocks. These help developers try out actions that may or may not succeed, handle failures if they occur, and clean up unwanted resources, respectively.

Questions

1. By default, the main method of your code block runs as which of the following?
    1. Worker thread
    2. Primary thread
    3. Background thread
    4. None of the above

2. What action needs to be performed to move a thread to the run state when suspended?
    1. Interrupt
    2. Resume
    3. Abort
    4. Suspended

3. What is the correct keyword to use while working on synchronization code regions?
    1. Lock
    2. Release
    3. Getlock
    4. Unlock

4. A task may or may not return a value.
    1. True
    2. False

5. When working with PLINQ, the results are returned in order.
    1. True
    2. False

Answers

1. **Primary thread**
2. **Resume**
3. **Lock**
4. **True**
5. **False**

Further reading

In this chapter, we talked about many features that .NET Framework offers that we can use in our applications. However, we didn't cover this topic in detail. Therefore, it may be useful for you to go through a couple of MSDN articles so that you can understand more about these concepts. Take a look at the following links:

- More on application domains can be found at `https://docs.microsoft.com/en-us/dotnet/framework/app-domains/application-domains#application-domains-and-threads`.
- More on threads and processes can be found at `https://docs.microsoft.com/en-us/windows/desktop/procthread/processes-and-threads`.
- The following documentation on parallel programming will help you understand some of the topics that we didn't cover in this chapter: `https://docs.microsoft.com/en-us/dotnet/standard/parallel-programming/for-further-reading-parallel-programming`.
- One of the concepts that you'll need to understand while working with tasks is task schedulers: `https://docs.microsoft.com/en-us/dotnet/api/system.threading.tasks.taskscheduler?view=netframework-4.7.2`.
- The following article about async provides more information about all the moving pieces that are used when asynchronous operations are performed: `https://docs.microsoft.com/en-us/dotnet/standard/async-in-depth`.

7
Implementing Exception Handling

Exception handling helps developers structure their programs in a way that helps them handle both expected and unexpected scenarios. Often, application logic may throw some form of unhandled exception, for example, a code block trying to write to a file on a system that ends up with a file with a use exception. Such scenarios can be handled if proper exception handling is in place.

Exception handling uses the `try`, `catch`, and `finally` keywords to allow us to write code that may not succeed and can be handled when required, as well as to help us clean up resources once the `try` block has been executed. These exceptions can be thrown by CLR, .NET Framework, or by external libraries that are used in your code.

In this chapter, we will try to understand how we can use, create, and throw exceptions by looking at the following topics:

- Exceptions and handling exceptions in code
- Compiler-generated exceptions
- Custom exceptions

After reading this chapter, you will be able to structure an application program and handle all sorts of exceptions that may be thrown from your application logic.

Technical requirements

The exercises in this chapter can be practiced using Visual Studio 2012 or above with .NET Framework 2.0 or newer. However, any new C# features from C# 7.0 and above require that you have Visual Studio 2017.

If you don't have a license for any of the aforementioned products, you can download the community version of Visual studio 2017 from `https://visualstudio.microsoft.com/downloads/`.

The same code for this chapter can be found on GitHub at `https://github.com/PacktPublishing/Programming-in-C-sharp-Exam-70-483-MCSD-Guide/tree/master/Chapter07`.

Exceptions and handling exceptions in code

Exceptions are types that are derived from the `System.Exception` class. We use the `try` block around statements that may throw an exception. When an exception occurs, control jumps to the `catch` statement, where CLR collects all the required stack trace information before terminating the program and displaying a message to the user. If exception handling is not done, the program just terminates with an error. While handling exceptions, it is important to understand that if we cannot handle an exception, we should not catch it. This ensures that the application will be in a known state. When you define a `catch` block, you define an exception variable that can be used to obtain more information, such as the origin of the exception, which line in the code threw this exception, the type of exception, and so on.

A programmer can create and throw exceptions from the application logic using the throw keyword. Each `try` block may or may not define the `finally` block, which will be executed whether an exception is thrown or not. This block helps us release resources that have been used in the code block. Alternatively, if you want a piece of code to execute in all scenarios, it can be placed in the `finally` block.

In the upcoming sections, we will look at how we can use exceptions, the syntax of the `try-catch-finally` block, using the `finally` block, when we can dispose of unused objects, different types of system exceptions, and creating our own exceptions.

Using exceptions

As we mentioned previously, errors in C# programs are propagated at runtime using exceptions. When application code encounters an error, it throws an exception, which is then caught by another block of code that collects all the information about the exception and pushes it to the calling method, where the `catch` block was provided. A dialog box will be displayed by the system if you're using a generic exception handler for any uncaught exceptions.

In the following example, we are trying to parse an empty string into an `int` variable:

```
public static void ExceptionTest1()
{
    string str = string.Empty;
    int parseInt = int.Parse(str);
}
```

When executed, the runtime throws a format exception with a message stating **Input string was not in a correct format**. As this exception wasn't caught, we can see the generic handler displaying this error message in a dialog box:

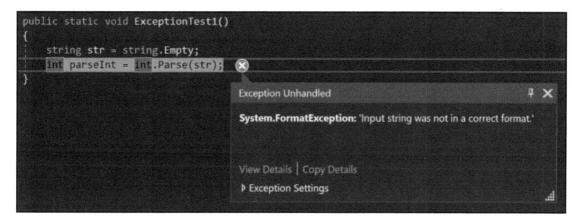

Here are the exception's details:

```
System.FormatException occurred
  HResult=0x80131537
  Message=Input string was not in a correct format.
  Source=<Cannot evaluate the exception source>
  StackTrace:
   at System.Number.StringToNumber(String str, NumberStyles options,
NumberBuffer& number, NumberFormatInfo info, Boolean parseDecimal)
   at System.Number.ParseInt32(String s, NumberStyles style,
NumberFormatInfo info)
   at System.Int32.Parse(String s)
   at Chapter7.ExceptionSamples.ExceptionTest1() in
C:\Users\srini\source\repos\Programming-in-C-Exam-70-483-MCSD-
Guide2\Book70483Samples\Chapter7\ExceptionSamples.cs:line 14
   at Chapter7.Program.Main(String[] args) in
C:\Users\srini\source\repos\Programming-in-C-Exam-70-483-MCSD-
Guide2\Book70483Samples\Chapter7\Program.cs:line 13
```

Each `catch` block defines an exception variable that gives us more information about the exception that is being thrown. The `exception` class defines multiple properties, all of which hold the following extra information:

Property	Description
Data	Gets custom-defined details about the exception in a key/value pair collection.
HelpLink	Gets or sets a help link related to an exception.
HResult	Gets or sets HRESULT, a number value that is associated with the exception.
InnerException	Gets the instance of the exception that triggered the exception.
Message	Gets detailed information from the exception.
Source	Gets or sets the application/instance name or the object/variable that caused the error.
StackTrace	Gets a call stack in a string format.
TargetSite	Gets the method that triggered the exception.

Now, we will try to handle the format exception and see what each property will provide us with. In the following example, we have a `try` block where the string is being parsed into an integer and a `catch` block that is being used to catch the format exception. In the `catch` block, we are displaying all the properties of the exception that we've caught:

```
public static void ExceptionTest2()
{
    string str = string.Empty;
    try
    {
        int parseInt = int.Parse(str);
    }
    catch (FormatException e)
    {
        Console.WriteLine($"Exception Data: {e.Data}");
        Console.WriteLine($"Exception HelpLink: {e.HelpLink}");
        Console.WriteLine($"Exception HResult: {e.HResult}");
        Console.WriteLine($"Exception InnerException:
                        {e.InnerException}");
        Console.WriteLine($"Exception Message: {e.Message}");
        Console.WriteLine($"Exception Source: {e.Source}");
        Console.WriteLine($"Exception TargetSite: {e.TargetSite}");
        Console.WriteLine($"Exception StackTrace: {e.StackTrace}");
    }
}
```

We are trying to parse a string into an integer variable. However, this is not allowed, and so the system throws an exception. When we catch the exception, we are displaying each property of the exception to observe what it stores:

```
C:\Users\srini\source\repos\Programming-in-C-Exam-70-483-MCSD-Guide2\Book70483Samples\Chapter7\bin\Debug\Chapter7.exe    —    □    ×
Exception Data: System.Collections.ListDictionaryInternal
Exception HelpLink:
Exception HResult: -2146233033
Exception InnerException:
Exception Message: Input string was not in a correct format.
Exception Source: mscorlib
Exception TargetSite: Void StringToNumber(System.String, System.Globalization.NumberStyles, NumberBuffer ByRef, System.G
lobalization.NumberFormatInfo, Boolean)
Exception StackTrace:    at System.Number.StringToNumber(String str, NumberStyles options, NumberBuffer& number, NumberF
ormatInfo info, Boolean parseDecimal)
   at System.Number.ParseInt32(String s, NumberStyles style, NumberFormatInfo info)
   at System.Int32.Parse(String s)
   at Chapter7.ExceptionSamples.ExceptionTest2() in C:\Users\srini\source\repos\Programming-in-C-Exam-70-483-MCSD-Guide2
\Book70483Samples\Chapter7\ExceptionSamples.cs:line 23
Press any key to exit.
```

Each exception is inherited from the `System.Exception` base case, which defines the type of exception and details all the properties that provide more information about the exception. When you need to throw an exception, you need to create an instance of the exception class, set all or some of these properties, and throw them using the `throw` keyword.

You can have more than one `catch` block for a `try` block. During execution, when an exception is thrown, a specific `catch` statement that handles the exception executes first and any other generic `catch` statements are ignored. Therefore, it is important to organize your `catch` blocks by placing them in order, that is, from the most specific to the least specific:

```
public static void ExceptionTest3()
{
    string str = string.Empty;
    try
    {
        int parseInt = int.Parse(str);
    }
    catch (ArgumentException ex)
    {
        Console.WriteLine("Argument Exception caught");
    }
    catch (FormatException e)
    {
        Console.WriteLine("Format Exception caught");

    }
    catch (Exception ex1)
```

```
        {
            Console.WriteLine("Generic Exception caught");
        }
    }
```

When the program executes, although there are multiple `catch` blocks present, the system identifies an appropriate `catch` block and consumes the exception. Due to this, you will see a `Format Exception caught` message in the output:

```
Format Exception caught
Press any key to exit.
```

The `finally` block is checked before invoking a `catch` block. When using resources in a `try-catch` block, there is a chance that these resources will move to an ambiguous state and aren't collected until the framework's garbage collector is invoked. Such resources can be cleaned up by the programmer via the use of `finally` blocks:

```
public static void ExceptionTest4()
{
    string str = string.Empty;
    try
    {
        int parseInt = int.Parse(str);
    }
    catch (ArgumentException ex)
    {
        Console.WriteLine("Argument Exception caught");
    }
    catch (FormatException e)
    {
        Console.WriteLine("Format Exception caught");

    }
    catch (Exception ex1)
    {
        Console.WriteLine("Generic Exception caught");
    }
    finally
    {
        Console.WriteLine("Finally block executed");
    }
}
```

As you can see, the `finally` block was executed, but not before an exception was raised and caught using the respective `catch` block:

```
Format Exception caught
Finally block executed
Press any key to exit.
```

Although we had three different `catch` blocks, the format exception was executed and the `finally` block was executed after.

Exception handling

Programmers partition application logic that may throw exceptions into a `try` block, followed by a `catch` block to handle these exceptions. An optional `finally` block, if present, is executed, regardless of whether an exception is thrown by a `try` block. You cannot just have a `try` block—it has to be accompanied by either a `catch` block or a `finally` block.

In this section, we will look at different code blocks in order to understand the usage of the `try-catch` statement, the `try-finally` statement, and the `try-catch-finally` statement.

You can use a `try-catch` statement without a `finally` block like so:

```
try
{
    //code block which might trigger exceptions
}
catch (SpecificException ex)
{
    //exception handling code block
}
```

The system also allows you to use a `try` block with a `finally` block—there's no need for the `catch` exception. This is shown in the following code:

```
try
{
    // code block which might trigger exceptions
}
finally
{
    // Dispose resources here.
    //Block you want to execute all times irrespective of try block is
executed or not.
```

```
    }
```

Last but not least, there's the `try-catch-finally` block:

```
try
{
    // Code that you expect to throw exceptions goes here.
}
catch (SpecificException ex)
{
    // exception handling code block
}
finally
{
    // code block that you want to run in all scenarios
}
```

A compile-time error is thrown if the runtime identifies incorrect syntax in a `try` block; for example, a `try` block without a `catch` or `finally` block during the compilation of the code. When you don't provide a `catch` or `finally` block, the compiler puts a red mark next to the closing bracket of `try` and an error is thrown, as shown in the error list window in the following screenshot:

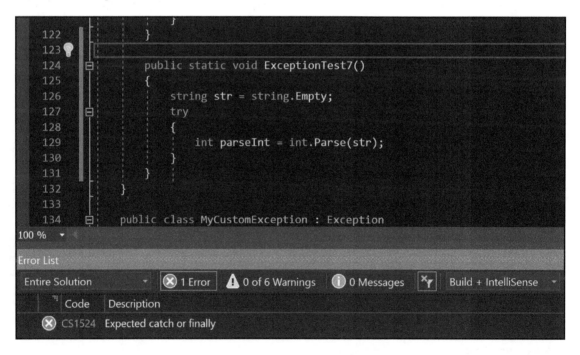

Exception filters are a type of exception that's used to catch in a `catch` block. `System.Exception` is the base class for any exception type class. As this is the base class, it can hold any exception in the code. We use this when we have code that handles every exception or when we are throwing an exception while calling `method()`.

We've already discussed that a `try` block can have multiple `catch` blocks with different exception filters. When the runtime evaluates the `catch` block, it takes a top-to-bottom approach and executes the most specific `catch` block that suits the exception that's been caught. If the `exception` filter in the `catch` block matches the exception that's been thrown or matches the base class of the exception that's been thrown, it's executed. As an exam tip, always remember to place the most specific `catch` statements on top and place the generic ones at the bottom.

Understanding the importance of exception handling helps you write proper code that handles every possible scenario and executes it without unexpected behavior occurring. For example, let's say your program is trying to open and write into a file and you receive an exception such as `File not found` or `File-in-Use`. Exception handling allows us to handle these scenarios. In the first case, the prompt asks the user to provide a correct filename, while in the second case, the prompt checks whether it is OK to create a new file.

In the following example, a `for` loop is throwing an index is out of range exception:

```
public static void ExceptionTest5()
{
    string[] strNumbers = new string[] {"One","Two","Three","Four" };
    try
    {
        for (int i = 0; i <= strNumbers.Length; i++)
        {
            Console.WriteLine(strNumbers[i]);
        }
    }
    catch (System.IndexOutOfRangeException e)
    {
        Console.WriteLine("Index is out of range.");
        throw new System.ArgumentOutOfRangeException(
                "Index is out of range.", e);
    }
}
```

The code handles it and displays a message on the screen before throwing it so that the invoking method can handle it, like so:

```
C:\Users\srini\source\repos\Programming-in-C-Exam-70-483-MCSD-Guide2\Book70483
One
Two
Three
Four
Index is out of range.
```

However, our main program doesn't handle the exception system. Instead, it uses the default and displays a dialog box:

```
public static void ExceptionTest5()
{
    string[] strNumbers = new string[] {"O
    try
    {
        for (int i = 0; i <= strNumbers.Le
        {
            Console.WriteLine(strNumbers[i
        }
    }
    catch (System.IndexOutOfRangeException
    {
        Console.WriteLine("Index is out of
        throw new System.ArgumentOutOfRang
            "Index is out of range.", e);
    }
}
```

Exception Unhandled

System.ArgumentOutOfRangeException: 'Index is out of range.'

Inner Exception
IndexOutOfRangeException: Index was outside the bounds of the array.

View Details | Copy Details
▷ Exception Settings

The `finally` block releases any variables or objects that were created in the `try` block. This block executes last and always runs if present:

```
public static void ExceptionTest6()
{
    FileStream inputfile= null;
    FileInfo finfo = new FileInfo("Dummyfile.txt");
    try
    {
        inputfile = finfo .OpenWrite();
        inputfile.WriteByte(0xH);
```

```
    }
    finally
    {
        // Check for null because OpenWrite() method might return null.
        if (inputfile!= null)
        {
            inputfile.Close();
        }
    }
}
```

In the preceding example, we created a file object in a `try` block and tried to write some bytes to it. When the runtime completes the execution of the `try` block, it executes a `finally` block and releases the `file` object that was created in the `try` block.

Compiler-generated exceptions

Let's go over a few runtime-generated exceptions that .NET Framework supports. The framework uses these exceptions on valid statements that are being executed. Then, based on their type, an exception from the following table is thrown. For example, if the compiler tries to execute a division operation and if the denominator is zero, `DividebyZeroException` is thrown:

Exception	Description
`ArithmeticException`	An exception that's triggered while performing arithmetic operations can be caught.
`ArrayTypeMismatchException`	When the value and type of the array don't match, this exception is thrown.
`DivideByZeroException`	When an attempt to divide an integer value by zero is made, this exception is thrown.
`IndexOutOfRangeException`	When an array is accessed with an index outside of its boundaries, this exception is thrown.
`InvalidCastException`	Converting a base type into an interface or derived type will cause this exception at runtime.
`NullReferenceException`	When you try to access an object that is `null`, this exception is thrown.
`OutOfMemoryException`	When the available memory for CLR is utilized, the new operator throws such exceptions.

OverflowException	While performing a division operation, for example, if the output is long and you try to push it to int, this exception is thrown.
StackOverflowException	Recursive calls usually cause such exceptions and indicate a very deep or infinite recursion.
TypeInitializationException	If you try to instantiate an abstract class, for example, this exception is thrown.

Now that we've looked at compiler-generated exceptions, let's take a look at custom exceptions.

Custom exceptions

All exceptions are derived from the System.Exception class in .NET Framework. So, in a scenario where these predefined exceptions don't suit our requirements, the framework allows us to create our own exceptions by deriving our exception class from the Exception class.

In the following example, we are creating a custom exception and inheriting from the Exception class. We can use different constructors for this:

```
public class MyCustomException : Exception
{
    public MyCustomException():base("This is my custom exception")
    {

    }

    public MyCustomException(string message)
            : base($"This is from the method : {message}")
    {

    }

    public MyCustomException(string message, Exception innerException)
        : base($"Message: {message}, InnerException: {innerException}")
    {
    }
}
```

When you create your own exception class, derive from the `System.Exception` class, and implement the base class, you get four constructors; implementing the three mentioned is the best practice. In the first instance, the base class message property is initialized by default and a message is displayed. However, in the second and third scenarios, the method that's throwing this custom exception needs to pass these values.

Summary

In this chapter, we looked at how we can use the exception class in a program, how we can create custom exceptions to meet our requirements, and different types of exceptions. We also learned about industry standards regarding how to plan and implement exceptions in an application.

In the next chapter, we will understand types and how to create and consume types.

Questions

1. C# supports `try` blocks without `catch` and `finally` blocks.
    1. True
    2. False
2. `catch` blocks need to be used in a most-generic-to-least-generic pattern.
    1. True
    2. False
3. If present, a `finally` block always executes.
    1. True
    2. False

Answers

1. **False**
2. **False**
3. **True**

Further reading

While implementing exception handling in your application code, it is important to understand industry standards. Please take a look at the following link to understand these best practices: `https://docs.microsoft.com/en-us/dotnet/standard/exceptions/best-practices-for-exceptions`.

Creating and Using Types in C# 8

Types are the building blocks of a C# program. Even while writing a basic C# program, we must use the right types while creating our program. In Chapter 2, *Understanding Classes, Structures, and Interfaces*, we learned the basics of types in a C# program. We learned about the value and reference type variables that are present in a C# program.

In addition to awareness of the different types, we should also understand that it's quite important for us to use each type in the best possible circumstance or situation. We also should be aware of the best practices regarding the creation and usage of these types. We will be going through this in this chapter.

We will walk through the following topics in this chapter:

- Creating types
- Consuming types
- How to use properties to enforce encapsulation
- Using of optional and named parameters
- Creating indexed properties
- Different operations related to string manipulation in C#

We will have an overview of **reflection** and try to understand how it can help us find, execute, and create types at runtime. In Chapter 10, *Find, Execute, and Create Types at Runtime Using Reflection*, we will do a deep dive into reflection.

Technical requirements

Like in the previous chapters covered in this book, the programs explained in this book will be developed in Visual Studio 2017.

The sample code for this chapter can be found on GitHub at `https://github.com/ PacktPublishing/Programming-in-C-Exam-70-483-MCSD-Guide/tree/master/ Book70483Samples`.

Creating types

When we create a variable in C#, it provides us with plenty of options to choose the appropriate type of the variable. For example, we can choose the following:

- We can choose an `enum` type if we would like the variable to acquire a defined set of variables. For example, if we define `Day` as an `enum` type, it can acquire the values `Monday`, `Tuesday`, `Wednesday`, `Thursday`, `Friday`, `Saturday`, and `Sunday`.
- Similarly, if we choose an `int` type, we tell **common language runtime** (**CLR**) that it cannot have decimal digits.

Hence, while defining types for any variables, we have to analyze the usage of the variable logically and then declare its type in C#. In the next section, we will just do a brief revision of the different types that we covered in the *Data types in C#* section in `Chapter 2`, *Understanding Classes, Structures, and Interfaces*.

Types in C#

In `Chapter 2`, *Understanding Classes, Structures, and Interfaces*, we learned that a variable can acquire the following types of values:

- **Value types**: In value types, the variables contain the actual value of the variable. This basically implies that if any change is made to a value type variable in a different scope of the program, the change is not reflected back once the control shifts to the calling function.

- **Reference types**: The data member contains the exact address of the variable in memory. As the variable just contains a reference to a memory address, two separate reference type variables can point to the same memory address. Therefore, if a change is made in a reference type variable, the change is made directly at the memory location of the variable and hence is carried forward to the different scopes present in the program execution.
- **Pointer types**: Pointers are another type of variable possible in C#. The pointer type is used to save the memory address of variable allowing us to any operation involving the memory location of the variable.

In the next section, we will do a deep dive into pointers and understand the implications and benefits of using them in our application.

Unsafe code and the use of pointer types

In languages such as C or C++, developers have the features to create *pointers* or *, which is an object that stores the memory address of another variable. This object allowed very low-level access of the memory to the application. However, due to the possibility of *dangling pointers*, the performance of the application suffers greatly. A dangling pointer is a potential situation that could exist in C when a pointer object is still pointing to a memory location that is no longer allocated in the application. Please refer to the following diagram:

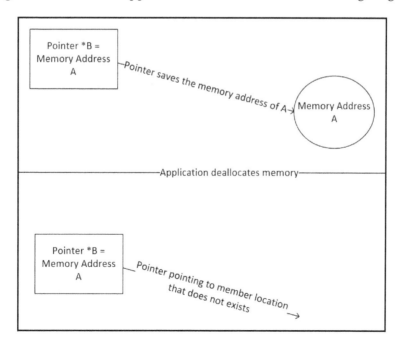

In the diagram, we have an application running in C or C++ that declared **Pointer B** and pointed it to the memory address of variable **A**. The pointer saves the memory address of the variable. Hence, in other words, **Pointer B** will not contain the memory address of variable **A**. Now, at some point during the program run, memory location **A** was released by the application. Even though the memory was released, there could be circumstances when we do not explicitly clear out the contents of the pointers containing the respective memory address. Due to this mistake or oversight, **Pointer B** was not updated to point to a new block of memory or pointing it to null. As a result, the pointer is still referring to a memory location that no longer exists in the application. This situation is called **dangling pointers**.

C# removes the possibility of dangling pointers because, explicitly, it does not allow the use of pointers. Instead, it encourages people to use *reference types*. The memory management of *reference types* is managed by a garbage collector.

 In Chapter 9, *Managing the Object Life Cycle*, we will look further at how the garbage collector works in .NET.

However, there are still some circumstances when developers feel the need to use pointers in their C# application. This is useful in scenarios where we need to do some operations with the underlying operating system, such as Windows or Linux, in which the application is running. In such circumstances, we will need pointers. To cater to such scenarios, C# has the concept of unsafe *code* in which it allows developers to use pointers in their code. The code that uses pointers must be classified clearly with an identifier of unsafe. This keyword conveys the message to **Common Language Runtime (CLR)** that the code block is unmanaged or unsafe—or, in other words, has used pointers. Let's go through a code example to see how we use pointer types in C#.

In the code example, we are creating a function block in which we are using a pointer variable. We will be saving the address of an `int` type in an `int` pointer type variable. Please refer to the following screenshot. Note that the user gets an error when they try to compile the program:

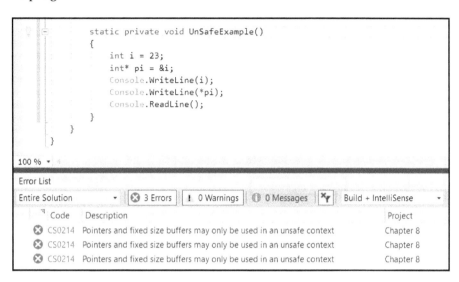

The reason is that, by default, the C# compiler will not allow any code containing a pointer or `unsafe` code block to be executed. We can override this behavior of C# by using the `unsafe` keyword in the function block:

```
class Program
{
    static void Main(string[] args)
    {
        UnSafeExample();
    }
    unsafe static private void UnSafeExample()
    {
        int i = 23;
        int* pi = &i;
        Console.WriteLine(i);
        Console.WriteLine(*pi);
        Console.ReadLine();
    }
}
```

To allow the compilation of `unsafe` code, we will need to change the build setting in Visual Studio. To update the settings, we need to right-click on the **Project** and click on **Properties**. Now, navigate to the **Build** section. Please refer to the following screenshot, which highlights the Visual Studio setting that we need to specify to allow compilation of `unsafe` code:

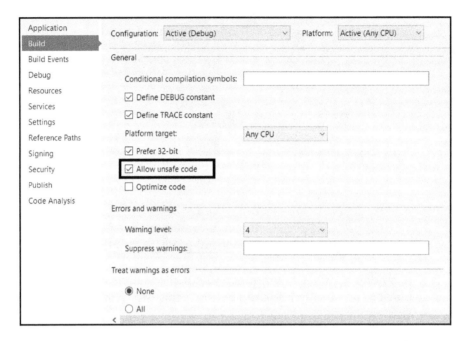

Now we have revisited the different types possible in C#. The next section explains the guiding principles that help us select a particular variable type over another.

Choosing the type of variable

In `Chapter 2`, *Understanding Classes, Structures, and Interfaces*, in the *Data types in C#* section, we saw the different data types that are possible for both value and reference types. We also did a code implementation to see the difference in the behavior of `Struct`, which is a value type, and `Class`, which is a reference type. In this section, we will do a deep dive and see this difference in behavior and how it can help us to choose the correct type for our variable.

Let's analyze how the following code statements for value and reference types and see how they differ in implementation:

```
// Value Type
int x = 10;
int y = x

// Reference Type
Car c = new Car();
Car c2 = c;
```

In the preceding code, we have declared the value type variables x and y. While declaring, the x variable has been assigned a value. In the next step, we are assigning x to y. Similarly, we have a class named Class and we have created an object of c. In the next statement, we have declared another object of the same class and have assigned c to c2.

Please refer to the following diagram, which shows how these types are implemented and managed inside memory:

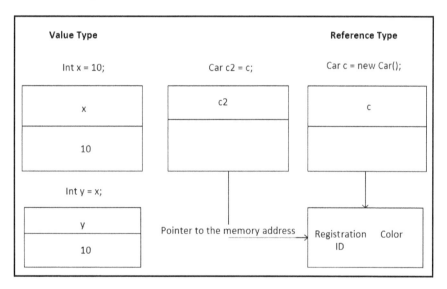

In the preceding diagram, we have declared variable x as an `int` data type and c as an object of the `Car` class. Now, we know that `int` is a value type, while `Class` is a reference type. So let's try to analyze why the behavior differs for both of them:

- For x, in the first statement, that is, `int x = 10`, a block of memory is reserved by the application. The rectangular block below the declaration conveys that.
- Now, when we execute the `int y = x` statement, we are declaring another variable, y, and it is assigned the value currently in x. What it does internally is it allocates another block of memory for y in memory. Therefore, as x and y are not pointing to the same memory location, they will hold different values.
- On the other hand, if we look at the `Car` class, we have just declared two attributes in it: the registration number and color. Now, when we use the `new` statement, what it does is that it creates an object for the class and allocates it memory. However, as against the value type implementation, it does not save the value in the object. Instead, in the object, it just saves a reference to the allocated memory block. In the rectangular shape in the preceding diagram, you will see that, once the c object is created for the `Car` class, a pointer is saved in the created object.
- Now, when we execute the `Car c2 = c;` statement, internally, it creates a new object, c2, but does not allocate a new memory block for the object. Instead, it just saves a reference to the memory location shared with the object, c.

As illustrated by the preceding implementation, whenever a new value type variable is declared, a new block of memory is reserved by the application, which is different from reference type variables.

Hence, in much simpler terms, the following factors can help us to choose between value and reference type:

- **A value type variable is logically immutable**: In very simple terms, it means that on every declaration of the value type, a new block of memory is reserved by the application. As they are different memory allocations, it implies that if we execute any operation on one memory location, the change is not transmitted across to the other memory location.
- **Whether there are lots of objects**: If there lots of objects being created in the application, it might be better to not create them as value type as it would exponentially increase the memory requirements of the application.

- **Whether the object is small**: If the object is small, then it may make sense to have them as value type variables. However, if we think that the object is bound to have too many properties, a reference type variable will make more sense.
- **Memory management**: Value type variables are managed on a stack whereas reference type variables are managed on a heap. When we move to Chapter 9, *Manage the Object Life Cycle*, we will look further into memory management and how the garbage collector works.

Now that we have a fair understanding of how we can create and consume different data types in a C# application, we will be looking at some of the features of C# that help us to set correct behavior for the different types we use in the application. In the next section, we will be looking at static variables and how they are implemented in C#.

Static variables

When we went over the section on value type versus reference type, we understood that all of the objects created in C# have a definite scope in the program execution. However, there could be some circumstances when we would like to have a variable acquire a constant value that is consistent across all instances of the objects. We can do this using the Static keyword. A Static keyword in a modifier in C# ensures that just one instance of the variable is created and its scope is throughout the entire run of the program. We can use a Static variable against a class, its member variable, and its member methods and constructors.

Let's now look at code examples involving the Static keyword.

Static member variables

In this section, we will look at how we can use the Static keyword against a class and its member variables. In the following code example, we have created a Static class called Configuration. Just for the sake of explanation, we will not be using the Static keyword for a member variable present in it:

```
internal static class Configuration
{
    public string ConnectionString;
}
```

Let's try to compile the program. We get an error stating that
the `ConnectionString` member variable must be declared `static` as well:

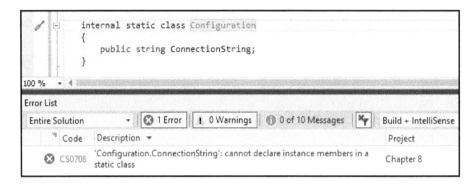

Once we use the `static` keyword against the `ConnectionString` member variable as
well, the error goes away. This is the correct representation of the class:

```
internal static class Configuration
{
    public static string ConnectionString;
}
```

If we need to use `Set/Get` value in the member variable, we can access it directly by using
the name of the class. Here is the code snippet for this:

```
Configuration.ConnectionString = "Sample Connection String";
```

In the preceding code example, we had a `Static` class `Configuration` in which it was
mandatory to have the `static` modifier against all of the member variables and properties.
However, there could be some circumstances when we don't want the entire class to be
static but just a particular member variable present inside it.

We can achieve this in C# by using the `static` modifier not against the class but against
the particular member variable. If we need to use this in the preceding code, the following
would be the updated code:

```
internal class Configuration
{
    public static string ConnectionString;
}
```

However, there will be no change in the way we access this property. It can still be done by
using the name of the class.

Static methods

In C#, a class can have two types of methods: static methods and non-static methods. Static methods are shared across the different instances of the class objects, whereas non-static methods are unique for each instance. Just like static member variables, we can declare a method as static by the use of the `static` keyword and can access them by directly using the class name.

The following code example indicates how we create a `static` method in a class:

```
internal class Configuration
{
    public static string ConnectionString;
    public static void CreateConnectionString()
    {
    }
}
```

To execute a static method, we can use the following code snippet:

```
Configuration.CreateConnectionPath();
```

In the next section, we will look at constructors and how they are implemented in C#.

Constructors

Constructors are called whenever an object is created for a `class` or `struct` type. They can help us to set some default values against the member variables present in these types.

In `Chapter 2`, *Understanding Classes, Structures, and Interfaces*, while understanding the difference between a `class` and `struct` type, we mentioned that, unlike classes, structs do now have a default constructor. That constructor, in programming terms, is known as a **parameter less constructor**. If a programmer does not specify any constructor for the class, then whenever an object is created for the class the default constructor triggers and sets default values against the member variables present in the class. The default values are set in accordance with the default values of the type of those member variables.

In terms of syntax, a constructor is just a method the name of which is the same as that of its respective type. In the method signature, it has got a parameter list that can be mapped to the member variables present in the type. It does not have any return type.

Please note that a class or struct can have multiple constructors each differing with each other based on the parameter list present in the method.

Let's look at a code example in which we will implement constructors:

```
public class Animal
{
    public string Name;
    public string Type;

    public Animal(string Name, string Type)
    {
        this.Name = Name;
        this.Type = Type;
    }
}
```

In the preceding code example, we have declared an `Animal` class with two member variables, `Name` and `Type`. We have also declared a two-parameter constructor in which we are passing `Name` and `Type` as string parameters. Using the `this` operator, we are then assigning the values passed to the member variables present in the class.

We can use the following code implementation to call this constructor:

```
Animal animal = new Animal("Bingo", "Dog");
```

In the next section, we will look at how named parameters are implemented in C#.

Named parameters

Named parameters were introduced in C# 4.0, and they allow us to pass arguments to a method/constructor/delegate/indexer using parameter names instead of the sequence in which the parameters are passed.

Using named parameters, developers no longer need to be concerned about the sequence in which they need to pass parameters. As long as they associate the values being passed with the right parameter name, the sequence will not matter. The parameter names are compared against the names of the parameters in the method definition. Let's look at the following code example to understand how it works:

```
internal Double CalculateCompoundInterest(Double principle, Double
interestRate, int noOfYears)
```

```
{
    Double simpleInterest = (principle) * Math.Pow((1 +
      (interestRate)/100), noOfYears);
    return simpleInterest;
}
```

In the preceding code example, we are calculating compound interest by passing the principal amount, interest rate, and number of years for which the amount was put in the bank.

If we call the method without using named parameters, we would use the following code snippet:

```
Double interest = CalculateCompoundInterest(500.5F, 10.5F, 1);
```

If we look closely at the preceding example, while calling the function, the developer will need to be fully aware of the sequence of the principle and interest rate parameters. That's because if the developer makes a mistake while calling the function, the resultant output will be incorrect.

With named parameters, we can call the method using the following syntax:

```
Double namedInterest = CalculateCompoundInterest(interestRate: 10.5F,
noOfYears: 1, principle: 500.5F);
```

Note that, in the preceding code, we are not passing values to the parameters in the sequence there are defined in the method. Instead, we are using parameter names to map the passing values with the parameters declared in the method. In the next section, we will look at another feature, *optional parameters,* which was introduced in C# 4.0 along with named parameters.

Optional parameters

Optional parameters in C# allow us to define a method in such a way that some of the parameters are optional. In other words, while defining the function for the optional parameters, a default value is specified.

If, while calling the method, no value is passed for the optional parameter, it assumes a default value. Let's look at a code example to understand how optional parameters work in C#:

```
static float MultiplyNumbers(int num1, int num2 = 2, float num3 = 0.4f)
{
    return num1 * num2 * num3;
```

```
}
```

In the preceding code example, we have defined a `MultiplyNumbers` method with three parameters, `num1`, `num2`, and `num3`. The `num1` parameter is mandatory, while the other two parameters, `num2` and `num3`, are optional.

 Please note that, while defining the function, the optional parameters, if any, must come after all of the required parameters have been specified in the sequence.

If we need to execute the preceding method, we can use any of the following code snippets:

```
float result = MultiplyNumbers(2); // output = 1.6f
float result1 = MultiplyNumbers(2, 5); // output = 4f
float result2 = MultiplyNumbers(2, 4, 5); // output = 40f
```

Note that there would be no compiler errors and if any optional parameters are not passed, the default value defined in the function declaration would be used. In the next section, we will look at how generic types are implemented in C#.

Generics types

Generics allow us to design classes and methods without the notion of data types. In simpler terms, when we talk about methods, generics allow us to define methods without specifying the type of the input variables.

Let's go through the following code implementation and see how it can help us. In the following example, we have created a function that compares the values between two `int` variables, `A` and `B`. If the value is the same, it returns `true`; however, if the value is not same, it returns `false`:

```
static private bool IsEqual(int A, int B)
{
    if(A== B)
    {
        return true;
    }
    else
    {
        return false;
    }
}
```

Now, let's say we try to pass a variable with a data type that is not `int`. In the following screenshot, we are trying to pass `string` instead of `int`, to which the compiler gives us an error:

```
    IsEqual("string", "string");
}
static private bool IsEqual(int A, int B)
{
    if (A == B)
    {
        return true;
    }
    else
    {
        return false;
    }
}
```

As illustrated in the following screenshot, it will give us the following error:

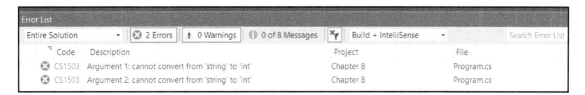

As illustrated by the preceding screenshot, the `IsEqual` function is accepting inputs of the `int` type. However, while calling the function, we are passing variables of the `string` type. Due to the type mismatch, the compiler is showing the error.

To correct this error, we need to make the `IsEqual` function generic. We can do this by altering the function so that instead of accepting the input variables of the `int` type, it can accept the input variables of the `object` type.

Please note that all of the variables in C# inherit from `object`.

In this code example, we are calling the `IsEqual` function twice and are passing different input parameters. In the first call, we are passing `string`; however, in the second call, we are passing `int`. Note that when we compile the project, no compile time error is retrieved and the function compares the passed variables irrespective of type:

```
static void Main(string[] args)
{
    UnSafeExample();
    IsEqual("string", "string");
    IsEqual(10, 10);
}

static private bool IsEqual(object A, object B)
{
    if (A == B)
    {
        return true;
    }
    else
    {
        return false;
    }
}
```

Although the preceding code implementation will be generic for all of the data types, it will lead to the following issues:

- **Performance degradation**: In the `IsEqual` function definition, the data types of variables is `object`. Due to this, for all calls being made to this function, the variables will need to be converted from their original type, that is, `int` or `string`, into `object`. This conversion will be an extra load for the application, which will lead to performance degradation. In programming terms, this conversion is known as **boxing and unboxing**, which we will cover shortly in this chapter.
- **Type unsafe**: This approach will not be type unsafe. For example, I will call the function by passing the following variables:

```
IsEqual(10, "string");
```

If I do so, the compiler will not give any error, even though we understand that the call makes no sense. To avoid these issues while still providing us with the capability of making the calls generic, C# provides us with the tool of using *generic types*.

Using generic types, we can avoid specifying any data type to the input variables of the functions. Hence, the implementation of `IsEqual` will look like this:

```
static private bool IsEqual<T>(T A, T B)
{
    if (A.Equals(B))
    {
        return true;
    }
    else
    {
        return false;
    }
}
```

In the preceding code example, please note that we are using `T` to illustrate the data type, hence making it generic for all data types.

As we are not using `object`, there will be no boxing and unboxing of variables. If we still try to pass incorrect data types to this function, as illustrated in the following screenshot, the compiler will give us an error:

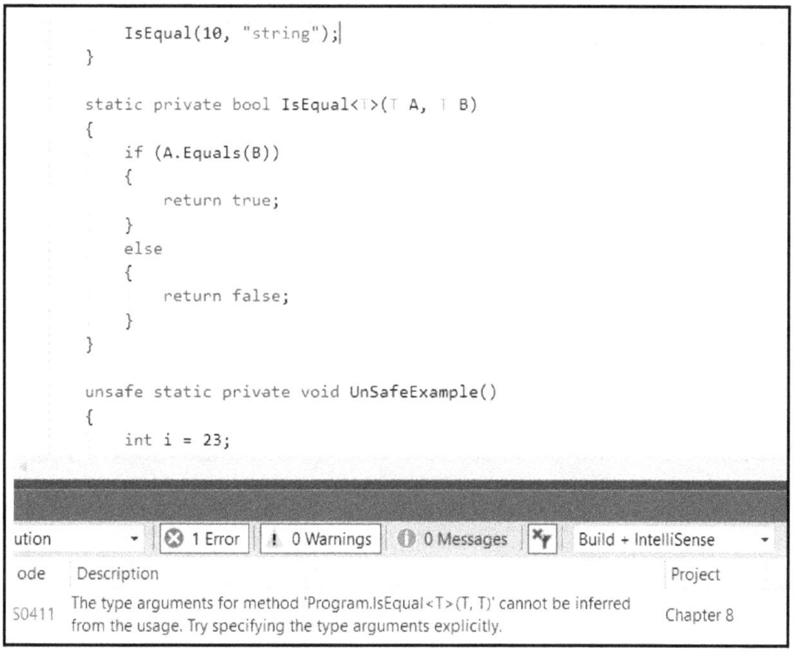

In the next topic, we will not go through the different concepts C# uses to work on the types of the data variables. We will go through how we can use boxing and unboxing in C# to convert one data type into another and the different things we should keep in mind when we are consuming variables of different types.

Consuming data types in C#

C# is a strongly-typed language. This basically means that, when we declare a variable with a particular data type, as in the following example, we cannot declare the x variable again:

```
int x = 5;
```

In addition to this, we cannot assign to this x variable any value that is not an integer. Hence, the following statement will give us an error:

```
x = "Hello";
```

To overcome this strongly typed feature, C# provides some capabilities when we are consuming a type. This includes boxing and unboxing of value type variables, use of the dynamics keyword, and implicit and explicit conversion of a variable of one data type to a variable of a different data type. Let's go through each of these concepts and understand how they work in C#.

Boxing and unboxing

In C#, boxing means converting a value type variable into a reference type variable. Unboxing is the opposite of boxing. It refers to the conversion of a reference type variable into a value type variable. Boxing and unboxing are detrimental to the performance of the application as they are an overhead to the compiler. As developers, we should try to avoid them as much as possible; however, it's not always possible and there are several instances that we encounter during programming that make us use this concept.

Let's look at the following example to see how boxing and unboxing works:

```
static private void BoxAndUnBox()
{
    int i = 3;
    // Boxing conversion from value to reference type
    object obj = i;
    // Unboxing conversion from reference type to value type
    i = (int)obj;
}
```

In the code implementation, we can see the following:

- We have declared a variable, `i`, of the `int` type and have assigned it a value of `3`. Now we know that, being `int`, this is a value type reference.
- Next, we declare an `obj` variable of the `object` type and have assigned it the value in `i`. We know that `object` is a reference type variable. Therefore, internally, the CLR will undergo boxing and convert the value into the `i` variable into a reference type variable.
- Next, in the third statement, we are doing the reverse. We are trying to assign the value in a reference type variable, that is, `obj`, to a value type variable, `i`. At this stage, the CLR will do the unboxing of the value.

Please note that, while doing boxing, we do not need to explicitly cast the value type to a reference type. However, when we are doing the unboxing, we need to explicitly specify the type into which we are converting the variable. This approach of explicitly specifying the type into which we are converting a variable is known as casting. To do casting, we can use the following syntax:

```
i = (int)obj;
```

What it basically means is that there are possibilities that this conversion can lead to an exception of the `InvalidCastException` type. For example, in the preceding example, we know that the value in `obj` is `10`. However, if it were to acquire a value that cannot be cast to an `int` value, for example, `string`, the compiler will give us a runtime error.

Now, in the next section, we will look at the different techniques C# provides us with for converting between data types.

Type conversions in C#

Type conversion in C# basically implies converting a variable from one data type into another. Now we will look into the different types of conversions available in C#.

Implicit conversion

Implicit conversion is done by the compiler automatically. It's done by the compiler without any intervention or command from the developer. The following two conditions must be fulfilled for a compiler to execute implicit type conversion:

- **No data loss**: The compiler must determine that if it executes the conversion implicitly, there will be no data loss. In Chapter 2, *Understanding Classes, Structures, and Interfaces*, in the *Data Types* section, we saw that each data type acquires a space in memory. Therefore, if we try to assign a variable with the type as float, which acquires 32 bytes of memory, to double, which acquires 64 bytes of memory, we can be sure that there won't be any data loss in the conversion.

- **No chance of cast exception**: The compiler must determine that there is no chance of an exception during the casting of the value from one data type to another. For example, if we try to set a string value to a float variable, the compiler will not do the implicit conversion as it would be an invalid cast.

Now, let's look at the following code implementation to see how implicit conversion works in C#:

```
int i = 100;
float f = i;
```

In the preceding code example, we have declared a variable, i, of the int type and have assigned it a value of 100. In the next statement, we have declared a variable, f, of the float type and have assigned it the value in i.

Now, the compiler would determine that both the required conditions for implicit conversions are being met, that is, float acquires more memory than int and there is no chance of an invalid cast exception—an int value is also a valid value in a float variable. Hence, the compiler gives no error and does the implicit conversion.

However, if we do the reverse, which is trying to assign a `float` value in `int`, the compiler will determine that the conditions are not being fulfilled and will give us a compile-time error. Please refer to the following screenshot:

However, in certain circumstances, even if there is a chance of data loss, we would still like to have those conversions. C# provides us with *explicit conversion*, which allows us to explicitly instruct the compiler to let the conversion take place. Let's go through how *explicit conversion* takes place.

Explicit conversion

When the compiler is not able to implicitly change the type of variables, but we still want the conversion to happen, we need to explicitly instruct the compiler to convert the value. This is referred to as *explicit conversion*.

There are two ways to do explicit conversion in C#:

- **Using a type cast operation**: In this, we use the base data type to instruct the compiler to do explicit conversion. For example, for the code implementation that we were trying in the preceding example, the following would be the syntax:

```
float k = 100.0F;
int j = (int)k;
```

In the preceding code, we are explicitly telling the compiler to do type conversion by using the `int` class conversion before the float variable.

- **Using the** `Convert` **class**: C# provides us with the `Convert` class, which we can use to do type casting between multiple data types. If we were to use the `Convert` class instead of the `int` keyword, the following would be the syntax:

```
float k = 100.0F;
int j = Convert.ToInt32(k);
```

Convert class can be used for type casting among different data types. Please refer to the following screenshot to get an idea of the different options that are available in the `Convert` class. Depending on the usage, we can use the appropriate method in the `Convert` class:

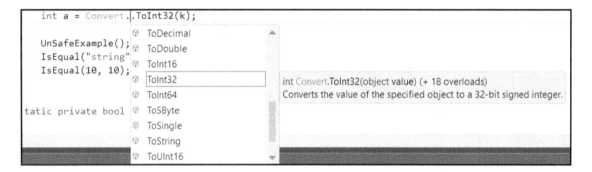

Hence, the overall implementation of the program will look like this:

```
float k = 100.67F;
int j = (int)k;
int a = Convert.ToInt32(k);
Console.WriteLine(j);
Console.WriteLine(a);
Console.ReadLine();
```

Now, let's try to run this program to see the output it gives:

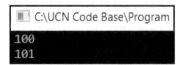

It implies that when we use the type cast keyword, that is, `(int)k`, the compiler tried to extract the integer component from the `float` variable, k, which turned out to be `100`.

On the other hand, when we used the `Convert` class, that is, `Convert.ToInt32(k)`, it tried to extract the nearest integer to the float variable, k, which turned out to be `101`. This is one of the key differences that developers need to be aware of while deciding between using type casting and the `Convert` class.

While we are looking at explicit type conversions, we need to be aware of two helper methods that help us do conversions:

- `Parse`
- `TryParse`

Both the `Parse` and `TryParse` methods are used to convert `string` into a different data type. However, there is a slight difference in the way invalid case exceptions are handled. Let's look at the following example to see how they work and the difference between them:

```
string number = "100";
int num = int.Parse(number);
```

In the preceding example, we have declared a string object and have assigned it a value of `100`. Now, we are trying to convert the value into an integer using the `Parse` method. When we run the program, we see the following output:

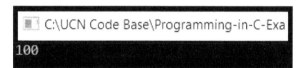

It implies that the parse method converts the string into its integer equivalent and assigns the value to another variable, `num`.

Now, let's suppose the value in the number is `100wer`. Now, it's evident that the value in the `number` string cannot be converted into `int` because it has some characters that cannot be categorized in an integer object. When we run this program, we get the following exception:

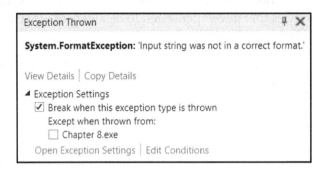

To avoid such situations, we use `TryParse`. In `TryParse`, CLR tries to convert the string object into the specified data type. However, if the conversion returns an error, `TryParse` returns `false` or, in other words, *the conversion failed*. In other cases, it returns true. Hence, if we were to write the same implementation with `TryParse`, we would do the following:

```
string number = "100wer";
int num;
bool parse = int.TryParse(number, out num);
if(parse)
{
    Console.WriteLine(num);
}
else
{
    Console.WriteLine("Some error in doing conversion");
}
Console.ReadLine();
```

In the preceding program, we have declared a variable of the `string` type and we are using `TryParse` to convert this value into a variable of the `int` type. We are checking whether the conversion is a success. If it's a success, we print out the number and in other cases, we print a statement to show that there was an error during the type conversion. When we run the program, we get the following output:

```
Some error in doing conversion
```

As we see from the output, the compiler tells us that there was an error doing the `TryParse`; however, it does not throw an exception in the application as opposed to the `Parse` method, which threw an invalid case exception in the same scenario.

In the next section, we will do a quick recap of encapsulation, which we covered in `Chapter 3`, *Understanding Object-Oriented Programming*, and we'll see how
to implement properties for class member variables objects, allowing us to consume them without worrying about the hidden complexities.

Enforcing encapsulation

Previously, we went through the following concepts in `Chapter 2`, *Understanding Classes, Structures, and Interfaces*, and `Chapter 3`, *Understanding Object-Oriented Programming*:

- Accessing modifiers and how they help us to control access to methods and fields in the same class, in the same assembly, and in the derived classes
- Encapsulation and how it helps us to group together related fields and methods together in the same object

However, there is another concept in encapsulation called properties, which makes sure that no one can have direct access to the data fields outside the class. This helps us to make sure that we have control over the modification of the data fields.

A property is very similar to the field of a class. Just like the field of a class, it has a type, name, and access modifier. However, what makes it different is the presence of accessors. Accessors are the `get` and `set` keywords that allow us to set and retrieve values from a field.

The following is what the syntax of a property looks like:

```
class SampleProperty
{
    private string name;
    public string Name
    {
        set { if(value != null)
            {
                this.name = value;
            }
            else
            {
                throw new ArgumentException();
            }
```

```
            }
        get { return this.name; }
    }
}
```

In the preceding code, please note the following:

- For the `SampleProperty` class, we have declared a `name` field and a `Name` property.
- The `name` field has been marked `private`, hence it won't be accessed outside the `SampleProperty` class.
- The `Name` property has been marked `public` and has the `get` and `set` accessors.
- In the `set` method, we are checking whether the value passed is null or not. If it's null, we are raising an argument exception. Therefore, we are putting rules around the value that can be set on the `name` field.

In this way, properties help us in consume the fields of a class.

Manipulating strings

Strings are a very important data type in C#. The string data type is used for saving text as `string`. In programming terms, it's a sequence of characters. String is a reference type variable unlike other basic data type variables, such as `int`, `float`, and `double`, which are value type variables. Also, strings are immutable in nature, that is, the values present in them cannot change. In this section, we will look at different operations related to this data type.

So, look at the following code example:

```
string s = "Hello";
s = "world";
```

When we are assigning a `Test` value to the already declared `string` objects, internally, CLR allocates a new memory block for the modified `string` object. Hence, for every operation that we do on a string, instead of modifying of the same `string` object, a new `string` object is declared in CLR. Due to this, we need to be very careful while doing operations on `string`, for example, if we execute the following loop operation on a string object:

```
string s = String.Empty;
for(int z = 0; z < 100; z++)
{
```

```
    s = + "a";
}
```

In the preceding code, we are concatenating the string object, s, with a character, a, in the loop. This loop will run 100 times. Therefore, the CLR will go on allocating more and more memory for the string object. Hence, due to memory usage, performance-wise, the preceding operation is not good.

To help to improve this feature in string, C# provides us with two built-in classes, Stringbuilder and StringWriter, which we will discuss next. We will also look at some of the features available with us for executing string searching in C#.

StringBuilder

Stringbuilder is an internal class provided by C# that helps us to improve string manipulation functions. To explain the idea, we will be executing a for loop from 0 to 100 and will be concatenating the resultant output in each loop with the letter a. Internally, a string builder uses a buffer to modify the string value instead of allocating memory on every string manipulation. The following code example shows how we can use string builder for string manipulation operations:

```
StringBuilder sb = new StringBuilder(string.Empty);
for (int z = 0; z < 100; z++)
{
    sb.Append("a");
}
```

In the preceding code, we are declaring a StringBuilder object, sb, and are appending its value with a in the loop. Internally, instead of allocating memory on every concatenation, StringBuilder will use an internal buffer to manage these operations.

StringReader and StringWriter

The StringReader and StringWriter classes derive from the TextReader and TextWriter classes respectively. TextReader and TextWriter are used for dealing with APIs such as reading from an XML file, generating an XML file, or reading from a file.

 We will study the TextReader and TextWriter classes more in Chapter 14, *Performing I/O Operations*.

Using the `StringReader` and `StringWriter` classes, we can interact with these I/O operations by manipulating the objects of strings and string builders.

Let's go through the following example in order to understand the methods better. In the following example, using `StringWriter`, we are firstly creating an extract of an XML file and then we will pass the resultant XML representation to `StringReader`, which will try to read an element present in it.

In the following code example, we are using `XMLWriter` to create an XML file with the start element as `Student` and an attribute of `Name`. We are saving the string representation of the XML file using `StringWriter`:

```csharp
static private string CreateXMLFile()
{
    string xmlOutput = string.Empty;
    var stringWriter = new StringWriter();
    using (XmlWriter writer = XmlWriter.Create(stringWriter))
    {
        writer.WriteStartElement("Student");
        writer.WriteElementString("Name", "Rob");
        writer.WriteEndElement();
        writer.Flush();
    }
    xmlOutput = stringWriter.ToString();
    return xmlOutput;
}
```

Suppose we print the output of the program; we will get the following result:

```
🔲 C:\UCN Code Base\Programming-in-C-Exam-70-483-MCSD-Guide\Book70483Samples\Chapter 8\bin
<?xml version="1.0" encoding="utf-16"?><Student><Name>Rob</Name></Student>
```

Now, in the following code snippet, we will use `StringReader` to read through this XML file:

```csharp
static private void ReadXMLFile(string xml)
{
    var stringReader = new StringReader(xml);
    using (XmlReader reader = XmlReader.Create(stringReader))
    {
        reader.ReadToFollowing("Name");
        string studentName = reader.ReadInnerXml();
        Console.WriteLine(studentName);
    }
```

```
        }
```

Please note that we are passing a string parameter to the function, which is first converted into a `StringReader` object. From that `StringBuilder` object, we are creating an `XmlReader` object.

The `ReadToFollowing` function reads the XML file until it finds an element with the respective name, which is passed as a parameter to the function. In the preceding code example, we are passing a parameter of `Name` to the `XmlReader` object. Based upon the XML file we have passed to it, it will take us to the element `Rob`. To read the text representation of the element, we can use the `ReadInnerXml` function on the `reader` object. Hence, in the preceding example, the `studentName` variable will be assigned the value of `Rob`. If we execute the code snippet, we will get the following output:

```
Rob
```

In the next section, we will go through some functions we can use to search for particular characters in a string object.

String searching

As the name suggests, string searching involves searching the presence of a particular letter or string in another string. C# provides several methods for doing this.

 Please note that C# is a case-sensitive language. Therefore, searching for a character, let's suppose *C*, is not the same as searching for the character *c* in the string.

Please refer to the following different types of searching that are possible with the `string` object:

- `Contains`: When we want to check whether a particular character exists in the string, we use the `Contains` function. The following example checks whether a character, `z`, exists in the string object. If it exists, it returns `true`; otherwise, it returns `false`.

  Let's take a look at the following example:

  ```
  string s = "hello australia";
  var contains = s.Contains("z");
  if(contains)
  ```

```
{
    Console.WriteLine(" z is present in it.");
}
else
{
    Console.WriteLine(" z is not present");
}
```

In the preceding code, using the `Contains` function, we are checking whether z occurs in the string against which we are calling the function. As we are calling it for a variable with the value `hello australia`, it will return the `false` value as z does not occur in the string. Hence, we get the following output when the code is executed:

```
False z is not present
```

- `IndexOf`: We use this function if we want to find out the index in the string at which a particular character is present.

  For example, in the following code example, we are finding the first and the last index of occurrence of the a character in the string `hello australia`:

  ```
  string s = "hello australia";
  var firstIndexOfA = s.IndexOf("a");
  Console.WriteLine(firstIndexOfA);
  var lastIndexOfA = s.LastIndexOf("a");
  Console.WriteLine(lastIndexOfA);
  ```

When we execute the program, we will get the first occurrence as **6** and the last occurrence as **14**. The `IndexOf` function retrieves the index the first appearance of a character or a string in the string against which we are using the function. Please also note that it does not ignore spaces. Hence, the whitespace is also counted as a character. Similarly, the `LastIndexOf` function retrieves the last index of the appearance of the respective character or string:

Please note that in C#, for any array or string, the index of the first character is zero.

- StartsWith/EndsWith: We use this function if we want to check whether a string starts or ends with a particular character.

The following code example shows a scenario in which we are checking whether the same string object used previously starts with h and ends with h. In the following code, in the first statement, we are checking whether the s string variable starts with h. Based on the evaluation, we print the output in the console window. Similarly, in the next statement, we are checking whether the same string variable ends with h. Based on the evaluation, we print the output in the console window again:

```
if(s.StartsWith("h"))
{
    Console.WriteLine("It Starts with h.");
}
else
{
    Console.WriteLine("It does not starts with h.");
}

if (s.EndsWith("h"))
{
    Console.WriteLine("It ends with h.");
}
else
{
    Console.WriteLine("It does not ends with h.");
}
```

Please refer to the following output for the preceding code example:

```
It Starts with h.
It does not ends with h.
```

- Substring: We use this function if we want to extract a substring from a particular string object. There are two variants of substring possible in C#. In one, we specify just the start index and extract the substring from that particular index. In another variant, we specify both the start and end index and extract the characters present in that substring.

Here is a code example of this:

```
string subString = s.Substring(3, 6);
string subString2 = s.Substring(3);
Console.WriteLine(subString);
Console.WriteLine(subString2);
```

In the preceding code example, we are finding two substrings of a string object, `hello australia`.

In the first substring, we have passed the start index as 3 and the end index as 6. Therefore, the substring will return us the values, `lo aus`.

In the second substring, we are just passing the start index, 3. Hence, it will return the entire string from this index. The following is the screenshot of the output from this execution:

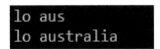

These are the different string manipulation functions available in C#. In the next section, we will go through an overview of reflection and learn how it helps us to get structure—in other words, classes and their methods and properties—from an assembly.

Overview of reflection

Reflection in C# means inspecting the contents of an assembly at run time. It returns the metadata for each class present in the assembly—so, it returns the following:

- The name of the class
- All of the properties present in the class
- All of the methods along with their return types and function parameters
- All of the attributes present in the class

In `Chapter 10`, *Find, Execute, and Create Types at Runtime Using Reflection*, we will do a deep dive on reflection; however, in this chapter, we will just go through a code sample of how we can implement reflection in C# to decode all of the metadata present in the assembly.

To use reflection, we need to include the `System.Reflection` namespace, which helps us to use required classes such as `Assembly`. Please refer to the following function, which reads a particular assembly based on its path and reads all of the classes, methods, and parameters present in the assembly:

```
static private void ReadAssembly()
{
    string path = @"C:\UCN Code Base\Programming-in-C-Exam-70-483-
     MCSD-Guide\Book70483Samples\Chapter8\bin\Debug\ABC.dll";
    Assembly assembly = Assembly.LoadFile(path);
    Type[] types = assembly.GetTypes();
    foreach(var type in types)
    {
        Console.WriteLine("Class : " + type.Name);
        MethodInfo[] methods = type.GetMethods();
        foreach(var method in methods)
        {
            Console.WriteLine("--Method: " + method.Name);
            ParameterInfo[] parameters = method.GetParameters();
            foreach (var param in parameters)
            {
                Console.WriteLine("--- Parameter: " + param.Name + " :
                 " + param.ParameterType);
            }
        }
    }
    Console.ReadLine();
}
```

In the preceding code base, we have declared a fully qualified path for an assembly in C#. Next, we have declared an object of the `Assembly` class and have retrieved an array of all `Types` present in the assembly. Then, we are looping through each type and finding out the methods in each of those types. Once we have a list of methods for each of the types, we retrieve the list of parameters present in that method and their parameter types.

Summary

In this chapter, we learned how to manage types in C#. We had a recap of the different data types available in C#. We did a deep dive into value and reference types in C#. We also had a review of the pointer data type and learned how it works. We had a look at some of the practices a user can use to choose the type of a variable. We had a look at generic types and learned how they help us to improve the performance of a system.

Then, we looked at the different techniques we use to consume a type declared in C#. We learned how boxing and unboxing work in C#. We then had a look at how to we consume these data types. We also looked at type conversions, both implicit and explicit, and learned how they help us to convert one data type into another.

Then, we had a look at `Properties` and how it helps us to have more control over setting and retrieving values from the field attributes of a class. Then, we worked on strings and learned how they work. We looked at the immutable nature of strings. We looked at using `StringBuilder`, `StringWriter`, and `StringReader`, which help us to improve the performance aspect of using strings. We then looked at the different functions in C# that help us to do different manipulation functions on a string. Finally, we did a high-level review of reflection and, using a code example, we learned how we can retrieve the metadata present in an assembly.

In the next chapter, we will look at how garbage collection is performed in C#. We will look at how the CLR manages memory for different data types in C#. We will look at how C# allows us to manage "unmanaged resources" or the "pointer types" that we saw in this chapter. We will also look at how we implement the `IDisposable` interface to manage unmanaged resources.

Questions

1. What is the keyword we use in the program function when we are using a pointer declaration?
   1. Sealed
   2. Safe
   3. Internal protected
   4. Unsafe

2. What would be the output of the following code snippet?

```
float f = 100.23f;
int i = f;
Console.WriteLine(i);
```

    1. 100

    2. Compile-time error

    3. 101

    4. Runtime error

3. What would be the output of the following code snippet?

```
string s = "hello australia";
var contains = s.Contains("A");
if(contains)
{
    Console.WriteLine("it's present");
}
else
{
    Console.WriteLine("it's not present");
}
```

    1. It's present

    2. It's not present

Answers

1. **Unsafe**
2. **Compile-time error**
3. **It's not present**

Managing the Object Life Cycle 9

C# is a managed language. Unlike other languages, such as C++, where we need to explicitly manage memory cleanup, in C# we do not need to worry about it. The garbage collector in the .NET Framework manages the allocation and release of memory for us.

The garbage collector ensures that, as long as we use managed types, that is, value and reference type variables, then we don't have to explicitly destroy an object in order to free its memory. However, as we discovered in `Chapter 8`, *Creating and Using Types in C#*, C# also gives us the freedom to utilize the capabilities of pointer object types in it. In C#, we must declare that code using the unsafe syntax. Apart from that, for variables declared in unsafe code, we also need to manage the release of memory.

In this chapter, as well as looking into memory management for unsafe code we will delve into the following topics:

- The differences between managed and unmanaged code in C#
- How garbage collection works in C#
- How a garbage collector uses a managed heap to allocate memory to objects during application execution
- Understanding the mark-compact algorithm used by the garbage collector
- How to manage unmanaged resources in C#
- Understanding finalization and the performance implications of using the finalize method
- Understanding the `IDisposable` interface and how it helps overcome the shortcomings of the finalize method
- Understanding how we can combine the `Dispose` method with the finalize method to ensure the best performance of our applications
- Understanding using the `using` block for all classes that implement the `IDisposable` interface

Technical requirements

As with the previous chapters in this book, the programs explained here will be developed in VS 2017.

The example code for this chapter can be found on GitHub at `https://github.com/ PacktPublishing/Programming-in-C-Sharp-Exam-70-483-MCSD-Guide/tree/master/ Book70483Samples`.

Managed code versus unmanaged code

In this section, we will understand the difference between managed and unmanaged code. Recall that we also studied this in `Chapter 1`, *Learning the Basics of C#*. Therefore, for a quick recap, we will just revise the concepts that we covered there.

These concepts apply not just to the C# language, they are also relevant to all languages written in the .NET Framework. The following are some of the differences between managed and unmanaged code:

- Managed code is executed by the **Common Language Runtime** (**CLR**). Due to this, the code is independent of the underlying OS. On the other hand, unmanaged code is code that is executed by the OS directly.
- In the case of managed code, the code is independent of the underlying framework or the OS. CLR compiles the code into an **Intermediate Language** (**IL**) code, which is then compiled to machine code. IL code consists of an underlying system or the OS on which the program is executing. On the other hand, in the case of unmanaged code, the code is directly compiled to the underlying machine code.
- As managed code is executed by the CLR, the .NET Framework provides several built-in capabilities such as garbage collection and type checking exceptions. However, for unmanaged code, as we will learn in this chapter, a programmer needs to explicitly manage memory cleanup activities, which are otherwise done by the garbage collector.

Now, before we learn how a programmer can manage memory for unmanaged code, let's first understand how garbage collection works in C# and how useful it is.

Garbage collection

Garbage collection is a functionality, provided by CLR in .NET, which helps us to clean up the memory occupied by managed objects. It is a thread that executes in the .NET Framework and, at regular intervals, checks whether there is any unused memory in the application. If it does find memory, then it reclaims that memory and destroys the underlying object.

Suppose we have implemented a .NET web application in C#. Now, let's assume that during any interval of time, there are several people who are trying to access this .NET application. The following is one particular scenario that will give us an idea of why garbage collection is a very important part of C# or, for that matter, any .NET application:

- When a user browses the application, they can execute a number of functionalities, such as accessing their profile or executing operations (for example, creating, updating, and deleting information).
- This information can be stored in different sources such as SQL, Oracle, or more.
- To access this information and to execute these operations, the application will require the creation of different objects during the application runtime.
- Assuming a scenario where memory is just being allocated to different objects but is not being cleaned up, over the course of time we will end up with a system that has too much unused memory. Memory cleanup is logical when the object declared in the memory is no longer required. For example, suppose that a user, after performing the intended operations in the application, logs out. In this case, the memory that was allocated for the operations of that particular user is no longer required. Therefore, that memory can be reclaimed.
- A the memory allocated to the application could be limited, this will lead to performance degradation over time.

Garbage collection in the .NET Framework ensures that such situations never arise for managed code. This thread runs in the background of the application and, at set intervals, reclaims the memory.

 Please note that garbage collection can only reclaim the unused memory of managed code. For unmanaged code, which we will learn about later, we need to explicitly write code to ensure that no memory leaks occur in the application.

The garbage collector in .NET executes the following tasks in an application:

- **Allocation of memory**: Each application running on .NET maintains a memory block required for its execution in a managed heap. The garbage collection manages the allocation of memory from this heap structure to the objects used in the program. In upcoming sections, we will learn more about managed heaps.
- **Deallocation of memory**: The garbage collector runs at set time periods during the application runtime and looks for objects that are no longer required by the application. It then destroys those objects and reclaims the memory for future use.

  The garbage collector reclaims the memory when one of the following three conditions occurs during the execution of a program:

  - **The application has low memory**: Each application running in .NET requires memory for its successful execution. If CLR determines that the application is getting free low memory from the OS, it tells the garbage collector to free any unused memory.
  - **The relocation of memory**: Garbage collection in C# is based on generations. Generations are simply divisions in the managed heap used by the application. In C#, we can have three generations: generation 0, generation 1, and generation 2. In upcoming sections, we will learn how generations are classified. The garbage collector tries to optimize the performance of the system by classifying the objects used in the application among the three generations of a managed heap. In generation 0, it keeps the newly created objects in the application run. In comparison, in successive runs it identifies the objects that are being used for a longer period in the application execution. It classifies them as generation 1 and generation 2 and then loops through these generations less extensively than it does for generation 0. This, therefore, results in better performance.
  - **When the Collect method is called**: As programmers, we hardly need to call the garbage collector method explicitly, as .NET is smart enough to ensure that garbage collection occurs at regular intervals. However, there could be certain scenarios where we would need to call this method explicitly. In such cases, we can do it by calling the `GC.Collect` method. In this chapter, we will look at a program implementation in which we do this.

Now, let's go through some of the basic structures that garbage collection works with in C#. We will start with a managed heap, which we will explore in the next section.

Managed heap

When an application is executed in the .NET Framework, the garbage collector allocates a section of memory to store and manage the objects declared during the application execution.

This memory is referred to as the managed heap. It's called "managed" because it's used to save the managed variables. The following diagram illustrates what a typical heap structure looks like:

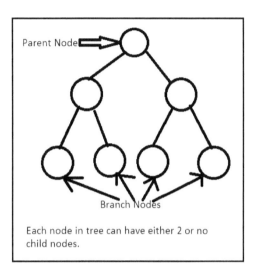

The preceding diagram is a typical example of what a heap structure looks like. At the top of the structure, we have a root node. Each node can have two child nodes. The address of the child node is saved in the parent node itself.

The garbage collector allocates and deallocates memory on this managed heap. The heap is referred to as the managed heap. When an object is allocated in the application, the object is stored in the heap. The object then saves the reference to the next object in the heap.

While allocating the memory, the CLR checks whether any free memory is available in the heap. If memory is available, it allocates it from the heap. However, every so often, the garbage collector performs a check on all of the objects present in the managed heap and checks whether the object is being used in the application. The garbage collector loops through the heap and finds out which objects are not associated with the application root as well as those that are not referred to anywhere in the heap. These objects are classified as dead objects. The garbage collector then removes such dead objects from the heap.

Before we can begin to understand the phases in which the garbage collector works, let's understand how the garbage collector segregates the managed heap into different divisions called **generations**.

Generations

The garbage collector segregates the managed heap into three divisions or generations:

- Generation 0
- Generation 1
- Generation 2

The idea behind this is to optimize the application by handling long-lived and short-lived objects in memory separately. For example, if we have determined that object a is a long-term object used during the application execution, then, ideally, the garbage collector would not want to check through this object on every occasion in order to see whether it is still valid.

Instead, the garbage collector classifies short-term objects in generation 0 and long-term objects in generation 1 or 2. Only objects present in generation 0 are checked during every run of the garbage collection.

On the other hand, the objects present in higher generations are not checked as frequently. Therefore, this avoids unnecessary checks and improves the performance of the overall application.

Generation 0 is the youngest generation and all new objects are allocated to generation 0. Generation 1 objects contain objects that live longer. Similarly, generation 2 consists of the longest living objects in the application execution. Let's go through the following example to see how generations help in optimizing application performance.

Let's say we have an application, *A*, which is declaring different objects during execution. The square brackets indicate the different divisions or generations maintained by the garbage collector. Each of the following steps indicates a particular stage during the application execution.

 Please note that the following example is just for explanation purposes only. The garbage collection calls will depend on different factors and are not necessarily be based upon the scope of the function execution.

Let's take a look at the following code example and see how it works. In the code example, we have declared a private `ReturnResult` function, which does not have any input parameter and returns an output parameter of the `object` type. In this function, just for the sake of explanation, we have declared some variables and are returning back one variable, a, to the calling function. Now, let's execute the code as follows:

```
static void Main(string[] args)
{
    object a = ReturnResult();
}

static private object ReturnResult()
{
    object a = new object();
    object b = new object();
    object c = new object();
    object d = new object();
    object e = new object();
    return a;
}
```

When the application execution begins, the application calls the `ReturnResult` function. Then, in the function, when the execution encounters the `new` keyword, the garbage collector gets triggered. As all the variables are newly created variables, these variables will be added to generation 0:

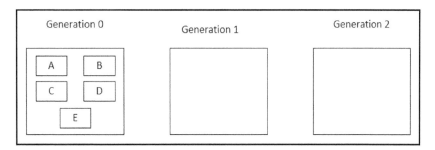

Now, suppose that in the next statement, we return the execution to the main function and pass object a. By doing so, the program execution shifts to the main operation. However, as we are just returning a, all the other b, c, d, and e objects will no longer be required in the application.

Additionally, we are also declaring new objects, f, g, and h, in the main program.

If the garbage collector is called during this time, it will identify that object a is still required in the program execution but all other objects can be released. Therefore, the garbage collector will reclaim the memory in the variables b, c, d, and e. The new objects, f, g, and h, will be added to generation 0. For object a, the garbage collector will assume that it's a long-lived object and this will be moved to the generation 1 division.

This is what the generations now look like:

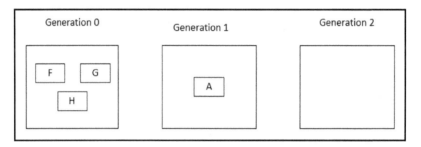

Now, let's suppose that, again, the main program calls for another ReturnResultFinal function passing object a. The newly added program does not return anything back. The following is the code implementation for this:

```
static void Main(string[] args)
{
    object a = ReturnResult();
    ReturnResultFinal(a);
}
static private object ReturnResult()
{
    object a = new object();
    object b = new object();
    object c = new object();
    object d = new object();
    object e = new object();
    return a;
}
static private void ReturnResultFinal(object a)
{
}
```

At this stage, the garbage collector can determine that all the other variables can be removed from the memory except a. During this time, it can also determine that this object can be promoted to generation 2. This is what the generations now look like:

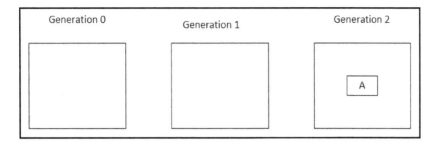

Before we move on to the next topic, let's briefly go through the mark-compact algorithm, used by the garbage collector.

The mark-compact algorithm

The mark-compact algorithm is used by the garbage collector to maintain the memory. Essentially, it can be classified into three phases:

- **The mark phase**: In the mark phase, the garbage collector loops through the different objects in the heap and identifies the one that is being referenced by a root item. A root item can be either the starting point of the program execution or a particular function. If the element is being referenced, it marks the object. All other objects, which are not referenced, are then classified as **dead** objects.
- **The relocating phase**: In the relocating phase, the garbage collector moves all the objects that are being referenced, groups them together, and then updates the memory address for each of the next objects in the memory heap.
  In addition to this, the garbage collector also classifies objects that are being used in the application to one of the different generations.
- **The compacting phase**: In the compacting phase, the garbage collector destroys the dead objects classified in the previous phase and reclaims their memory.

The entire process that the garbage collector undertakes can lead to a performance impact on the application. This is due to the fact that during the program execution, the garbage collector needs to make sure that the references in the heap are not changed during its run. This means that all the other threads of the application are paused while the run is in progress.

Fortunately, this situation does not arise often as the garbage collector starts cleaning only when the memory available for the application execution is low. Therefore, while the memory is high, the collection algorithm does not kick in. Additionally, as explained while we were discussing generations, when the garbage collection starts, it first checks the generation 0 heap objects. If they survive the cleanup, they are promoted to the next generation. For objects in the higher generations, the garbage collector assumes that the objects in higher generations will probably be used in the application for a longer period of time.

In the next section, we will look at how we can explicitly call the garbage collection method in C#.

Calling garbage collection

Although it's not recommended, and we hardly find any reason or circumstance where we seldom need to call the garbage collector explicitly during the program execution, we can use the following syntax to execute the Collect method in garbage collection. The following is the code implementation for this:

```
GC.Collect();
GC.WaitForPendingFinalizers();
```

GC is present in the system namespace. The Collect method executes the mark-compact algorithm, which we discussed in the previous section. The WaitForPendingFinalizers method pauses or suspends the current thread until the garbage collector finishes its execution.

Now that we have a fair understanding of how garbage collection works in C#, we will look at how we can perform memory management for unmanaged objects or unmanaged code.

Managing unmanaged resources

The garbage collection provided by the .NET Framework is good enough when we are dealing with managed objects. However, there are several instances in which we need to use unmanaged resources in our code. Some of these instances include the following:

- When we need to access OS memory using pointers
- When we are doing I/O operations related to file objects

In each of these circumstances, the garbage collector does not explicitly free up the memory. We need to explicitly manage the release of such resources. If we do not release such resources, then we may end up with problems related to memory leaks in the application, locks on OS files, leaks on connection threads to resources such as databases, and more.

To avoid these situations, C# provides finalization. Finalization allows us to cleanup unmanaged code in a class before the garbage collector is invoked.

 Please note that when using finalization, we cannot control when the code specified in finalization will be called. It's up to the garbage collector to determine when the object is no longer required. However, what we are sure of is that the finalization code will be called before the object gets cleaned up by the garbage collector.

To declare a finalizer in a class, we use the ~ syntax. The following is the code implementation we use to declare a finalizer for a particular class in C#:

```
public class SampleFinalizerClass
{
    ~SampleFinalizerClass()
    {

    }
}
```

In the preceding code example, we have declared a `SampleFinalizerClass` syntax. In order to clean up unmanaged resources in the class, we have declared a finalizer. The name of the finalizer is the same as that of the class but is appended with a ~.

In Finalizer, we can do things such as destroying pointer objects, releasing connections on files, releasing connection threads to databases, and more.

Now, although using the `Finalizer` keyword does clean up unmanaged code before the object is destroyed by the garbage collector, it does introduce some extra overhead for the garbage collector. Let's examine the following example in order to understand the reason behind this overhead.

The finalization mechanism

In this section, we will understand how the garbage collector performs finalization in the .NET Framework. To do finalization, it maintains two queues in the system:

- **The finalization queue**: The finalization queue is a data structure maintained by the garbage collector, which contains a reference to all the objects in a managed heap that have implemented the finalize method. Using this queue, the garbage collector essentially identifies all the objects that it needs to call the finalize method for in order to clean up the unmanaged code before the object can itself be destroyed.

- **The fReachable queue**: The `fReachable` queue is a data structure maintained by the garbage collector. It contains a reference to all the objects in the managed heap, which, even though they don't have any reference with the application root, can be deleted. However, before deleting them, it must call the finalize method to clean up the unmanaged code.

Let's try and understand this with the following example. Suppose we have an application wherein we have declared an object class, A, which has the finalize method. All other objects don't have the finalize method.

Please refer to the following representational diagram of the different structures that could be in the garbage collector:

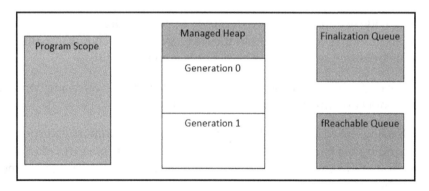

These structures can be described as follows:

- **Program Scope**: This represents the different objects that may be in the scope of the application root or, in other words, are being used in the particular block of the program.
- **Managed Heap**: This represents the heap memory structure maintained by the garbage collector to allocate memory to the objects present in the program scope. There are two divisions in the managed heap. One is **Generation 0**, which is used for newly created short-lived objects, and another is **Generation 1**, which is used to save long-lived objects.
- **Finalization Queue**: As indicated previously, this will contain a reference to all the objects in a managed heap that have an implementation of the finalize method.
- **fReachable Queue**: As indicated previously, this will contain a reference to all the objects in a managed heap for which, although they are not used in the program scope, the garbage collector needs to call the finalize method before their memory can be reclaimed.

Take a look at the following steps:

1. Declare the following two classes: `SampleFinalizeClass` and `SampleNoFinalizeClass`. Please note that the `SampleFinalizeClass` class has a finalize method:

```
public class SampleFinalizerClass
{
    ~SampleFinalizerClass()
    {
    }
}
public class SampleNoFinalizeClass
{
}
```

2. Create three objects; one for `SampleFinalizerClass` and two for `SampleNoFinalizerClass`:

```
SampleFinalizerClass b = new SampleFinalizerClass();
SampleNoFinalizeClass c = new SampleNoFinalizeClass();
SampleNoFinalizeClass d = new SampleNoFinalizeClass();
```

As objects b, c, and d are newly created objects, they will be added to generation 0 in the managed heap. While doing so, the garbage collector will also recognize that object b needs to have an additional call of the finalize method before it can be cleared. It will make this entry in the finalization queue by adding a reference to object b. The following diagram indicates what this would look like:

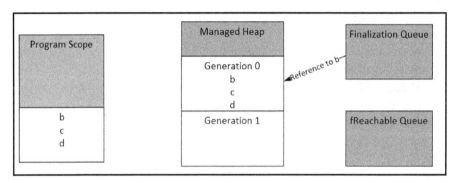

3. Pass the execution to another function by passing it to object c. The following is the code snippet for this:

```
GarbageCollectorFinalize(c);
// Please note that in the example cs file, these two lines will be
in the different blocks of the program
static private void GarbageCollectorFinalize(SampleNoFinalizeClass
a)
{
}
```

Now, suppose that, during program execution when the control is at the `GarbageCollectorFinalize` function, the garbage collector gets called. The garbage collector will identify that object d is no longer required and, therefore, its memory can be reclaimed. However, object c is being still referenced. Therefore, it will make an assumption that this could be a long-lived object and will thus promote the object to generation 1.

For object b, it will recognize that it's not referenced now; however, it does have a finalize method and so cannot be cleaned. Therefore, it keeps object b in memory for now. However, it removes the entry in the **Finalization Queue** and adds an entry in the **fReachable Queue** so that the variable can be cleared later.

Object b, as it cannot be removed from memory in the same way as object c, will also be promoted to **Generation 1**. The following shows this:

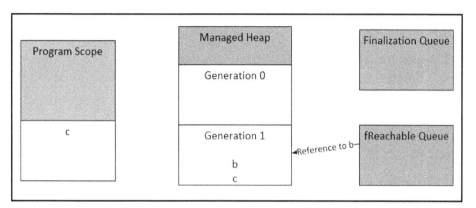

This illustrates the following:

- Even though object b may not still be required, it will be persisted for a longer period of time in the memory.
- As in the previous example, the garbage collector will need to execute another iteration in order to clear these objects from the memory.
- Unused objects that are implementing finalize may be moved to a higher generation.

Due to these reasons, it's highly advisable that whenever we need to declare an object that has the finalize method, we must implement the IDisposable interface.

Before we go on to look at the IDisposable interface, let's take a look at the following code implementation illustrating how the Finalizer function works in C#:

1. Consider the following code implementation, in which we declare a Finalizer class and then add a Finalizer function to it:

```
public class Finalizer
{
    public Finalizer()
    {
        Console.WriteLine("Creating object of Finalizer");
    }
    ~Finalizer()
    {
        Console.WriteLine("Inside the finalizer of class Finalizer");
```

```
    }
  }
```

Note that we have added text in both the `Finalizer` class constructor and in the `Finalizer` method.

2. Use the following code snippet to create an object of this class. Additionally, note that we have set a `null` value to the object. Setting a `null` value signifies that the object is no longer required in the application:

```
Finalizer f = new Finalizer();
f = null;
Console.ReadLine();
```

Note that, by using the `Console.ReadLine()` syntax, we are preventing the application from terminating. We have done this to analyze the output coming from the program. When we execute `.exe`, we get the following output:

```
C:\UCN Code Base\Programming-in-C-Exam-70-483-MCSD-Guide\Book70483Samples\Chapter 9\bin\Debug>Chapter9.exe
Creating object of Finalizer
```

In the preceding output, we are only getting the message from the constructor of the `Finalizer` class. Even though the object has been set as `null`, the finalizer of object `f` has not been executed yet.

This is due to the fact that we cannot specify when the garbage collector kicks in. Now, press *Enter* in the `.exe` execution. Notice that the program stops the execution; however, before it terminates, the finalizer is called to reclaim the memory of object `f`:

```
C:\UCN Code Base\Programming-in-C-Exam-70-483-MCSD-Guide\Book70483Samples\Chapter 9\bin\Debug>Chapter9.exe
Creating object of Finalizer

Inside the finalizer of class Finalizer
```

This proves we were right about finalizers, which we discussed earlier in this section. Even though object `f` was no longer needed in the application, it was still kept in the managed heap memory until the garbage collector executed the `Finalizer` method.

3. Now, add the following code to implicitly call the garbage collector and note that the finalize method is called immediately:

```
Finalizer f = new Finalizer();
f = null;
GC.Collect();
Console.ReadLine();
```

If we execute the program now, we will see the output from the finalizer of the `Finalizer` class, illustrating that the garbage collector immediately reclaimed the memory:

When we call the `GC.Collect()` method, internally, it calls the finalizers for all the objects that are no longer required. Thus we get the message, **Inside the finalizer of class Finalizer**.

In the preceding code example, we discovered that if we use `Finalizer`, we may have some performance implications in the program. Although we can use the `GC.Collect()` command to implicitly call the garbage collector, even that can cause some lag in the program. To overcome these issues, C# is capable of using the `IDisposable` interface in such circumstances. In the next section, we will understand how we can implement this interface and how it helps us achieve better performance.

The IDisposable interface

The finalize method, which we examined in the preceding section, has some performance implications for the system. With the `Finalizer` method, we are not sure of when the memory will be reclaimed by the garbage collector even after the object is no longer required. This implies that there is a possibility that unused memory will be persisted in a managed heap for longer than the desired amount of time.

With the `IDisposable` interface, we can assume control over when the memory is reclaimed for unmanaged resources in the application. The `IDisposable` interface in C# only has one method, which is `Dispose()`.

In this method, we can perform the same cleanup of unmanaged resources that we did in the Finalizer method. The following is the code implementation of the IDisposable interface:

```
public class DisposeImplementation : IDisposable
{
    public DisposeImplementation()
    {
        Console.WriteLine("Creating object of DisposeImplementation");
    }
    ~DisposeImplementation()
    {
        Console.WriteLine("Inside the finalizer of class
                          DisposeImplementation");
    }
    public void Dispose()
    {
    }
}
```

Notice that in the preceding example, we have declared a DisposeImplementation class and have implemented a IDisposable interface in this class.

As we are implementing the IDisposable interface, we have defined a Dispose function in the same class.

With the Dispose method, we need to clear all the unmanaged resources we are using in this class. While this approach is reliable in terms of when the resources will be reclaimed, there are some points we need to understand:

- It's the programmer's responsibility is to ensure that the Dispose method is called to reclaim the memory.
- If the programmer misses calling the Dispose method, there is a chance that the unmanaged resources will not be cleared.

Therefore, as a good programming practice, we should use both the Finalize and Dispose methods together in any implementation related to unmanaged resources. This will ensure that if the programmer has missed calling the Dispose method, then the Finalize method will always be there to reclaim the memory of the unmanaged resources.

Additionally, in order to ensure that we do not duplicate the work in Finalize and Dispose, we can use the approach illustrated in the following example.

For the same class that we used in the preceding implementation, we will declare an isDisposed field. The value of this field is set to false. In the Dispose method, we will reset its value to true to indicate that the cleanup for the unmanaged resources has occurred.

Now, to make sure that we do not do a cleanup of the resources a second time, we will check the value of this property in the Finalize method. If the Dispose property is set to true, indicating that cleanup has already occurred, then nothing will happen. If the Dispose property is set to false, indicating that cleanup has not occurred, then finalize will do a cleanup of the resources just as before. The following is the code implementation for this:

```
public class DisposeImplementation : IDisposable
{
    private bool isDisposed = false;
    public DisposeImplementation()
    {
        Console.WriteLine("Creating object of DisposeImplementation");
    }
    ~DisposeImplementation()
    {
        if(!isDisposed)
        {
            Console.WriteLine("Inside the finalizer of class
                            DisposeImplementation");
            this.Dispose();
        }
    }
    public void Dispose()
    {
        isDisposed = true;
        Console.WriteLine("Inside the dispose of class
                        DisposeImplementation");
        /// Reclaim memory of unmanaged resources
    }
}
```

Now, let's demonstrate these classes in two ways. First, we will call the Dispose method before calling the GC.Collect() method.

Call the `Dispose` method as follows:

```
DisposeImplementation d = new DisposeImplementation();
d.Dispose();
d = null;
GC.Collect();
Console.ReadLine();
```

In the preceding code, in the `Dispose` method we are setting the value in the flag to `true`. Apart from setting the flag, we will also be reclaiming memory from unmanaged resources. Therefore, when we call the finalize method, as the value in the flag is already set to `true`, the block inside the finalize method does not get executed.

The following is the output:

```
C:\UCN Code Base\Programming-in-C-Exam-70-483-MCSD-Guide\Book70483Samples\Chap
Creating object of DisposeImplementation
Inside the dispose of class DisposeImplementation
```

Now, let's consider another scenario in which the programmer forgets to call the `Dispose` method explicitly. The following is the code snippet for this:

```
DisposeImplementation d = new DisposeImplementation();
//d.Dispose();
d = null;
GC.Collect();
Console.ReadLine();
```

In the preceding code, we are not calling the `Dispose` method, so the value in the flag is set to `false`. Therefore, when the garbage collector executes the finalize method in object d, it also executes the code block to explicitly call the `Dispose` method for the same object.

The following is the output for this:

```
C:\UCN Code Base\Programming-in-C-Exam-70-483-MCSD-Guide\Book70483Samples\Chapter 9\bin\Debug\Chapter9.exe
Creating object of DisposeImplementation
Inside the finalizer of class DisposeImplementation
Inside the dispose of class DisposeImplementation
```

There is also a property that we can use to suppress calling the finalize method in the `Dispose` method. We can use this when we are sure that we don't need to verify the resources in the finalize method. The following is the syntax we can use to suppress calling the finalize method:

```
public void Dispose()
{
    isDisposed = true;
    GC.SuppressFinalize(this);
    Console.WriteLine("Inside the dispose of class
                       DisposeImplementation");
    /// Reclaim memory of unmanaged resources
}
```

In the preceding code block, we have used `GC.SupressFinalize()` for the current object. This will remove the references from the finalization queue, ensuring that the finalize method is never triggered for the current object. Therefore, if we execute the same input, we get the following output:

```
C:\UCN Code Base\Programming-in-C-Exam-70-483-MCSD-Guide\Book70483Samples\Chapter 9\bin\Debug>Chapter9.exe
Creating object of DisposeImplementation
Inside the dispose of class DisposeImplementation
```

Using this pattern, we can ensure that unmanaged resources are released from memory without compromising the performance of the application.

In the next section, we will look at using the `using` block as a good practice for when we are dealing with any classes implementing the `IDisposable` interface.

The using block

Any program is bound to have errors. There could be several unforeseen circumstances where our written logic will throw exceptions.

If we are using unmanaged resources, then unhandled exceptions can be very harmful. They can lead to issues related to dangling memory, unclosed connections to file objects, and more.

For example, consider the preceding example, where we have written a `Dispose` method to free up the memory. Let's say we have a scenario in which the application throws an exception before the `Dispose` method is called. In this case, the application will never have a chance to reclaim the memory occupied by the unmanaged resources.

To avoid such scenarios, C# lets us use the `using` block in our code. When we use the `using` block, no matter what happens inside the `using` block, the `Dispose` method is always called. Let's understand this with the following code implementation:

```
using (DisposeImplementation d = new DisposeImplementation())
{

}
Console.ReadLine();
GC.Collect();
Console.ReadLine();
```

Note that in the preceding code block, we are using the same `DisposeImplementation` class but are using it inside the `using` block. We are not explicitly nullifying the `d` object, to indicate to the garbage collector that it's no longer needed. Additionally, we are not explicitly calling the `Dispose` method to free up the unmanaged resources. Yet, when we run the program, we get the following output:

```
C:\UCN Code Base\Programming-in-C-Exam-70-483-MCSD-Guide\Book70483Sample
Creating object of DisposeImplementation
Inside the dispose of class DisposeImplementation
```

The `using` block handles it automatically. The `using` block ensures that as soon as the control is out of the `using` block, it will call the `Dispose` method for the object.

Now, let's consider a scenario in which we get an error in the `using` block. For the sake of explanation, we will introduce an error manually by throwing an exception.

The following is the code snippet for this:

```
using (DisposeImplementation d = new DisposeImplementation())
{
    throw new Exception("in here");
}
```

If we execute the code, we get the following result:

```
C:\UCN Code Base\Programming-in-C-Exam-70-483-MCSD-Guide\Book70483Samples\Chapter 9\bin\Debug>Chapter9.exe
Creating object of DisposeImplementation

Unhandled Exception: System.Exception: in here
    at Chapter_9.Program.Main(String[] args) in C:\UCN Code Base\Programming-in-C-Exam-70-483-MCSD-Guide\Book70483Samples\Chapter 9\Program.cs:line 25
Inside the dispose of class DisposeImplementation
```

Now, in the code, we have thrown an exception that is not being handled. However, even then, the `Dispose` method of the `DisposeImplementation` object is called before the application errors out due to the exception. If we don't use the `using` block, this will not happen. To illustrate this, remove the `using` block and throw the same exception in the application. The following is the code implementation for this:

```
DisposeImplementation d = new DisposeImplementation();
throw new Exception("in here");
```

In the preceding block, we have removed the `using` statement and are throwing an unhandled exception after the object is created. If we execute the code, we get the following output:

```
C:\UCN Code Base\Programming-in-C-Exam-70-483-MCSD-Guide\Book70483Samples\Chapter 9\bin\Debug>Chapter9.exe
Creating object of DisposeImplementation

Unhandled Exception: System.Exception: in here
    at Chapter_9.Program.Main(String[] args) in C:\UCN Code Base\Programming-in-C-Exam-70-483-MCSD-Guide\Book70483Samples\Chapter 9\Program.cs:line 29
```

As you can see in the preceding screenshot, during the program execution the `Dispose` method is never called for the `DisposeImplementation` object. This illustrates that, as a best practice, we must always use a `using` block for classes implementing the `IDisposable` interface.

Summary

In this chapter, we learned about memory management for unmanaged resources in C#. We revised the differences between managed code and unmanaged code in C#. We then looked at garbage collectors and delved into how they work. We learned about the memory storage structure of a managed heap, which it uses internally to allocate memory to different objects created during program execution. We learned about the internal divisions of generations, which the garbage collector uses internally to improve the performance of the system. We also learned about the mark-compact algorithm, which the garbage collector uses. We then explored how we can invoke garbage collection implicitly.

Following this, we went on to understand concepts about memory management for unmanaged objects. We learned about the `Finalize` method and how it facilitates memory management of an unmanaged object. We learned about the performance implications of using the `Finalize` method, and then we went on to understand how the `IDisposable` interface helps overcome its shortcomings. We learned about how we implement the `IDisposable` interface in a class and how we can combine both the `Dispose` and `Finalize` methods to improve the performance of the system. Finally, we learned about using the `using` block for classes that implement the `IDisposable` interface.

In the next chapter, we will look at how reflection works in C#.

Questions

1. A garbage collector can reclaim memory for unmanaged resources used in C# code.
    a. True
    b. False

2. Which of the following can be used to make sure the `Finalize` method is not called?
    a. `GC.Collect();`
    b. `GC.SupressFinalize(this);`
    c. `GC.WaitForPendingFinalizers();`
    d. None of these

3. Which one of the following statements is incorrect?

    a. `Finalize` can lead to performance implications due to the object remaining in memory longer than required.
    b. Generation 0 is used to save objects that are short-lived.
    c. Even if we use the `IDisposable` interface, we will not be able to suppress the calls that the garbage collector performs to execute the code in the `Finalize` method.
    d. The `using` block ensures that the `Dispose` method is called by the garbage collector automatically.

Answers

1. **b**
2. **b**
3. **c**, using SupressFinalize method we will be able to remove the reference from the finalize queue thus the finalize method will not be executed.

10
Find, Execute, and Create Types at Runtime Using Reflection

The .NET Framework contains not just code but metadata as well. Metadata is data about assemblies, types, methods, properties, and so on used in a program. These assemblies, properties, types, and methods are classes defined within the C# programming language. These classes, types, and methods are retrieved at runtime to parse a developer's application logic for execution. Attributes allow us to add extra information to these programs as well as methods that can be used during runtime while executing application logic.

The .NET Framework also allows developers to define this metadata information during development. It can be read during runtime using reflection. Reflection enables us to create an instance of the type retrieved and to invoke its methods and properties.

In this chapter, we will understand how the .NET Framework allows us to read and create metadata, and we will also learn how to use reflection to read metadata and process it during runtime. In the *Attributes* section, we will focus on using attributes, creating custom attributes, and learn how to retrieve attribute information at runtime. The *Reflection* section supplies an overview of how we can use reflection to create types, access properties, and invoke methods. Reflection also allows us to retrieve attribute information; for example, this could be extra information that we provided to .NET Runtime to be processed while executing the application logic.

In this chapter, we will look at the following topics:

- Attributes
- Reflection

Technical requirements

The exercises in this chapter can be performed using Visual Studio 2012 and later with the .NET Framework 2.0 and later. However, any new C# features from C# 7.0 and later require you to have Visual Studio 2017.

If you don't have a license for any of these products, then you can download the Community Version of Visual Studio 2017 from `https://visualstudio.microsoft.com/downloads/`.

The sample code for this chapter can be found on GitHub at `https://github.com/PacktPublishing/Programming-in-C-sharp-Exam-70-483-MCSD-Guide/tree/master/Chapter10`.

Attributes

Metadata or declarative information on types, methods, and properties can be associated using attributes. Metadata refers to what types are defined in a program. For instance, a class is a type: each class defines certain properties and methods, each property is of a type, and each method accepts certain data types and returns certain data types. All this information is referred to as metadata and can be accessed and retrieved during program execution.

Like any other method, while you define an attribute, you can define the parameters as well. You can define one or more attributes on an assembly, class, method, or property. Based on the program requirements, you can define what types of attribute your application needs and define them in your program. Once defined, you can read this information while executing your program and then process it.

In the following section, we will demonstrate how to use attributes and create custom attributes as per our requirements.

Using attributes

A declarative way of associating information to code can be done via attributes. However, only a few attributes can be used on every type. Instead, they are used for specific types. Attributes on any type can be specified by using square brackets, `[]`, on top of the type that we want to apply.

Let's take a look at the following code. Generally, we see the `Serializable` attribute when we want to serialize an object to the binary or XML formats. In real-world applications, when we need to transfer a large object over the wire, we serialize an object into one of the aforementioned formats and then send it. The serialize attribute on a class enables runtime to allow converting the object to binary or XML or any format required by the program:

```
[Serializable]
public class AttributeTest
{
//object of this class can now be serialized
}
```

Another common usage of attributes is in unit test projects. Observe the following code:

```
namespace Chapter10.Test
{
    [TestClass]
    public class UnitTest1
    {
        [TestMethod]
        public void TestMethod1()
        {
        }
    }
}
```

In the preceding code snippet, we create a new test project where two attributes are added to each class and method. By adding them in this way, we are letting the framework know that this class represents a test class and that the method is a test method.

As mentioned earlier, the use of attributes can be restricted to specific types. To achieve this, we will use attribute targets. By default, an attribute is applied to the preceding type. However, using a target, we can set whether the attribute applies to a class, method, or an assembly.

When the target is set to assembly, it means that the attribute is applied to the entire assembly. Similarly, a target can be set to a module, field, event, method, property, or type.

For example, an attribute can be set on a field to let the runtime know what type of input is accepted. Additionally, it can be set on a method to specify whether it is a normal method or a web method.

Some common attributes defined by the framework include the following:

- **Global**: Attributes that are applied at the assembly or module level are generally global attributes, for example, `AssemblyVersionAttribute`. You might have seen this in every .NET project that is created using Visual Studio.

  Let's take a look at the following example. Here, you can see the `assembly.cs` file created when you create any .NET project using Visual Studio. Every assembly contains the following code, which tells the runtime about the current assembly that is being executed:

  ```
  using System.Reflection;
  using System.Runtime.CompilerServices;
  using System.Runtime.InteropServices;

  [assembly: AssemblyTitle("Chapter10")]
  [assembly: AssemblyDescription("")]
  [assembly: AssemblyConfiguration("")]
  [assembly: AssemblyCompany("")]
  [assembly: AssemblyProduct("Chapter10")]
  [assembly: AssemblyCopyright("Copyright © 2019")]
  [assembly: AssemblyTrademark("")]
  [assembly: AssemblyCulture("")]

  [assembly: ComVisible(false)]

  // The following GUID is for the ID of the typelib if this project
  is exposed to COM
  [assembly: Guid("f8a2951a-4520-4d0f-ab30-7dd609db84d5")]

  [assembly: AssemblyVersion("1.0.0.0")]
  [assembly: AssemblyFileVersion("1.0.0.0")]
  ```

- **Obsolete**: This attribute allows us to mark an entity or a class that should not be used. Therefore, when applied, it generates a warning message that is provided while applying the attribute. This class defines three constructors: the first without any parameters, the second with one parameter, and the third with two parameters. From a code-readability perspective, it is recommended that we use constructors with parameters as they generate warning or error messages based on usage. Additionally, setting the second parameter to `true` while applying an attribute will throw an error, whereas `false` will generate a warning. In the following code, we will see how we can use an obsolete attribute.

In the following code snippet, we defined a class named `Firstclass`; later, a new class was created with the name `SecondClass`. When we want new users accessing our library to use the second class rather than the first class, then we can use an `Obsolete` attribute with a message so that new users will see it and act accordingly:

```
[System.Obsolete(Firstclass is not used any more instead use
SecondClass)]
class FirstClass
{
    //Do Firstthing
}

class SecondClass
{
    //Do Secondthing
}
```

- **Conditional**: When a conditional attribute is applied, the execution of the preceding code depends on the evaluation of the attribute. In a real-project scenario, while running a program in a live environment, you don't want to log information and messages and fill up your storage. Instead, you can have a conditional attribute on your log methods, which will allow you to write when a flag in your configuration file is set to `true`. In this way, you can actually implement selecting logging.

In the following code, we have a `LogMessage` method; however, the attribute above the class will let the runtime application know that, when the `LogErrorOn` attribute is set to `yes` or `true`, it should execute this method:

```
using System;
using System.Diagnostics;
Public class Logging
{
    [Conditional(LogErrorON)]
    public static void LogMessage(string message)
    {
        Console.WriteLine(message)
    }
}
public class TestLogging
{
    static void Main()
    {
        Trace.Msg("Main method executing...");
        Console.WriteLine("This is the last statement.");
```

```
        }
    }
```

- **Caller information**: The caller information attribute allows you to retrieve who is calling the method. They are `CallerfilePathAttribute`, `CallerLineNumberAttribute`, `CallerMemberNameAttribute`. Each one has its own purpose, as their names suggest. They allow us to get the line number, the method name, and the path of the file.

Creating custom attributes

C# allows you to define your own attributes. This is similar to normal C# programming where you define classes and properties. To define an attribute, the first thing you need to do is to inherit it from the `System.Attribute` class. The class and properties you define are used to store and retrieve data at runtime.

There are four steps that you need to complete in order to complete defining custom attributes:

- Attribute usage
- Declaring attribute class
- Constructors
- Properties

Attribute usage can be defined by using `System.AttributeUsageAttribute`. We already mentioned that there are restrictions on certain attributes, which define where they can be used—for example, in classes, methods, or properties. `AttributeUsageAttribte` allows us to define such restrictions. `AllowMultiple` specifies whether this attribute can be used more than once on a specific type. Inherited controls defining child classes form the current attribute class. The following is the general syntax for using the `AttributeUsage` class:

```
[AttributeUsage(AttributeTargets.All, Inherited = false, AllowMultiple =
true)]
```

As you might have observed, you can declare the `AttributeUsage` attribute using its constructor on top of the custom attribute you want to define with the three parameters. With `AtributeTargetsAll`, you can use `CustomAttribute` on any type of element that is a class, property, method, and so on. A full list of allowed values is defined at `https://docs.microsoft.com/en-us/dotnet/api/system.attributetargets?view=netframework-4.7.2#System_AttributeTargets_All`.

`Inherited` and `AllowMultiple` are both Boolean properties, which accept true or false.

Once we define `AttributeUsage`, we can now move on to declare our custom class. This should be a public class and must inherit from the `System.Attribute` class.

Now that we have our class declared, we can move on and define our constructors and properties. The framework allows us to define one or more constructors, covering all possible scenarios around a different combination of properties. Let's define a custom attribute. A constructor of these attributes accepts three parameters—`AttributeTargets`, `AllowMultiple`, and `Inherited`:

```
using System;

namespace Chapter10
{
    [System.AttributeUsage(System.AttributeTargets.Field |
System.AttributeTargets.Property, Inherited =false,AllowMultiple = false)]
    public class CustomerAttribute : Attribute
    {
        public CustomerType Type { get; set; }

        public CustomerAttribute()
        {
            Type = CustomerType.Customer;
        }
    }

    public enum CustomerType
    {
        Customer,
        Supplier,
        Vendor
    }
}
```

The preceding code defines a custom attribute named `CustomerAttribute`. We also defined a `CustomerType` enum that we want to use as an `Attribute` property. By not defining any parameters in the constructor and assigning the `Customer` type to a `Type` property, we are telling runtime, by default, when its value is a customer. Additionally, this attribute is set to be used on either a field or property so that it cannot be used at the class level.

Now, let's examine how we can use this attribute in our class:

```
namespace Chapter10
{
    internal class Account
    {
        public string CustomerName { get; set; }

        [Customer]
        public RatingType Rating { get; set; }
    }

    public enum RatingType
    {
        Gold =1,
        Silver =2,
        Bronze=3
    }
}
```

Here, we defined an `Account` class where we used our custom attribute. We applied an attribute without any parameters. This means that, by default, we create an account of the customer type. In the following section, we will demonstrate how we can retrieve these attributes and use them in our application logic.

Retrieving metadata

As you are aware of OOP concepts, retrieving attribute information is as simple as creating an instance of the attribute that we want to retrieve, and then invoking the `GetCustomAttribute` method of the `System.Attribute` class.

In the following example, we define a new attribute called `ChapterInfo` and define a constructor to mark two of its properties as required parameters:

```
[System.AttributeUsage(System.AttributeTargets.Class, Inherited
=false,AllowMultiple = false)]
    public class ChapterInfoAttribute : Attribute
    {
        public string ChapterName{ get; set; }
        public string ChapterAuthor { get; set; }

        public ChapterInfoAttribute(string Name, string Author)
        {
            ChapterName = Name;
            ChapterAuthor = Author;
```

```
        }
    }
```

`ChapterName` and `ChapterAuthor` are the two required parameters that the developer has to define when using this attribute.

As you can see, in the following code the attribute is being defined over the `Program` class with two values: `Name` and `Author`. In the main method, `GetCustomAttribute` is invoked to read its properties, as you would do for any other class type variable:

```
namespace Chapter10
{
    [ChapterInfo("SAMPLECHAPTER", "AUTHOR1")]
    class Program
    {
        static void Main(string[] args)
        {
            ChapterInfoAttribute _attribute =
(ChapterInfoAttribute)Attribute.GetCustomAttribute(typeof(Program),
typeof(ChapterInfoAttribute));
            Console.WriteLine($"Chapter Name is: {_attribute.ChapterName}
and Chapter Author is: {_attribute.ChapterAuthor}");
            // Keep the console window open in debug mode.
            System.Console.WriteLine("Press any key to exit.");
            System.Console.ReadKey();
        }
    }
}
```

Observe the following output:

```
//Output
Chapter Name is: SAMPLECHAPTER and Chapter Author is: AUTHOR1
Press any key to exit.
```

As you can see, the (`[ChapterInfo("SAMPLECHAPTER", "AUTHOR1")]`) values passed in the attribute definition over the program class were retrieved and displayed.

Reflection

Reflection is a way to query metadata at runtime from the application program. Reflection supplies type information from the assemblies loaded into memory that you can use to create an instance of the class and also access properties and methods of the class.

For example, your application code executes a query and returns a dataset object, but your frontend accepts a custom class or model, and the model is defined during runtime. Based on the request received, reflection can be used to create the required model/class at runtime, access its properties or fields, and set their value by traversing through the resulting dataset.

Additionally, in previous sections, we learned how we can create custom attributes. So, in a scenario where you create an attribute to restrict numbers in a specific property, you can then use reflection to read the attribute, get the preceding property, implement application logic to restrict numbers, or display a message to users.

We can also use reflection to create a type at runtime and access its methods and properties. Reflection works with `System.Types` to query information about assemblies that are currently loaded into memory and are being executed.

The **Common Language Runtime (CLR)** manages application domains with boundaries around objects that are of the same scope. This process includes loading assemblies into these domains and controlling them as required.

In the .NET world, assemblies contain modules, modules contain types, and types contain members. An assembly class is used to load assemblies. Modules are used to identify information about classes in the assembly as well as global and non-global methods.

There are many methods available in the `Reflection` class, such as `MethodInfo`, `PropertyInfo`, `Type`, `CustomAttribute`, and many more. These methods help developers to retrieve information at runtime. In the previous example, we used the `GetCustomAttribute` method to retrieve attribute information and displayed it.

Invoking methods and using properties

In this section, we'll take a look at how we can access the properties and methods of a custom class at runtime using reflection.

This example serves to give you an idea of how we can access methods and properties using reflection at runtime. However, based on your requirements, you can dynamically access properties, their types and methods, and their parameters.

We created a new custom class where we defined two integer type properties: `Number1` and `Number2`. Then, we defined a public method that accepts a parameter and returns a number to be added or subtracted:

```
internal class CustomClass1
    {
        public int Number1 { get; set; }
        public int Number2 { get; set; }

        public int Getresult(string action)
        {
            int result = 0;
            switch (action)
            {
                case "Add":
                    result = Number1 + Number2;
                    Console.WriteLine($"Sum of numbers {Number1} and
{Number2} is : {result}");
                    break;

                case "Subtract":
                    result = Number1 - Number2;
                    Console.WriteLine($"Difference of numbers {Number1} and
{Number2} is : {result}");
                    break;
            }
            return result;
        }
    }
```

Then, we created a simple method where we could access the properties and methods of the custom class that we created previously. In the first line, we retrieved the type information of the custom class. Using this type, we created an instance of the class using the `Activator.CreateInstance` method. Now, using the `Getproperties` method of the type we retrieved, we accessed all the properties and set a value to each of them based on the property name.

In the next line, using the `Type` information of the object, we retrieve `MethodInfo` using the `GetMethod` method. Then, we invoked the `public` method of the custom class twice with two different actions called `Add` and `Subtract`:

```
public static void GetResults()
        {
            Type objType = typeof(CustomClass1);
            object obj = Activator.CreateInstance(objType);
            foreach (PropertyInfo prop in objType.GetProperties())
```

```
    {
        if(prop.Name =="Number1")
            prop.SetValue(obj, 100);
        if (prop.Name == "Number2")
            prop.SetValue(obj, 50);
    }

    MethodInfo mInfo = objType.GetMethod("Getresult");
    mInfo.Invoke(obj, new string[] { "Add" });
    mInfo.Invoke(obj, new string[] { "Subtract" });
}
```

If you run the program and debug every line, you will see that each property has been retrieved and values have been set. The following is the output of the program:

```
Sum of numbers 100 and 50 is : 150
Difference of numbers 100 and 50 is : 50
Press any key to exit.
```

This sample is a simple one, as we created two properties, both of the integer type. However, in real time, such simple scenarios may not exist. Therefore, at runtime, you need to use the GetType method in order to understand the type of property retrieved.

Additionally, in the example we were able to get the type of the Custom class where we hardcoded it. Using generics, we can even pass the class at runtime and get the info type.

Summary

In this chapter, we learned how we can use system attributes, create custom attributes, retrieve attributes, and then use them in our application logic. Using reflection to retrieve attribute information, we also looked at how we can create types, access properties, and invoke a method.

In the next chapter, we will gain an understanding of why is it important to validate application input, the type of information that flows into our application, and how can we handle it.

Questions

1. While creating custom attributes, a target can be set to restrict the usage of an attribute?
    1. True
    2. False

2. _____ is the method used to retrieve attribute information.
    1. `GetAttributeValue`
    2. `GetCustomAttribute`
    3. `GetMetadata`
    4. `GetAttributeMetadata`

3. The system allows you to retrieve property information from the object?
    1. True
    2. False

Answers

1. **True**
2. **GetAttributeValue**
3. **True**

11
Validating Application Input

When working on real-world projects, there may be scenarios where different kinds of users access your application and enter information in to it. In the event that any aspect of the scenario was not handled properly, or any input data was not properly parsed, this can cause your application to crash or result in the corruption of your application data. Even though you validate all the input data used and accessed within your application when deployed in production, input data can interact with other external applications, which can place your application in jeopardy.

The purpose of this chapter is to understand the importance of validating input data in your application. Different validation techniques are available in the .NET Framework to validate JSON data and XML data.

In upcoming sections, we will focus on why it is important to validate input data, how we can manage data integrity, how to use framework-provided parsing statements and regular expressions, and how to validate JSON and XML data. After reading this chapter, you will be able to create application logic to validate incoming data and also handle scenarios where exceptions might occur.

In this chapter, we will cover the following topics:

- The importance of validating input data
- Data integrity
- Parsing and converting
- Regular expressions
- JSON and XML

Technical requirements

Exercises in this chapter can be implemented using Visual Studio 2012 or above with .NET Framework 2.0 or above. However, any new C# features from C# 7.0 and above require you to have Visual Studio 2017.

If you don't have a license for any of the products, you can download the community version of Visual Studio 2017 from `https://visualstudio.microsoft.com/downloads/`.

The sample code for this chapter can be found on GitHub at `https://github.com/ PacktPublishing/Programming-in-C-Exam-70-483-MCSD-Guide/tree/master/ Book70483Samples/Chapter 11`.

The importance of validating input data

Creating and running an application in isolation mode makes your application run without any issues. However, when working on a real project, your application will be executing in an environment where many external interfaces may interact. In such scenarios, is your application capable of handling such communications? Can it handle all kinds of data from these external applications? There will be many users who will try to use your system; some may use it properly, and others may try to break your system. Can your application tolerate such interactions?

There may be problems with both types of user. Those who use your system properly may make mistakes by entering incorrect data or may forget to provide the requisite data. In the event your application has logic based on the user's date of birth and the user enters some text data, your application might throw an exception and crash.

In a scenario where users try to break your application by providing data that doesn't match any of the types that your application expects, this may crash your application and a significant amount of time may be devoted to recovering it.

Any of these aforementioned actions can cause temporary damage to your application or may constitute a major issue. When it corrupts your database, recovering your application may entail more time and effort.

Creating an application using .NET Framework involves the provision of some built-in features that can be utilized to validate some of the input data, be it from internal or external users or external applications. Framework allows you to add attributes over each property that can validate data for you. These are available when you use ASP.NET or the Entity Framework, and so on. As you learned in previous chapters, you can define custom attributes and perform validation on the data entered by users.

In the next section, we will see a variety of data integrity scenarios that are important to understand while working on data validations in your applications.

Data integrity

While working on any application, it is very important to design it in such a way that it handles all scenarios, or at least provides user-friendly messages to users on what went wrong. We have already learned about exception handling in `Chapter 7`, *Implementing Exception Handling*, which can be handy in such scenarios.

While working on a database or distributed applications, data integrity plays a vital role.

Data integrity applies differently in different scenarios:

- For example, if you are creating an application and storing user information in a table, one of the principles you may adopt might be to not maintain duplicate users in the table so that they are uniquely identifiable. This is termed **entity integrity**.

- In a scenario where you are collecting demographic information, you may allow certain values, or ranges of values, in specific fields. This is termed **domain integrity**. In other words, you are making sure that the data entered in each record/entity is valid.

- There may be a scenario where you have to enter data into multiple tables with a parent-child relationship. In such cases, your application should maintain these relationships while saving information to the database. This is called **referential integrity**.

- Last but not least, in a business scenario, in order to achieve the desired outcome based on a business process, your application may enforce certain constraints. This is called **user-defined** integrity, or **business-defined** integrity.

There are many real-world examples. These include any eCommerce applications or any banking applications. How critical is it to validate and control input and program flow? In a banking application, what would happen in the event of a power outage? In an eCommerce application, how would a shopping cart be maintained between multiple sessions, when the user closes their browser, or in the event that a clean-up job kicks in?

Many of these data integrity options are available in the latest databases and frameworks, which enable us to utilize these options to validate and control the flow of our program.

One of the ways to validate data is to use the data annotations assembly, which is available in .NET Framework 3.5 and above. Data annotations talk about adding more information about an attribute or property in a class. You can use data annotations by referring to the `System.ComponentModel.DataAnnotations` namespace. These data annotations fall into three categories:

- Validation attributes
- Display attributes
- Modeling attributes

Each of these attributes is used for a specific purpose: validation attributes enforce the validation of data; display attributes are used as display labels on the user interface, and modeling attributes represent the recommended use of the relevant attribute.

In the following class, we will reference `System.ComponentModel.DataAnnotations` and use validating attributes, display attributes, and modeling attributes on the three available properties:

```
using System;
using System.ComponentModel.DataAnnotations;

namespace Chapter11
{
    public class Student
    {
        [Required(ErrorMessage = "Fullname of the student is
         mandatory")]
        [StringLength(100,MinimumLength =5,ErrorMessage ="Name should
         have minimum of 5 characters")]
        [DataType(DataType.Text)]
        public string FullName { get; set; }

        [DataType(DataType.EmailAddress)]
        [EmailAddress]
        public string EmailAddress { get; set; }
```

```
        [DataType(DataType.Date)]
        [Display(Name ="Date of Birth")]
        public DateTime DOB { get; set; }
    }
}
```

On the name property, we have a required field attribute and string length restrictions as validation attributes. The data type set to text is a data modeling attribute that tells the system that the name attribute only accepts text values. On the DOB property, we have a display attribute. However, display properties can be used in either ASP.NET applications or WPF applications.

Now, we create an instance of the Student class and try to validate its data. Data annotations help us to define ValidationContext; when an object is validated, ValidationResult will be returned, which consists of all properties and their respective error messages. While defining properties in the Student class, we added attributes with messages. When ValidationContext returns results, it returns each of these properties with their respective attributes and messages:

```
Student st = new Student();
st.FullName = "st1";
st.EmailAddress = "st@st";
st.DOB = DateTime.Now;

ValidationContext context = new ValidationContext(st, null, null);
List<ValidationResult> results = new List<ValidationResult>();
bool valid = Validator.TryValidateObject(st, context, results, true);
if (!valid)
{
    foreach (ValidationResult vr in results)
    {
        Console.Write("Student class Property Name :{0}",
          vr.MemberNames.First());
        Console.Write(" :: {0}{1}", vr.ErrorMessage,
          Environment.NewLine);
    }
}
```

When you create a ValidationContext instance, we use the constructor that takes three parameters. These are as follows:

- An instance of an object that we want to validate
- An object that implements the IServiceProvider interface, which means that you need to create an instance using the GetService method
- A dictionary of a key/value pair to consume

Also, while trying to validate an object, we passed `true` as the last parameter, which represents the validation of all properties of the object.

When you execute the program, you should see the following output. The student's name should have a minimum of five characters and the email address should be in a valid format:

```
Student class Property Name :FullName :: Name should have minimum of 5
characters
Student class Property Name :EmailAddress :: The EmailAddress field is not
a valid e-mail address.
Press any key to exit.
```

In the next section, we will look at the different features available in C# to validate our data.

Parsing and converting

Entity integrity and domain integrity involve allowing valid values into our application for further processing. Valid values include manipulating or managing input provided by a user, rendering it as data that is acceptable to the application. This process may including parsing specific types of data to the type our application accepts, converting data types, and so on.

`Parse` and `TryParse` are two statements available across multiple data types within the .NET Framework, for example if you are writing a console application and you want to accept parameters as command-line arguments. In a console application, command-line parameters are always of the string type. So, how do you parse these arguments from the string type to another required type?

In the following example, we know that our first parameter is a Boolean value, but is passed as a string. When we are certain of the value passed, we can use the parse method to convert the string to a Boolean. `Parse` compares to with static string values and returns either `true` or `false`. When invalid data is passed, an exception is thrown—`Input string is in an invalid format`.

Let's start with an example. Define two methods that each take a parameter of the string type. We want to parse it into Boolean and integer values. Parsing a Boolean is as simple as using the parse method of a Boolean type. However, for the integer type, there are two approaches. One is to use parse, as we did when parsing a Boolean, and the other is TryParse. When we are not sure if the string parameter provided is an integer or not, then we can use the TryParse method, which will then give us a bool result on which we can set up our logic. In the following example, we are showing both ways. This will allow us to handle exceptions and provide the user with a meaningful message:

```
internal class ParseSamples
    {
        internal void ProcessBool(string boolValue)
        {
            if (bool.Parse(boolValue))
            {
                Console.WriteLine($"Parsed bool value is :
                {bool.Parse(boolValue)}");
            }
        }

        internal void ProcessInteger(string intValue)
        {
            int processedValue =int.MinValue;
            if (int.TryParse(intValue, out processedValue))
            {
                Console.WriteLine($"Parsed int value is :
                {processedValue}");
            }
            else
            {
                Console.WriteLine("Parsed value is not an integer");
            }
            Console.WriteLine($"Parsed int value is :
             {int.Parse(intValue)}");
```

Now that our sample class is ready, let's invoke it using our main method. Here, we have a switch statement to check the length of the arguments passed to the main method. If it is 1, call the processbool method; if it is 2, call both methods, otherwise, a message is displayed:

```
static void Main(string[] args)
        {
            ParseSamples ps = new ParseSamples();
            switch (args.Length)
            {
```

```
        case 1:
            ps.ProcessBools(args[0]);
            break;
        case 2:
            ps.ProcessBools(args[0]);
            ps.ProcessIntegers(args[1]);
            break;
        default:
            Console.WriteLine("Please provide one or two
             command line arguments");
            break;
    }


    // Keep the console window open in debug mode.
    System.Console.WriteLine("Press any key to exit.");
    System.Console.ReadKey();
}
```

To invoke this method, because we are trying to read command-line arguments in our program, these need to be passed at runtime or from the **Properties** window, which will then be read at runtime. Parameters are passed from the **Properties** window as follows. Right-click on **Project**, select **Properties**, and then navigate to the **Debug** tab, where you can set these parameters:

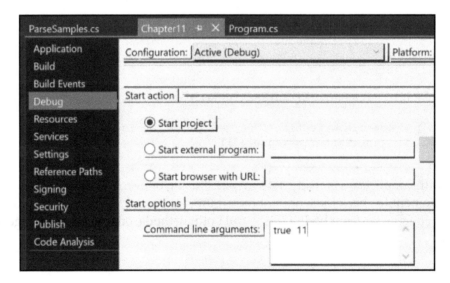

When you run the program, as you pass 1 or 2 arguments, the respective case statements get executed and the output will be presented on the screen:

```
//Command line argument true
Parsed bool value is : True
Press any key to exit.

//Command line argument true 11
Parsed bool value is : True
Parsed int value is : 11
Parsed int value is : 11
Press any key to exit.

//Command line arguments true Madhav
Parsed bool value is : True
Parsed value is not an integer
```

Here, in the last output, `TryParse` statements are processed, but `Parse` will throw an error as follows. Because `Parse` expects a proper string to be passed, when a non-string value is passed, or when your statement doesn't correspond to the value passed, it throws an error. However, if we handle this statement using `try..catch`, we won't see any issues. Otherwise, your program will break and an exception dialog will appear as follows:

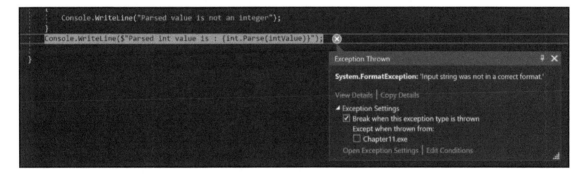

Another way to validate your input is to use the conversion method. `Convert` is a method defined in .NET Framework that casts a base type to another base type. Unlike `Parse`, `Convert` accepts an object of a type and converts it into another type. `Parse` accepts only string input. Also, when a `null` value is passed, `Convert` returns the minimum value of the target type. The `Convert` class has a few static methods that support conversion to and from different types in .NET Framework. Types supported by the `Convert` method are `Boolean`, `Char`, `SByte`, `Byte`, `Int16`, `Int32`, `Int64`, `UInt16`, `UInt32`, `UInt64`, `Single`, `Double`, `Decimal`, `DateTime`, and `String`.

When you apply the `Convert` method, you can expect any of the following output. The system either successfully converts the source type to the target type or throws one of the following exceptions: `FormatException`, `InvalidCastException`, or `ArgumentNull`. Let's look at an example:

```
internal void ConvertSample()
{
    try
    {
        string svalue =string.Empty;
        Console.WriteLine(Convert.ToInt32(svalue));
    }
    catch (FormatException fx)
    {
        Console.WriteLine("Format Exception : "+fx.Message);
    }
    try
    {
        double dvalue = 1212121212121212.12;
        Console.WriteLine(Convert.ToInt32(dvalue));
    }
    catch (OverflowException ox)
    {
        Console.WriteLine("OverFlow Exception : " + ox.Message);
    }
    try
    {
        DateTime date= DateTime.Now;
        Console.WriteLine(Convert.ToDouble(date));
    }
    catch (InvalidCastException ix)
    {
        Console.WriteLine("Invalid cast Exception : " + ix.Message);
    }
    double dvalue1 = 12.22;
    Console.WriteLine("Converted Value : " + Convert.ToInt32(dvalue1));
}
```

In the preceding example, we tried to convert different types. The important thing to note is that you can get any output while converting, and so you have to handle it accordingly in your application code. Also, while converting decimal or float values to integers, precise information is lost. However, no exception is thrown.

With same-type conversions, there won't be any exceptions or conversions. `FormatException` is thrown when you try to convert a string to any other type. `String` to `Boolean`, `String` to `Char`, or `String` to `DateTime` may throw this exception.

`InvalidCastException` occurs when a conversion between specific types is not valid, as in the following examples:

- Conversions from `Char` to `Boolean`, `Single`, `Double`, `Decimal`, or `DateTime`
- Conversions from `Boolean`, `Single`, `Double`, `Decimal`, or `DateTime` to `Char`
- Conversions from `DateTime` to any other type except `String`
- Conversions from any other type, except `String`, to `DateTime`

`OverflowException` is thrown in the event of loss of data, for example, when converting a huge decimal to an integer, as shown in our example. In our example, we are converting a double value to an `int` value. The `int` type variable in C# has a minimum and maximum value. If the number passed is outside this range, an overflow exception is raised:

```
Format Exception : Input string was not in a correct format.
OverFlow Exception : Value was either too large or too small for an Int32.
Invalid cast Exception : Invalid cast from 'DateTime' to 'Double'.
Converted Value : 12
Press any key to exit.
```

Regular expressions

When talking about validating input data, it is important to have an understanding of regular expressions, which is a powerful way to process text. It employs a pattern-matching technique to identify a pattern of text in input texts and validates it to the required format. For example, if our application wants to validate an email, regular expressions can be used to identify whether the email address provided is in a valid format. it checks for `.com`, `@`, and other patterns and returns if it matches a required pattern.

`System.Text.RegularExpressions.Regex` acts as a regular expression engine in .NET Framework. To use this engine, we need to pass two parameters, the first a pattern to match and the second text where this pattern matching happens.

The regex class comes up with four different methods – `IsMatch`, `Match`, `Matches`, and `Replace`. The `IsMatch` method is used to identify a pattern in the input text. The `Match` or `Matches` methods are used to get all occurrences of text that match a pattern. The `Replace` method replaces text that matches a regular expression pattern.

Now, let's jump into some examples to understand regular expressions:

```
public void ReplacePatternText()
{
    string pattern = "(FIRSTNAME\\.? |LASTNAME\\.?)";

    string[] names = { "FIRSTNAME. MOHAN", "LASTNAME. KARTHIK" };
    foreach(string str in names)
    {
        Console.WriteLine(Regex.Replace(str, pattern, String.Empty));
    }
}

public void MatchPatternText()
{
    string pattern = "(Madhav\\.?)";

    string names = "Srinivas Madhav. and Madhav. Gorthi are same";
    MatchCollection matColl = Regex.Matches(names, pattern);
    foreach (Match m in matColl)
    {
        Console.WriteLine(m);
    }
}

public void IsMatchPattern()
{
    string pattern = @"^c\w+";

    string str = "this sample is done as part of chapter 11";
    string[] items = str.Split(' ');
    foreach (string s in items)
    {
        if (Regex.IsMatch(s, pattern))
        {
            Console.WriteLine("chapter exists in string str");
        }
    }
}
```

The `ReplacePatternTest` method identifies `FirstName` and `LastName` from an array of strings and replaces them with an empty string. In the `MatchPatternText` method, we identify how many times `Madhav` exists in the string; in the third method, we use a pattern to identify a chapter word. The `^c\w+` pattern represents the beginning of the word, `c` represents a word starting with *c*, `\w` represents any characters, and + represents matches with the preceding token.

The following output shows the first two lines of the output from
the `ReplacePatternTest` method, where we replaced `Madhav` with an empty string. The
second output set identifies a pattern and displays it. The third set is where we identify a
chapter word in the string:

```
//ReplacePatternText method
MOHAN
 KARTHIK

//MatchPatternText method
Madhav.
Madhav.

//IsMatchPattern method
chapter exists in string str
Press any key to exit.
```

JSON and XML

With the extensive use of internet and cloud applications, JSON and XML are becoming
more important in terms of data transfer between applications. Using JSON and XML also
increases the number of data-related issues, unless the data is validated.

Schema validation can be used to validate an XML file, which will help us to identify
whether XML is inline with data types defined. However, to validate the actual data, you
may still be using the methods we discussed in this chapter. Visual Studio helps you to
create a schema file. The `Xsd.exe <XML file>` command will create a schema file. Here is
an example XML file.

This XML file has a `Students` root element, in which information is held in relation to
multiple students. Each `student` element has child elements that hold values
including `FirstName`, `LastName`, `School`, and `DOB`:

```
<?xml version="1.0" encoding="utf-8" ?>
<Students>
  <student>
    <FirstName>Student1</FirstName>
    <LastName>Slast</LastName>
    <School>School1</School>
    <DOB>23/10/1988</DOB>
  </student>
</Students>
```

Visual Studio allows us to create a schema for this XML. Open the XML file in Visual Studio and select the **XML** menu item. The **Create Schema** option will become available. Selecting this will create a .xsd schema:

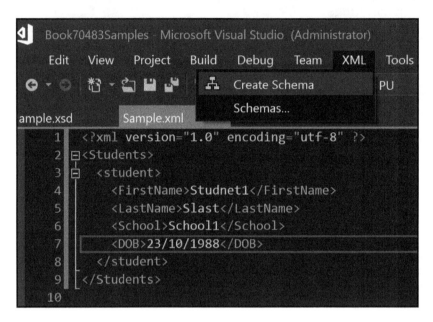

The content of the Sample.xsd file is as follows:

```xml
<?xml version="1.0" encoding="utf-8"?>
<xs:schema attributeFormDefault="unqualified"
elementFormDefault="qualified" xmlns:xs="http://www.w3.org/2001/XMLSchema">
  <xs:element name="Students">
    <xs:complexType>
      <xs:sequence>
        <xs:element name="student">
          <xs:complexType>
            <xs:sequence>
              <xs:element name="FirstName" type="xs:string" />
              <xs:element name="LastName" type="xs:string" />
              <xs:element name="School" type="xs:string" />
              <xs:element name="DOB" type="xs:string" />
            </xs:sequence>
          </xs:complexType>
        </xs:element>
      </xs:sequence>
    </xs:complexType>
  </xs:element>
</xs:schema>
```

As you can see, names are defined as a string, as are dates. So when you access this date element, we may need to convert it in order to use it in our application.

Now, we will jump to some sample code and observe how to validate an XML file using a schema:

```
static void LoadXML()
{
    var path = new Uri(Path.GetDirectoryName(System.
     Reflection.Assembly.
     GetExecutingAssembly().CodeBase)).LocalPath;
    XmlSchemaSet schema = new XmlSchemaSet();
    schema.Add("", path + "\\sample.xsd");
    XmlReader rd = XmlReader.Create(path + "\\sample.xml");
    XDocument doc = XDocument.Load(rd);
    Console.WriteLine("Validating XML");
    doc.Validate(schema, ValidationEventHandler);
    Console.WriteLine("Validating XML Completed");
}
static void ValidationEventHandler(object sender,
 ValidationEventArgs e)
{
    XmlSeverityType type;
    if (Enum.TryParse<XmlSeverityType>(e.Severity.ToString(), out
     type))
    {
        if (type == XmlSeverityType.Error) throw new
         Exception(e.Message);
    }
}
```

As we passed a valid XML file, we did not encounter any issues validating it. However, when you try to remove any elements from it, such as removing the school from the XML file, then you encounter an error message. Try it yourself when you practice this lab so as to understand validation in greater detail:

```
Validating XML
Validating XML Completed
Press any key to exit.
```

When executed, this method either writes a message on the console to the effect that validation is complete, or it may throw an exception in the event of an error in the XML.

Another format we discussed is JSON. .NET Framework provides us with JSON serializers, which can be used to validate JSON. This is like creating a C# class, using a JSON serializer to convert a C# object to JSON, and then deserializing back to the C# object. It is similar to the .NET Framework serialization concept. However, not every JSON has a schema to serialize or deserialize. In this case, we will work on validating the JSON format. In the following example, we create a class serializer to convert a JSON object and then deserialize it back to an object.

Here, we are creating a class called `Authors` with three properties: `AuthorName`, `Skills`, and `DOB`. We will use this object to serialize and deserialize this object:

```
public class Authors
{
    public string AuthorName { get; set; }
     public string Skills { get; set; }
     public DateTime DOB { get; set; }
}
```

In the next section, we created a new method where we used the `Newtonsoft.Json` namespace to convert the `Authors` object to JSON. You can get `NewtonSoft.Json` using NuGet packages:

```
static string GetJson()
{
    string result = string.Empty;
    Authors aclass = new Authors() { AuthorName = "Author1", Skills =
     "C#,Java,SQL", DOB = DateTime.Now.Date };
    result = JsonConvert.SerializeObject(aclass);
    Console.WriteLine($"JSON object : {result}");
    return result;
}
```

Next, we will convert JSON to the `Authors` object using the `JSON.Deserialize` method:

```
static Authors GetObject(string result)
{
    Authors aresult = JsonConvert.DeserializeObject<Authors>(result);
    Console.WriteLine($"Name: {aresult.AuthorName}, Skills =
     {aresult.Skills},
    DOB = {aresult.DOB}");
    return aresult;
}
```

Following is the program that invokes both these methods. Initially, we invoke the `GetJSON` method to get the `Json` string, and then use this string to convert it to an `Authors` object using the `GetObject` method. In the second line, we modify the string result that we got in the first line, and try to deserialize it. This operation will throw an exception.

In the following, we are trying to modify the `.json` results by concatenating text called `Test`. This is what happens when you modify the `.json` object and try to deserialize it to an `Authors` object:

```
string result = GetJson();
Authors a = GetObject(result);
string result1 = string.Concat(result, "Test");
Console.ReadLine();
Authors a1 = GetObject(result1);
```

The following output shows the JSON object that we converted from the `Authors` object, followed by the `Author` object that we deserialized from the JSON object:

```
JSON object :
{"AuthorName":"Author1","Skills":"C#,Java,SQL","DOB":"2019-03-31T00:00:00+1
1:00"}
Name: Author1, Skills = C#,Java,SQL, DOB = 3/31/2019 12:00:00 AM
Press any key to exit.
```

Here is the exception that the program throws when we modify JSON and try to deserialize it to an `Authors` object:

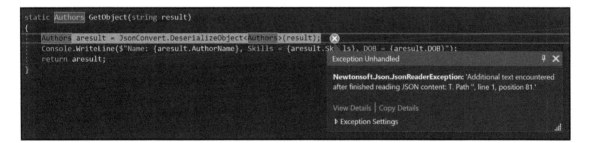

This is an example where we try to validate a JSON object. If it gets modified during transmission, this can be identified during the deserialization process.

Summary

In this chapter, we understood the importance of validating input data; different ways of validating input data in our application, including the `Parse` and `Convert` methods; and how we can use regular expressions and the data annotations namespace. We also looked briefly at how we can validate XML and JSON input.

In the next chapter, we will explore ways to secure our data, such as emails, passwords, and API keys, using encryption techniques available in .NET Framework.

Questions

1. The `Parse` method always takes the __ type as input
    1. Any valid .NET type
    2. Object
    3. String
    4. None

2. When converting `DateTime` to `Double`, which exception is thrown?
    1. No exception is thrown; instead, it gets converted successfully.
    2. A Format exception is thrown.
    3. An Overflow exception is thrown.
    4. An Invalid cast exception is thrown.

3. Information about members of an object can be provided using the _____ namespace.
    1. `DataContract`
    2. `DataAnnotations`
    3. `System.Reflection`
    4. `System.XML`

Answers

1. **String**
2. **An Invalid cast exception is thrown**.
3. `DataAnnotations`

12
Performing Symmetric and Asymmetric Encryption

While working on distributed applications, it is very important to keep information secure, in particular, in the case of eCommerce applications, where user data, such as your personal and credit card-related information, is collected and transmitted over the internet. Cryptography enables us to encrypt and decrypt plain text. To understand it in simple terms, let's suppose that there is plain text in our application that can be transformed by adding a static value to each character in the text, thereby rendering it non-readable. This process is called **encryption**. Conversely, decryption is the process of transforming this unreadable text back into readable text.

When you encrypt text, it looks like random bytes, and is called **cipher-text**.

After reading this chapter, you will be able to understand how to encrypt and decrypt text, the different algorithms that are available to perform these encrypt and decrypt operations, and the options that .NET Framework affords us in terms of their application to actual projects.

The following topics will be covered in this chapter:

- Cryptography
- Symmetric encryption
- Asymmetric encryption
- Digital signatures
- Hash values

Technical requirements

The exercises in this chapter can be practiced using Visual Studio 2012 or above with .NET Framework 2.0 or above. However, any new C# features from C# 7.0 and above require Visual Studio 2017.

If you don't have a license for any of the products, you can download the community version of Visual Studio 2017 from `https://visualstudio.microsoft.com/downloads/`.

Sample code for this chapter can be found on GitHub at `https://github.com/PacktPublishing/Programming-in-C-sharp-Exam-70-483-MCSD-Guide/tree/master/Book70483Samples/Chapter12.`

Cryptography

When working with public networks involved with creating and managing web applications that are accessible over the internet, your application is at high risk of being intercepted and modified by unauthorized parties. Cryptography allows us to protect data from such unauthorized parties from being viewed or modified. Cryptography also provides ways to protect our data and assists in the transfer of data securely over the network. To perform such operations, we can use encryption algorithms to create cipher data prior to transmission. When intercepted by unauthorized parties, it will be difficult for them to decrypt this in order to read or modify this data.

To perform such operations, .NET framework is shipped with the `System.Secure.Cryptography` namespace, which comes with many algorithms, including the following:

- Secret key encryption
- Public key encryption
- Digital signatures
- Hash values

Let's jump into an example regarding where cryptography can be used. Suppose, as a customer, that I am trying to place an order for a laptop over the internet. For this, I am chatting with the company's representative. Once I am sufficiently satisfied with the quote, the discount offered, and the terms and conditions to place an order, I then need to provide personal and credit card information via this channel.

So, how can we ensure the following in this regard?

- That this information is unclear for anyone listening in on our conversation
- That there was no unauthorized access to the information transferred
- That the information received is from the company's representative

All of this can be achieved with the implementation of cryptographic algorithms. These algorithms facilitate confidentiality, data integrity, authentication, and non-repudiation.

Confidentiality protects the identity of users, data integrity protects data from being changed, authentication ensures that data is from an authenticated party, and non-repudiation prevents any party from denying that a message was sent.

.NET Framework provides different algorithms, as mentioned earlier. Although these are numerous, we will limit our discussion to four major ones in this chapter.

Secret-key encryption, which is also referred to as symmetric encryption, uses a single shared key to encrypt and decrypt data. In this regard, however, it is important to keep the secret information safe from unauthorized access because anyone in possession of this key can then access the data and misuse it. Because it uses the same key for both encryption and decryption, this works faster and is suitable for large amounts of data. There are different types of algorithm available, such as **DES** (short for **Data Encryption Standard**), triple DES, and **AES** (short for **Advanced Encryption Standard**). These algorithms encrypt blocks of data simultaneously, so they are also referred to as block ciphers. DES and Triple DES use 8 bytes as a block, while AES uses 16 bytes as a block, but also supports 24 and 32 bytes.

Public-key encryption, also referred to as asymmetric encryption, uses public/private keys to encrypt and decrypt data. Of these two keys, the private key must be kept secret from unauthorized access, as anyone with the private key can access your data. Public and private keys in this encryption technique are mathematically linked and use a fixed buffer size. These are slow compared to secret key encryption, and are useful for encrypting small amounts of data. Any data encrypted using a public key can only be decrypted using a private key. Also, if you sign data using a private key, it can only be verified using a public key.

Digital signing uses digital signatures that are unique to that party. As mentioned in public key encryption, a party can sign the data using a private key and, when the other party receives information and when the public key of the sending party is trusted, you can identify who sent the message and, in turn, maintain the integrity of the data.

Since the public key of the sending party is public, anyone in possession of the public key can process the message, meaning that your message is not secret. To keep it secret, you also need to encrypt the message.

Hash values map data of any length to a fixed-length byte sequence. When you have a block of text and change it prior to rehashing, it will produce a new hash. This way, we can maintain data integrity during transfer.

However, as has been discussed in relation to other cryptographic methods, this method does not authenticate the sender of the message.

Symmetric encryption

Symmetric encryption uses a single key and works on blocks of text. This method works quicker than others. While using this method, it is important to maintain the confidentiality of the secret key, and both the sender and receiver should use the same key, which is a disadvantage of this method.

Let's look at an example and understand how we can encrypt a message or block of text:

1. Here, we use the encrypt method, where we read a block of text from a file, encrypt it using a symmetric algorithm, and write the encrypted content to a different file.
2. The encrypt method accepts an instance of SymmetricAlgorithm, which is used to create an instance of ICryptoTransform by passing a key and initial vector. The system allows you to generate your own key or use the one it generates.
3. Then, we create a memory stream to store the buffer at runtime:

```
public static void EncryptSymmetric(SymmetricAlgorithm sem)
{
    //Read content from file
    string filecontent = File.ReadAllText("..\\..\\inputfile.txt");
    //Create encryptor using key and vector
    ICryptoTransform encryptor = sem.CreateEncryptor(sem.Key,
sem.IV);
    //create memory stream used at runtime to store data
    using (MemoryStream outputstream = new MemoryStream())
    {
        //Create crypto stream in write mode
        using (CryptoStream encStream = new
CryptoStream(outputstream, encryptor, CryptoStreamMode.Write))
        {
            //use streamwrite
            using (StreamWriter writer = new
StreamWriter(encStream))
            {
                // Write the text in the stream writer
```

```
            writer.Write(filecontent);
        }
    }
    // Get the result as a byte array from the memory stream
    byte[] encryptedDataFromMemory = outputstream.ToArray();
    // Write the data to a file
    File.WriteAllBytes("..\\..\\Outputfile.txt",
encryptedDataFromMemory);
    }
}
```

A cryptostream is created using the memory stream, `ICryptoTransform`, along with the write mode. A cryptostream is used to write to memory, which can then be converted into an array and written to an output file.

4. Once you execute the encrypt method, you can now open the output file from the solution and check the results.
5. Now, we will read the data from the output file and decrypt it to plain text:

```
public static string DecryptSymmetric(SymmetricAlgorithm sem)
{
    string result = string.Empty;
    //Create decryptor
    ICryptoTransform decryptor = sem.CreateDecryptor(sem.Key,
sem.IV);
    //read file content
    byte[] filecontent =
File.ReadAllBytes("..\\..\\Outputfile.txt");
    //read file content to memory stream
    using (MemoryStream outputstream = new
MemoryStream(filecontent))
    {
        //create decrypt stream
        using (CryptoStream decryptStream = new
CryptoStream(outputstream, decryptor, CryptoStreamMode.Read))
        {
            using (StreamReader reader = new
StreamReader(decryptStream))
            {
                //read content of stream till end
                result = reader.ReadToEnd();
            }
        }
    }
    return result;
}
```

The decrypt method uses the same signature as the encrypt method. However, instead of creating an `encryptor` class, we create a `decryptor` class, which implements the `ICryptoTransform` interface.

The following is the main program, where we create `SymmetricAlgorithm` of the `AESManaged` instance type, and then pass it to the encrypt and decrypt methods:

```
static void Main(string[] args)
{
    Console.WriteLine("Using AES symmetric Algorithm");
    SymmetricAlgorithm sem = new AesManaged();
    Console.WriteLine("Encrypting data from inputfile");
    EncryptDecryptHelper.EncryptSymmetric(sem);
    Console.WriteLine("Data Encrypted. You can check in outputfile. Press
any key to decrypt message");
    System.Console.ReadKey();
    Console.WriteLine("Decrypting content form outputfile");
    string message = EncryptDecryptHelper.DecryptSymmetric(sem);
    Console.WriteLine($"Decrypted data : {message}");
    // Keep the console window open in debug mode.
    System.Console.WriteLine("Press any key to exit.");
    System.Console.ReadKey();
}
```

Before executing the program, check the input file in the solution where you can change the content and execute it. Following encryption, the output file in the solution can be verified for the encrypted content:

```
Using AES symmetric Algorithm
Encrypting data from inputfile
Data Encrypted. You can check in outputfile. Press any key to decrypt message
Decrypting content form outputfile
Decrypted data : This is the text we are trying to encyrpt. we will wirte the output into outputfile.txt. THis seems to
be a small file so we will try to add more text in the file so we get more than 100 bytes when we read each time.
Press any key to exit.
```

When you practice this example, make sure that you have all the helper methods in one class, and the main method in another class, as specified in the sample code on GitHub. Now that you have all the methods, when you execute them, you see the preceding output.

Your encryption method uses the AES algorithm. It reads data from the input file, encrypts data using the AES algorithm, and then writes a message on the screen. Once you press any key, your decrypt method is initiated, decrypts the message, and writes to the output file. The same message is displayed on screen.

In a real-time scenario, when you want to perform secure transactions using file transfers, this is one way to do so. Because you will be using symmetric algorithms, it will be easy to encrypt or decrypt the content.

A sender encrypts the content of the file and sends it to the receiver. The receiver decrypts the file content and processes it. In this method, both the sender and receiver should be aware of the key used.

Asymmetric encryption

Asymmetric encryption uses two keys—a public key and a private key. Because of this, it runs bit slowly. Also, it is necessary to keep the private key safe at all times. Unless you have the private key, you cannot decrypt the message.

Now, let's jump into an example and try to understand how this is done. In this scenario, we will be using RSACryptoServiceProvider. This algorithm provides us with public and private keys that can be used to encrypt and decrypt messages. The encrypt method accepts a public key and text to encrypt, and we then convert the text to a byte array since the encrypt method accepts byte arrays. Then, we set the public key for the algorithm and invoke the encrypt method:

```
public static byte[] EncryptAsymmetric(string publicKey, string
texttoEncrypt)
{
    byte[] result;
    UnicodeEncoding uc = new UnicodeEncoding();
    byte[] databytes = uc.GetBytes(texttoEncrypt);
    using (RSACryptoServiceProvider rsa = new RSACryptoServiceProvider())
    {
        rsa.FromXmlString(publicKey);
        result = rsa.Encrypt(databytes, true);
    }
    return result;
}
```

In the decrypt method, we pass the byte array that needs to be decrypted along with a private key. Once a message is encrypted using a public key, it can only be decrypted using its corresponding private key:

```
public static string DecryptAsymmetric(string privateKey, byte[]
bytestoDecrypt)
{
    byte[] result;
    using (RSACryptoServiceProvider rsa = new RSACryptoServiceProvider())
```

```
        {
            rsa.FromXmlString(privateKey);
            result = rsa.Decrypt(bytestoDecrypt, true);
        }
        UnicodeEncoding uc = new UnicodeEncoding();
        string resultText = uc.GetString(result);
        return resultText;
    }
```

The following is the main method, where we create the RSACryptoproviderservice class to get public and private keys. rsa.ToXmlString(false) provides a public key, and setting it to true will give us a private key. We will use these keys to encrypt and decrypt messages:

```
static void Main(string[] args)
{
    #region asymmetric Encryption
    Console.WriteLine("Using asymmetric Algorithm");
    RSACryptoServiceProvider rsa = new RSACryptoServiceProvider();
  string publicKey = rsa.ToXmlString(false);
  string privateKey = rsa.ToXmlString(true);
    Console.WriteLine("Encrypting data ");
    byte[] resultbytes =
EncryptDecryptHelper.EncryptAsymmetric(publicKey,"This is a dummy text to
encrypt");
    Console.WriteLine("Data Encrypted. Press any key to decrypt message");
    System.Console.ReadKey();
    Console.WriteLine("Decrypting content");
    string resultText = EncryptDecryptHelper.DecryptAsymmetric(pricateKey,
resultbytes);
    Console.WriteLine($"Decrypted data : {resultText}");
    #endregion

    // Keep the console window open in debug mode.
    System.Console.WriteLine("Press any key to exit.");
    System.Console.ReadKey();
}
```

Execute the program by changing the input text, or you can try changing the algorithm. However, when you change the algorithm, you may need to apply any syntactical changes that are required in order for the program to run and work:

```
Using asymmetric Algorithm
Encrypting data
Data Encrypted. Press any key to decrypt message
Decrypting content
Decrypted data : This is a dummy text to encrypt
Press any key to exit.
```

When you execute the program, you see the preceding output. In the sample, you are using an asymmetric algorithm to encrypt content. As the control flows through the code, it display messages. Once the message is encrypted, it will ask you to press any key. Upon pressing any key, the program decrypts the message and displays it on screen.

In the scenario that we discussed under symmetric algorithms, where you want to perform secure transactions between two parties, you can use public-private key combinations.

A receiver performs encryption using a private key and sends the file or block of text to the receiver, where a public key is used to decrypt the content. In the event the public-private keys do not match, you cannot read or validate the data. This is one way to validate input data.

Digital signatures

Digital signatures can be used to sign the message that will authenticate the sender. However, signing a message doesn't prevent a third party from reading the message. To achieve this, we need to encrypt the message and sign it.

In the following example, we are using a public key and a private key (asymmetric algorithm). We use the sender's private key to sign the message and the receiver's public key to encrypt the message. If you observe the code, we also use hash computing in this example. After encrypting the message, we hash the message.

We are going to use RSACryptoServiceProvider, along with RSAPKCS1SignatureFormatter, which will be used to create a signature.

In the following program, we convert text to a byte array using UnicodeEncoding classes, encrypt the message using the receiver's public key and the symmetric or asymmetric algorithms we learned in previous sections, compute the hash of the content, and then digitally sign the message. Once all of these processes have been implemented, we transmit the data across, where we recompute the hash, verify the signature, and then decrypt the message using the keys.

In the following example, we are using public-private keys to perform encryption. As mentioned previously, simply signing the message doesn't secure the content of the message. Instead, it will allow you to authenticate the sender:

```
public static void DigitalSignatureSample(string senderPrivatekey, string
receiverspublickey, string texttoEncrypt)
{
 UnicodeEncoding uc = new UnicodeEncoding();
 Console.WriteLine("Converting to bytes from text");
 //get bytearray from the message
 byte[] databytes = uc.GetBytes(texttoEncrypt);
 Console.WriteLine("Creating cryptoclass instance");
 //Creating instance for RSACryptoservice provider as we are using for
sender and receiver
 RSACryptoServiceProvider rsasender = new RSACryptoServiceProvider();
 RSACryptoServiceProvider rsareceiver = new RSACryptoServiceProvider();
 //getting private and public key
 rsasender.FromXmlString(senderPrivatekey);
 rsareceiver.FromXmlString(receiverspublickey);
 Console.WriteLine("Creating signature formatter instance");
 //GEt signature from RSA
 RSAPKCS1SignatureFormatter signatureFormatter = new
RSAPKCS1SignatureFormatter(rsasender);
 //set hashalgorithm
 signatureFormatter.SetHashAlgorithm("SHA1");
 //encrypt message
 Console.WriteLine("encrypting message");
 byte[] encryptedBytes = rsareceiver.Encrypt(databytes, false);
 //compute hash
 byte[] computedhash = new SHA1Managed().ComputeHash(encryptedBytes);
 Console.WriteLine("Creating signature");
 //create signature for the message
 byte[] signature = signatureFormatter.CreateSignature(computedhash);
 Console.WriteLine("Signature: " + Convert.ToBase64String(signature));
 Console.WriteLine("Press any key to continue...");
 Console.ReadKey();
 //receive message then recompute hash
 Console.WriteLine("recomputing hash");
 byte[] recomputedHash = new SHA1Managed().ComputeHash(encryptedBytes);
 //signature deformatter
 Console.WriteLine("Creating signature dformatter instance");
 RSAPKCS1SignatureDeformatter signatureDFormatter = new
RSAPKCS1SignatureDeformatter(rsareceiver);
 signatureDFormatter.SetHashAlgorithm("SHA1");
 //verify signature
 Console.WriteLine("verifying signature");
 if (!signatureDFormatter.VerifySignature(recomputedHash, signature))
 {
```

```
    Console.WriteLine("Signature did not match from sender");
    }
    Console.WriteLine("decrypting message");
    //decrypt message
    byte[] decryptedText = rsasender.Decrypt(encryptedBytes, false);
    Console.WriteLine(Encoding.UTF8.GetString(decryptedText));
}
```

The following is the main program, where we create an instance of
the RSACryptoServiceProvider class and collect public and private keys. However, as
we are encrypting and decrypting the message in the same method, a single set of public
and private keys was used.

As part of this example, we perform both encryption and decryption. We can create
multiple RSA providers and use their public-private keys for senders and receivers. You
can create different console applications, one as a sender and the other as a receiver, and
simulate a real-world scenario. For simplicity's sake, I have used one pair of public-private
keys to perform operations:

```
static void Main(string[] args)
{
    #region Digital Signatures
    RSACryptoServiceProvider rsa = new RSACryptoServiceProvider();
    string publicKey = rsa.ToXmlString(false);
    string pricateKey = rsa.ToXmlString(true);
    EncryptDecryptHelper.DigitalSignatureSample(pricateKey, publicKey,"This
is a sample text for Digital signatures");
    #endregion

    // Keep the console window open in debug mode.
    System.Console.WriteLine("Press any key to exit.");
    System.Console.ReadKey();
}
```

Check the output by changing the input message and algorithms. However, as said earlier, you may need to take care of any syntactical changes before executing:

```
Converting to bytes from text
Creating crypoclass instance
Creating signature formatter instance
encrypting message
Creating signature
Signature: YyPXosYDBGsdRbA1ZsMGoEtpgIfKMqZ4SILWJGbN64mx8I6qqNxehNXnTHqjAWiQkb9OoV7UB/sT2io1DEynEFVFbmDWUxAR1UTTmg191ybzw
kD9UHcwp6nH+W526LoSLLpqnIV2ujpAxP6bDpbdLus2woKZipNB+UPji/25uxQ=
Press any key to continue...
▨recomputing hash
Creating signature dformatter instance
verifying signature
decrypting message
This  is  a  sample  text  for  Digital  signatures
Press any key to exit.
```

In a real-world scenario, suppose two entities are communicating via web services where such digital signatures are implemented. The sender will have a set of public and private keys, and the receiver will have public and private keys. Both parties should exchange their respective public keys to facilitate application communication.

Hash values

Computing a hash creates a fixed-length numeric value from a byte array. A hash maps a variable-length binary string to a fixed-length binary string. A hash cannot be used for two-way conversion. When you apply a hash algorithm, each character gets hashed into a different binary string.

In the following example, we use the SHA1Managed algorithm to compute the hash. We compute the hash twice to check whether the result is the same. As mentioned earlier, this method is used to maintain data integrity.

In the following code, we are using the UnicodeEncoding class to convert the text to a byte array, and the SHA1Managed algorithm to compute the hash for the byte array. Once converted, we display each and every hashed byte on the screen. To validate the hash, we recompute the hash on the string and compare the hash values. This is one way to validate input data:

```
public static void HashvalueSample(string texttoEncrypt)
{
    UnicodeEncoding uc = new UnicodeEncoding();
    Console.WriteLine("Converting to bytes from text");
    byte[] databytes = uc.GetBytes(texttoEncrypt);
    byte[] computedhash = new SHA1Managed().ComputeHash(databytes);
```

```
    foreach (byte h in computedhash)
    {
        Console.Write("{0} ", b);
    }
    Console.WriteLine("Press any key to continue...");
    byte[] reComputedhash = new SHA1Managed().ComputeHash(databytes);
    bool result = true;
    for (int x = 0; x < computedhash.Length; x++)
    {
        if (computedhash[x] != reComputedhash[x])
        {
            result = false;
        }
        else
        {
            result = true;
        }
    }

    if (result)
    {
        Console.WriteLine("Hash value is same");
    }
    else
    {
        Console.WriteLine("Hash value is not same");
    }
}
```

The main method for invoking the hash value example is as follows. Here, we just call the helper method that performs the hash compute on the text provided:

```
static void Main(string[] args)
{
    #region Hashvalue
    EncryptDecryptHelper.HashvalueSample("This a sample text for hashvalue
sample");
    #endregion


    // Keep the console window open in debug mode.
    System.Console.WriteLine("Press any key to exit.");
    System.Console.ReadKey();
}
```

When we compute the hash, we display the result and then we undertake a comparison to see whether the result from both calls is the same:

```
Converting to bytes from text
231 53 168 73 94 220 54 85 10 229 75 129 169 129 1 102 148 251 215 43 Press any key to continue...
Hash value is same
Press any key to exit.
```

The preceding screenshot shows the program where you compute the hash and display the hashed array. Also, when the program recomputes the hash and effects a comparison, you see the same hash value message.

Summary

In this chapter, we focused on understanding cryptography and how we can use symmetric and asymmetric algorithms. We also focused on how we can use these to validate senders, receivers, and the content of messages. We can use the techniques learned in the chapter to validate input data and perform similar operations when working with secure transactions. We also looked at how we can sign messages using digital signatures, and how can we maintain data integrity using hash values.

In the next chapter, we will focus on .NET assemblies, how we can manage them, and how we can debug C# applications.

Questions

1. Out of the four methods discussed in this chapter, which two can be used to authenticate the sender?
    1. Symmetric algorithm
    2. Asymmetric algorithm
    3. Hash values
    4. Digital signatures

2. When two parties need to communicate using an asymmetric algorithm, which key do they need to share?
     1. Private key
     2. Public key
     3. Both
     4. None

3. Which type of algorithm is used to encrypt large amounts of data?
     1. Symmetric
     2. Asymmetric
     3. Both
     4. None

Answers

1. **Digital signatures**
2. **Public key**
3. **Symmetric**

13
Managing Assemblies and Debugging Applications

In the last chapter, we learned about cryptography and how we can encrypt and decrypt using different techniques available in C#. In this chapter, we will focus on how we can manage .NET assemblies, debugging applications, and how to do tracing. Writing a .NET application appears to be relatively simple; however, it is important to make sure your program serves its purpose, maintains quality standards, doesn't crash on exceptions, and behaves properly in all circumstances. To achieve such a quality output, it is important to test your application and check the input source and values generated at runtime, which are used in the application logic for further processing and so on.

Assemblies are the fundamental units of .NET application deployment. They maintain the version, type, resources required, scope, and security details. We will discuss this in more detail in the upcoming sections.

Debugging is the process of stepping through each and every line of code that seems to be problematic or code that you believe will throw errors. During this process, we can observe the values in the variables and parameters and whether the program is running as expected.

It is also important to understand whether we are creating a library or an independent application to distribute to clients. Based on this, we can decide what type (`.exe` or `.dll`) of application needs to be created.

Tracing allows you to track through each and every line of code while it is executing.

After reading this chapter, you will be able to understand assemblies in .NET and how we can manage them, as well as versioning and signing. We will also look at a number of ways to debug an application and how to write trace messages when an exception occurs. In this chapter, we will cover the following topics:

- Assemblies
- Debugging a C# application
- Tracing

Technical requirements

You can practice the exercises from this chapter using Visual Studio 2012 or later with .NET Framework 2.0 or later. However, any new C# features from C# 7.0 and later require you to have Visual Studio 2017.

If you don't have a license for any of these products, you can download the Community version of Visual Studio 2017 from `https://visualstudio.microsoft.com/downloads/`.

The sample code for this chapter can be found on GitHub at `https://github.com/PacktPublishing/Programming-in-C-sharp-Exam-70-483-MCSD-Guide/tree/master/Chapter13`.

Assemblies

Assemblies in the .NET Framework can be of two types, `.exe` or `.dll`, and are termed as the building blocks of a .NET application.

These assemblies form the basic units of an application and allow a programmer to maintain versions, security, scope of usage, and reuse. Since an assembly contains all the information required to execute your application, it provides the runtime with information about what .NET types are used and what features of runtime are required to execute the application.

When you create an application in .NET using Visual Studio, it creates source code files (`.cs` files), properties of an assembly (`AssemblyInfo.cs`):

These projects allow programmers to associate other assemblies, which, in turn, allows them to create and maintain larger projects for multiple users to work on each project. When work on individual projects is completed, these projects can be created as one assembly unit to release for the customer.

When an assembly is created, each assembly creates a manifest file that details information about the following:

- Each file that has been used in creating this assembly
- If there are any references that have been used
- The version of the assembly with a unique name

Assembly contents and manifest

An assembly in the .NET Framework contains the following four elements:

- Assembly manifest
- Metadata
- MSIL code
- Resources

These elements can be grouped into one assembly, as shown in the following screenshot. Here, the runtime requires manifest information in order to get the type information, the dependent assembly information, the version, and the unique name of the assembly in order to execute:

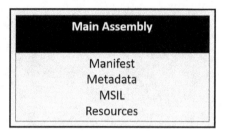

The .NET Framework also allows us to group the four elements of the assemblies into multiple modules and create an assembly to refer them while executing the program block. When you refer such modules in an assembly, it is the manifest file that maintains all the links required to refer to these resources:

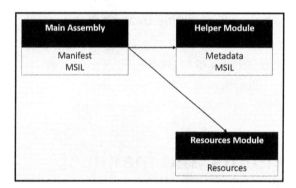

An assembly manifest contains the name of the assembly, the version of the assembly, which culture is used to build the assembly, the strong name information (that is, public key), the type information, a list of files and how they are associated with each other and the assembly, and, finally, a list of referenced assemblies and their versions. We can add more information by updating the `AssemblyInfo.cs` file.

A manifest file can be part of the **portable executable** (**PE**) file along with MSIL or a standalone PE file. Each assembly file contains all the files that are required for an assembly; it governs how the mapping between these files, resources, and assemblies are maintained, and it also contains referenced assemblies.

Target .NET Framework

When you create a C# application, you can specify which .NET Framework you want to target your application to. In a real-world scenario, not every customer updates their servers with the latest versions when new versions of the Framework are released. Additionally, when a new version is released, some of the old features might be deprecated and newer versions of the existing features are added. In these situations, your application should not fail. So, the .NET Framework allows you to target your application to a specific version of the .NET Framework.

You can target the .NET Framework version while creating a new project using Visual Studio, or change the target framework using the property pages of the project:

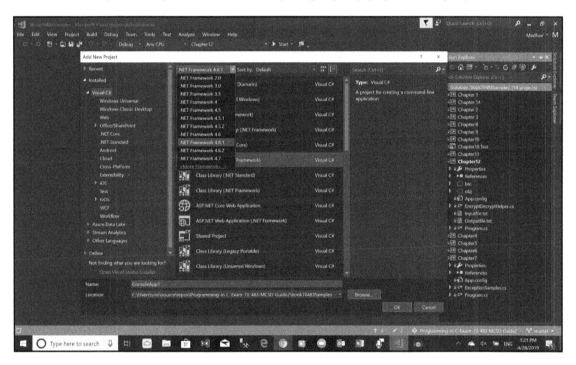

Alternatively, to change the target framework version using the property pages, select an existing project, right-click on it, and then navigate to **Properties**:

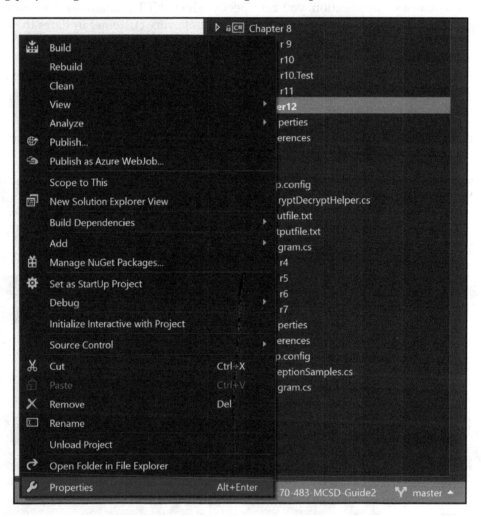

In the **Target framework** drop-down menu, select your required version:

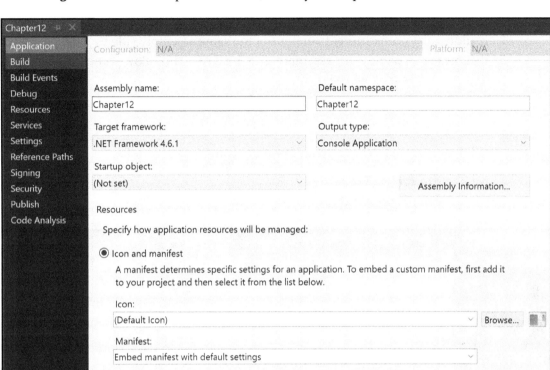

Signing assemblies

Creating a unique identity for an assembly is referred to as signing or strong-naming an assembly. Providing a unique identity for an assembly avoids assembly conflicts. Each assembly maintains hashes of the modules, resources, and file information in its manifest. When you sign an assembly, the following is captured:

- The name of the assembly
- The version number of the assembly
- If available, the culture (also called *locale* for code development) of the assembly
- The public key that is used to sign the assembly to the assembly manifest

Signing an assembly provides the following benefits:

1. It allows us to give a friend access to other signed assemblies.
2. It allows us to run different versions of the same assembly side by side.
3. It allows us to deploy our assembly into the GAC. This allows other applications to use our assembly as well.

You can sign an assembly in two ways: the first is by using Visual Studio, and the second is by using the command-line tool. Visual Studio makes it simple to sign the assembly.

Here, we will demonstrate how to sign an assembly using Visual Studio:

1. Navigate to **Project Properties.**
2. Navigate to the **Signing*** tab on the left side:

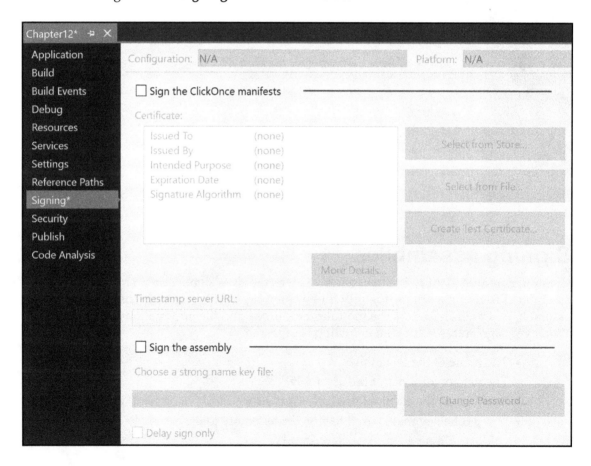

3. Select the **Sign the assembly** checkbox.
4. Choose **<New...>** in the drop-down menu, and then choose a strong key filename:

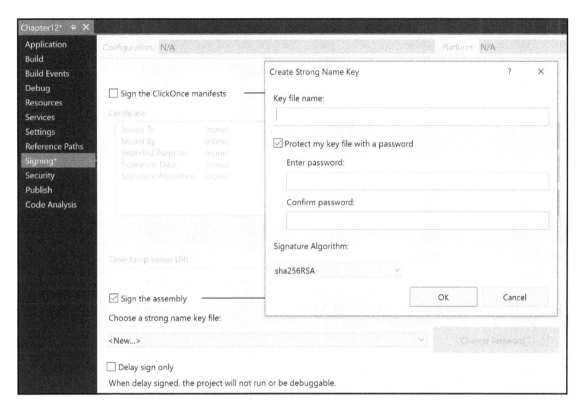

5. Give a key filename in the pop-up window.
6. Visual Studio allows you to choose an algorithm and provide a password for the key file.
7. The password is optional; an algorithm can be changed as per your requirements from the available list.

Alternatively, we can sign an assembly using Command Prompt and Visual Studio tools that come with the following installation steps:

1. Click the Windows button on your system.
2. Navigate through the installed programs.
3. Find the Visual Studio 20xx installation folder.
4. Select **Developer Command Prompt** for Visual Studio 20xx.

5. Use `sn.exe` to generate a strong name pair into a `.snk` file:

```
sn -k keyPair.snk
```

6. Once the key file is created, you can now use Visual Studio to sign the assembly or use the `al.exe` tool.

7. Use `al.exe` to link the assembly and key pair generated in the preceding steps:

```
al /out:chapter12.dll MyModule.netmodule /keyfile:keyPair.snk
```

More information about these commands is available on MSDN (`https://docs.microsoft.com/en-us/dotnet/framework/tools/sn-exe-strong-name-tool`).

Versioning assemblies

When you are ready with an assembly and have signed it, you can version it. When you version an assembly, the current assembly and all the dependent assembly versions are maintained in the assembly manifest. When a versioned assembly is deployed into an environment, then that becomes the default version of your application and the system throws an assembly manifest mismatch error when either the current assembly or dependent assemblies do not match the default version. There is a way to override this using a configuration file, which tells the runtime to use a specific version instead of the default version.

When an assembly is executed at runtime, it performs multiple steps to resolve assembly binding:

1. It checks the current assembly for the version information and a unique name.
2. It checks for configuration files to see whether any version override policies are defined.
3. In the case of any policy changes, the runtime identifies and loads the redirected assembly as per the policy.
4. It checks the GAC, or the path specified in configuration files, then the application directory, subdirectories, and serves the assembly binding request.

Version number

Every assembly maintains version information in two forms, identity and informational. The version number, name, and culture of the assembly form the identity of the assembly and the informational version is provided in a string format specified in the assembly info file and is for informational purposes.

The version number of an assembly is represented as a four-part string:

```
<Major version>.<Minor Version>.<Build number>.<revision>
```

For example, if an assembly version is set to 2.1.1234.2, this indicates that the major version of the assembly is 2, the minor version is 1, the build number is 1234, and the revision number is 2. When this version is created or updated, it is maintained in the manifest file along with a snapshot of all resources and dependent assembly files and their versions. In addition to this, versioning checks are applicable only when the assembly is signed.

One important thing to understand from a real-world scenario is that, when you build a product and release your assemblies for customers and later upgrade your assembly, then you have to maintain the previous versions. So, when a new version of an assembly is released, clients can still use the old version as long as it is supported.

Debugging the C# application

When you build a C# application, you will have two options, debug mode and release mode. Debug mode helps you to step through each and every line of your code to check for errors and fix them if required. Release mode doesn't allow us to step into code. Visual Studio makes it easy for developers by providing more tools, which allows us to `Step-in`, `Step-Over`, and `Step-Out` when a debug point is hit by the runtime. These tools are highlighted in a blue box in the following screenshot:

Apart from these tools, Visual Studio also allows us to view stack trace, inspect variables, and much more. Let's explore this further in order to understand more about debugging.

Let's start with the basics. To place a breakpoint, just click on the left margin next to the line of code you want to debug or place your cursor on the line and press the *F9* key on the keyboard. Another way to place a breakpoint is to select the **Debug** menu option and select a new breakpoint.

When you set a breakpoint, the entire line of code is highlighted in the color brown. When the program starts the execution with breakpoints, the control halts at the breakpoint and highlights the line in yellow, which means the highlighted line is set to execute next:

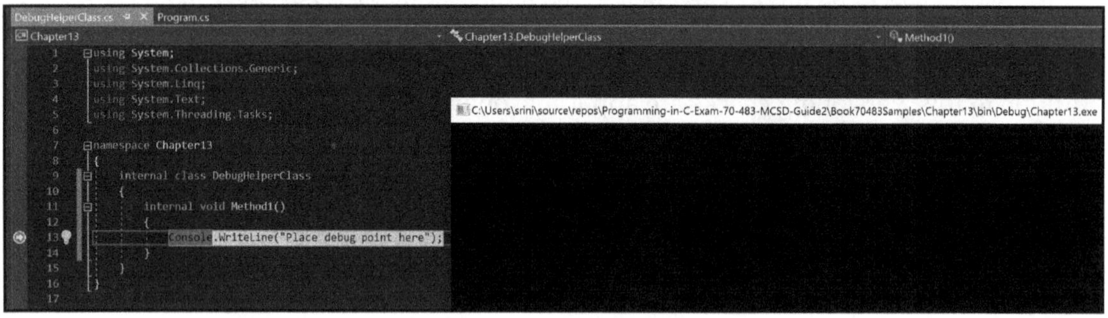

Observe the preceding screenshot; we have a breakpoint at line **13**. When you start the program, the control halted at line **13** where the breakpoint is placed. When we step-over, the output is printed on the screen but the control stays at line **14** as shown in the following screenshot:

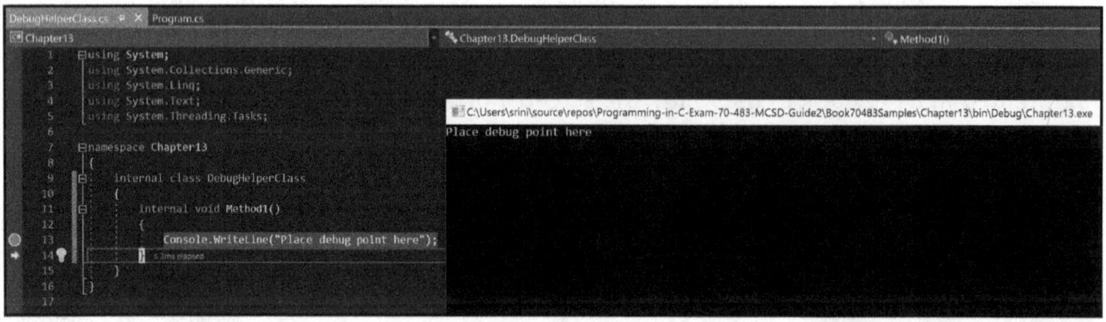

When a breakpoint is hit, though the application execution is halted, all the variables, functions, and objects remain in memory, allowing us to validate the values. When you want to debug an application, you build it in debug mode, which generates a .pdb file; this file is key for debugging. The .pdb file contains symbols (or source) that get loaded into memory to allow us to debug. If these symbols were not loaded, then you might see an error message stating that the symbols were not found. It is also important to maintain the versions of these pdb files, as any version mismatch between your assembly and the .pdb file will result in an assembly version mismatch error.

Let's jump into an example code and examine the different actions we can perform while debugging, as well as the features that Visual Studio provides us with.

The following is an example program that accepts two numbers and calculates the addition and subtraction of those numbers, and then invokes another method where 10 is added to the result. Let's debug this application by placing a couple of breakpoints in the code block:

```
internal void Method2()
{
    Console.WriteLine("Enter a numeric value");
    int number1 = Convert.ToInt32(Console.ReadLine());

    Console.WriteLine("Enter another numeric value");
    int number2 = Convert.ToInt32(Console.ReadLine());

    int number3 = number1 + number2;
    int number4 = number1 - number2;
    int number5 = Method3(number4);

}

internal int Method3(int number4)
{
    return number4+10;
}
```

Here, two breakpoints were placed on lines 18 and 21. When the program starts executing, it stops at line 18 for user input and when you select continue program execution, the control stops at line 21. One of the important things to observe in the following screenshot is that when the control stops at line 21, you can view the value of the `number1` variable by just hovering the cursor over it. You can see that the `number1` variable has a value of 23:

```csharp
DebugHelperClass.cs    X   Program.cs
Chapter13                                              Chapter13.DebugHelperClass
  1    using System;
  2    using System.Collections.Generic;
  3    using System.Linq;
  4    using System.Text;
  5    using System.Threading.Tasks;
  6
  7    namespace Chapter13
  8    {
  9        internal class DebugHelperClass
 10        {
 11            internal void Method1()
 12            {
 13                Console.WriteLine("Place debug point here");
 14            }
 15
 16            internal void Method2()
 17            {
 18                Console.WriteLine("Enter a numeric value");
 19                int number1 = Convert.ToInt32(Console.ReadLine());
 20                         number1 23
 21                Console.WriteLine("Enter another numeric value");  ≤ 5,130ms elapsed
 22                int number2 = Convert.ToInt32(Console.ReadLine());
 23
 24                int number3 = number1 + number2;
 25                int number4 = number1 - number2;
 26                int number5 = Method3(number4);
 27
 28            }
```

Visual Studio debugging tools allow us to watch a variable while the program is being executed in debug mode. You can right-click on a variable and select `Add Watch` to add the variable to the watch window. As you see can see at the bottom of the screen, there is a watch window where variable `number3` has been added, and we can see the value of 43, which is the output of the sum of `number1` and `number2`. The watch window allows you to view the values after the line of code executes. This comes in really handy when your application logic is performing complex calculations:

```
7    ☐namespace Chapter13
8     {
9       ☐    internal class DebugHelperClass
10           {
11      ☐        internal void Method1()
12               {
13                   Console.WriteLine("Place debug point here");
14               }
15
16      ☐        internal void Method2()
17               {
18                   Console.WriteLine("Enter a numeric value");
19                   int number1 = Convert.ToInt32(Console.ReadLine());
20
21                   Console.WriteLine("Enter another numeric value");
22                   int number2 = Convert.ToInt32(Console.ReadLine());
23
24                   int number3 = number1 + number2;
25                   int number4 = number1 - number2;   ≤ 1ms elapsed
26                   int number5 = Method3(number4);
```
100 %   ▾

Watch 1

Name	Value
⊗ Regex.IsMatch(str, pattern)	error CS0103: The name 'Regex' does not exist in the current context
● number3	43

Another window that comes in handy with debugging is **Immediate Window** (*Ctrl + Alt + I*), which can be opened by using the keyboard shortcut or the **Debug** menu. In contrast to the watch window, this window helps you to perform operations before executing the line of code. As you can see in the following screenshot, the control is at line 25 where the breakpoint was hit; however, if you look down, the **Immediate Window** was open where we performed the number1 - number2 operation to check the value before executing the line:

```
 4    using System.Text;
 5    using System.Threading.Tasks;
 6
 7  □namespace Chapter13
 8    {
 9  □    internal class DebugHelperClass
10       {
11  □        internal void Method1()
12           {
13               Console.WriteLine("Place debug point here");
14           }
15
16  □        internal void Method2()
17           {
18               Console.WriteLine("Enter a numeric value");
19               int number1 = Convert.ToInt32(Console.ReadLine());
20
21               Console.WriteLine("Enter another numeric value");
22               int number2 = Convert.ToInt32(Console.ReadLine());
23
24               int number3 = number1 + number2;
25               int number4 = number1 - number2;
26               int number5 = Method3(number4);
```

100 %

Immediate Window

```
number1-number2
3
```

When you place a breakpoint and hover your cursor over the breakpoint in the left margin, the system displays a cogwheel, which allows you to add conditions to your breakpoint; for example, your program has a `for` loop, but you want your breakpoint to hit when the loop variable is, say, 5:

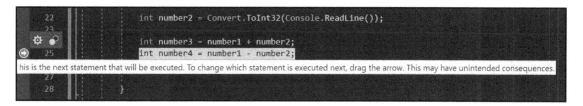

When you click on the cogwheel, you will be presented with the condition wizard where you can configure the condition of when the breakpoint should hit. By default, the condition is set to true, which can be changed by the developer. In the following screenshot, we selected `number4=3`, which means that this breakpoint will be hit when the number 4 value is equal to 3:

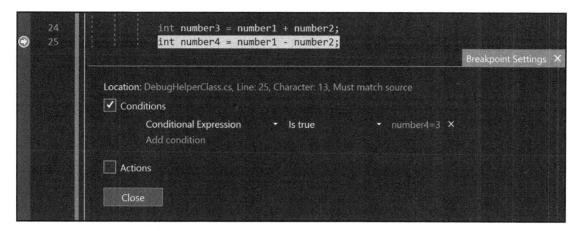

Another important feature to understand while debugging is that certain types of projects in Visual Studio allow you to change the variable values at runtime while debugging the application. When the following program was executed, we entered `60` as a numeric value to variable `number2`. You can see the value of variable 2 as follows:

```
 7    namespace Chapter13
 8    {
 9        internal class DebugHelperClass
10        {
11            internal void Method1()
12            {
13                Console.WriteLine("Place debug point here");
14            }
15
16            internal void Method2()
17            {
18                Console.WriteLine("Enter a numeric value");
19                int number1 = Convert.ToInt32(Console.ReadLine());
20
21                Console.WriteLine("Enter another numeric value");
22                int number2 = Convert.ToInt32(Console.ReadLine());
23
24                int number3 = number1 + number2;    ≤ 4,245ms elapsed
25                int number4 = number1 - number  number2 60
26                int number5 = Method3(number4);
27
28            }
```

Now, when you select the displayed value, the system allows you to change it (we changed it to 40), and then continue the execution of the block with the modified value. Please remember that not every project type will allow you to change values at runtime:

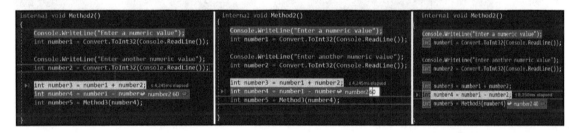

As discussed earlier, there are many tools available while debugging a C# application using Visual Studio and some of them are highlighted in the following screenshot. The **Continue** and **Stop Debugging** buttons enable the developer to continue executing once a breakpoint is hit, or to stop the execution.

There are buttons to **Step Into**, **Step Out**, and **Step Over**. These buttons allow you to step into each and every line of code once a breakpoint is hit, or skip the execution of a method and continue the execution in the same context, or step into an external method.

Once you debug your program block and fix all the issues you found, you can disable or delete all the breakpoints at once by using the **Delete All Breakpoints** or **Disable All Breakpoints** option in the **Debug** menu:

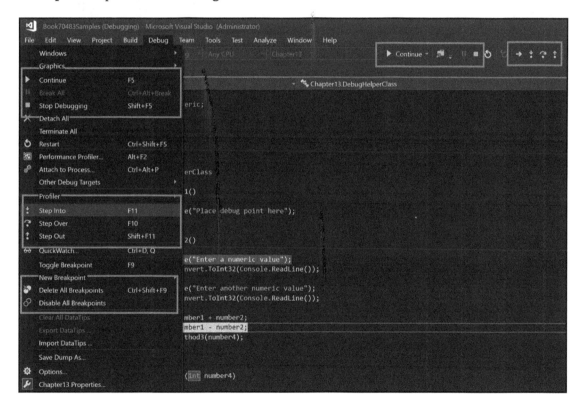

A few more options are highlighted in the following screenshot, such as **Attach to Process**, **QuickWatch...**, **Save Dump As...**, **Parallel Stacks**, **Immediate**, and **Watch** windows, **Call Stack**, and many more:

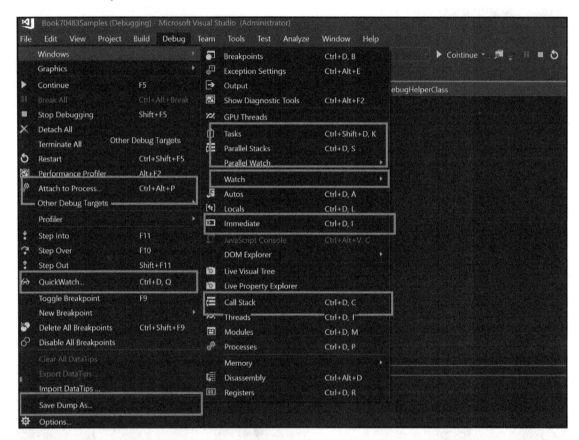

We structure our project in such a way that multiple assemblies are created, be it a helper or a dependent assembly. While debugging, it is important to load the symbols by attaching the process running those assemblies to the current debugging process using the **Attach to Process...** command. Otherwise, the system prompts that the source code is not available, so control cannot step into the code block.

In a real-project scenario, sometimes your application crashes suddenly; in such scenarios, you can save the memory dump and analyze the memory registers on what's happening. This might require you to have special skills to read and understand such dumps.

We read about parallel tasks and multithreading in previous chapters; when your code block is running a multithreaded application of parallel tasks, the **Debug** menu can help you understand the parallel stack and tasks.

Tracing

Tracing enables us to monitor an application while it is executing. When a program is executed, the runtime allows us to write messages to monitor the control flow of the program. This will enable us to identify any incorrect behavior of the application logic. In the case of exceptions, we can identify where exactly the code failed and what variable values caused issues in smooth execution. These messages can be created by the `System.Diagnostics.Debug` class. When such messages are created, by default, these messages are displayed in the output window of Visual Studio.

Apart from creating these messages, you can redirect these messages to a file or database using the `System.Diagnostics.Trace` class. You can register listeners using the trace class, which allows you to redirect your messages. Here, your debug class or trace class acts as the publisher and the listener class acts as a subscriber. We hope you remember Chapter 5, *Creating and Implementing Events and Callbacks*, where we learned about the publisher and subscriber model.

Let's take a look at an example to understand how we can use debug messages. In the following program, we are trying to accept two input parameters and perform actions such as addition and subtraction on those numbers. However, we added a few extra lines to monitor messages that record what's happening:

```
internal void Method4()
{
    Console.WriteLine("Enter a numeric value");
    int number1 = Convert.ToInt32(Console.ReadLine());
    Debug.WriteLine($"Entered number 1 is: {number1}");

    Console.WriteLine("Enter another numeric value");
    int number2 = Convert.ToInt32(Console.ReadLine());
    Debug.WriteLine($"Entered number 2 is: {number2}");

    int number3 = number1 + number2;
    Debug.WriteLineIf(number3>10, $"Sum of number1 & number 2 is :
{number3}");
    int number4 = number1 - number2;
    Debug.WriteLineIf(number4 < 10, $"Difference of number1 & number 2 is :
{number4}");
}
```

Because we used `Debug.WriteLine` to record the messages, these values are written in the output window. Observe the following output window where all `Debug.WriteLine` messages are written:

```
C:\Users\srini\source\repos\Programming-in-C-Exam-70-483-M

Enter a numeric value
56
Enter another numeric value
48

100 %    ▼

Output

Show output from:   Debug
 'Chapter13.exe'  (CLR v4.0.30319: Chapter13.exe):  Loaded
 'Chapter13.exe'  (CLR v4.0.30319: Chapter13.exe):  Loaded
 'Chapter13.exe'  (CLR v4.0.30319: Chapter13.exe):  Loaded
 Entered number 1 is: 56
 Entered number 2 is: 48
 Sum of number1 & number 2 is : 104
 Difference of number1 & number 2 is : 8
```

In the preceding code block, you can see the last two `Debug.WriteLine` statements in the program block, where `Debug.WriteLineIf` is used. The system checks the condition that we provided, and, if it returns true, the system writes the message to the output window.

Now, let's go a step further and see how we can use tracing listeners to redirect your message to different channels.

We are going to use the same program with five extra lines, where we add `Console.Out` and a `logfile.txt` file as two different trace listeners, and then attach these two listeners to the debug object. The last line is `Debug.Flush`, which pushes all messages from the object to the log file:

```
internal void Method5()
{
    TextWriterTraceListener listener1 = new
TextWriterTraceListener(Console.Out);
    Debug.Listeners.Add(listener1);

    TextWriterTraceListener listener2 = new
TextWriterTraceListener(File.CreateText("logfile.txt"));
    Debug.Listeners.Add(listener2);

    Console.WriteLine("Enter a numeric value");
    int number1 = Convert.ToInt32(Console.ReadLine());
    Debug.WriteLine($"Entered number 1 is: {number1}");

    Console.WriteLine("Enter another numeric value");
    int number2 = Convert.ToInt32(Console.ReadLine());
    Debug.WriteLine($"Entered number 2 is: {number2}");

    int number3 = number1 + number2;
    Debug.WriteLineIf(number3 > 10, $"Sum of number1 & number 2 is :
{number3}");
    int number4 = number1 - number2;
    Debug.WriteLineIf(number4 < 10, $"Difference of number1 & number 2 is :
{number4}");
    Debug.Flush();
}
```

Because we added `Console.Out` as one of the listeners, `Debug.WriteLine` messages are now written on the screen when we execute the program:

Additionally, as we added `logfile.txt` as one of the listeners, a new text file gets created in the program executing folder where `Debug.WriteLine` messages are written:

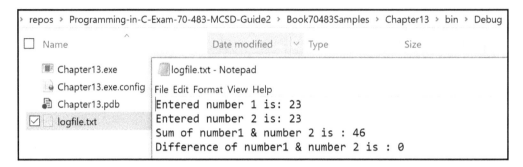

These listeners are not limited to text files and console. Based on the project requirement, you can add XML, database listeners, which might require some extra coding.

Summary

In this chapter, we learned how a C# assembly can be managed, how to debug an assembly or a program block, what features Visual Studio gives us in performing these actions, and how to use tracing.

In the next chapter, we will look at the different functionalities provided in C# to access and utilize the data present in file objects and external web services, focusing on performing I/O operations on file objects and the different helper classes available in the `System.Net` namespace, which helps us with I/O operations.

Questions

1. What does the version number of an assembly represent?
    1. Major version, minor version, build number, and revision.
    2. Major build, major version, assembly number, and date.
    3. Major build, major version, assembly number, and revision.
    4. All of the above.

2. What is the important benefit of strong naming an assembly?
    1. It allows you to share your assembly.
    2. It allows you to run more than two assemblies at the same time.
    3. It allows you to get it installed in GAC.
    4. All of the above.

3. What is the easiest way to log debug messages in a text file?
    1. Create a file and use a text stream object to write messages.
    2. Create a trace listener and attached it to the debug object.
    3. Use a third-party logging assembly.
    4. All of the above.

Answers

1. **Major version, minor version, build number, and revision**
2. **All of the above**
3. **Create a trace listener and attached it to the debug object**

14
Performing I/O Operations

In any programming language, all applications are dependent upon some sort of data. These applications interact with one another, passing data present in different sources such as file objects and external web services.

In this chapter, we will look at the different functionalities provided in C# to access and utilize data in file objects and external web services.

In this chapter, we will cover the following topics:

- Performing I/O operations on file objects
- Different helper classes available in the `System.Net` namespace that help us with I/O operations

Technical requirements

Like in the previous chapters covered in this book, the programs explained in this chapter will be developed in Visual Studio 2017.

Sample code for this chapter can be found on GitHub at `https://github.com/PacktPublishing/Programming-in-C-sharp-Exam-70-483-MCSD-Guide/tree/master/Chapter14`.

File I/O operations

File is a very crude term representing a collection of data stored on a disk at a particular directory path. While writing C# applications, there are several occasions when we will need to use file objects:

- To store data in an application or pass it across to another application
- To access configuration settings that are necessary for application execution
- To access files that are present in a directory path

These operations are called I/O operations. C# provides a namespace, `System.IO`, that has some helper classes. These helper classes help us execute I/O operations on file objects. In this section, we will look at those helper classes in C#.

Working with System.IO helper classes

The `System.IO` namespace contains a collection of classes that allow us to do file manipulation in C#. It includes classes that allow us to do operations such as the following:

- Read data from a file
- Write data to a file
- Create/delete new files

At different points during this chapter, through code examples, we will look at all of these I/O operations that we can perform on a file. However, before we start looking at those examples, we need to understand a very important concept, *Stream*, on which I/O operations are based.

A stream signifies a sequence of bytes exchanged between applications during an I/O operation. In C#, it's represented by an abstract class called `System.IO.Stream`. It provides a wrapper class to transfer bytes, and all classes that need to read/write bytes from any source must inherit from this particular class.

Before we move on to learn more about streams and how we deal with it them in C#, let's first look at how we deal with drives, directories, and some other basic operations with files.

Drives and directories

A drive represents a storage medium for the filesystem. It can be a hard drive, a CD, or any other storage type. In .NET Framework, we have a `DriveInfo` class in the `System.IO` namespace, which helps us access the filesystem information that is available on the drive. It provides methods that can help us access information such as name, size, and the free space available on the drive. Please refer to the following code implementation, in which we are looping through all the files available on the drive:

```
DriveInfo[] allDrives = DriveInfo.GetDrives();
foreach (DriveInfo d in allDrives)
{
    Console.WriteLine("Drive Name" + d.Name);
    Console.WriteLine(" Drive type " + d.DriveType);
    if (d.IsReady == true)
    {
        Console.WriteLine("Available space ", d.AvailableFreeSpace);
        Console.WriteLine("Total size in bytes ", d.TotalSize);
    }
}
Console.ReadLine();
```

In the preceding piece of code, we are browsing through all the drives (that is, C, D, E, and so on) available on the filesystem and are publishing information related to the following:

- The name of the drive
- The type of drive, that is, fixed, RAM, CD ROM, removable, and so on
- The total available memory size on the drive
- The total free memory available on the drive

If we execute the code, the execution will loop through all the drives that are present in the filesystem. Once a drive is retrieved, the execution will retrieve certain properties about the drive, such as free space, total size, and drive type. Thus, when we execute the program, we will get the following output. Please note that we may not get all the information as it also depends upon the security permissions on the directory:

In the system in which we are executing this program, we just have a C drive. Thus, while the program is executing, we are showing the properties of the C drive.

There are other properties on the `driveinfo` object as well. If we click on **Go to Definition** on the `DriveInfo` class, we can see the attributes of the class. Please visit the following link for more information: `https://docs.microsoft.com/en-us/dotnet/api/system.io.driveinfo?view=netframework-4.7.2`.

Each drive in a filesystem comprises directories and files. A directory in itself can comprise multiple sub-directories and files. If we need to do an operation on a particular directory, we do it using the `DirectoryInfo` class in C#. In the following code snippet, we are creating an object of the `DirectoryInfo` class, passing the location of a particular directory path:

```
DirectoryInfo directoryInfo = new DirectoryInfo("C:\\UCN Code
Base\\Programming-in-C-Exam-70-483-MCSD-Guide\\Book70483Samples");
foreach (DirectoryInfo f in directoryInfo.GetDirectories())
{
    Console.WriteLine("Directory Name is" + f.Name);
    Console.WriteLine("Directory created time is " + f.CreationTime);
    Console.WriteLine("Directory last modified time is " +
f.LastAccessTime);
}
```

For the `directoryInfo` object, we are then looping through all the child directories and are showing the information related to the following:

- Name of the directory
- Time the directory was created
- Time the directory was last modified

When we execute the preceding program, we do so on the `C:\\UCN Code Base\\Programming-in-C-Exam-70-483-MCSD-Guide\\Book70483Samples` file path. Please note that this is where we have been placing the codebase for the chapters we've got through in this book. Thus, when we execute this program, it will loop through the sub-folders of all those chapters and will fetch information such as `Directory Name`, `Directory created time`, and `Directory last modified time`. The following is the output that we will get for the program:

```
Directory Name is .vs
Directory created time is 10/02/2019 6:10:19 PM
Directory last modified time is 10/03/2019 3:04:55 PM
Directory Name is Chapter 1
Directory created time is 11/02/2019 11:47:47 PM
Directory last modified time is 10/03/2019 3:04:55 PM
Directory Name is Chapter 14
Directory created time is 10/03/2019 12:56:48 PM
Directory last modified time is 10/03/2019 3:34:11 PM
Directory Name is Chapter 2
Directory created time is 10/02/2019 6:11:25 PM
Directory last modified time is 10/03/2019 3:04:55 PM
Directory Name is Chapter 3
Directory created time is 10/02/2019 6:11:25 PM
Directory last modified time is 10/03/2019 3:04:55 PM
Directory Name is Chapter 8
Directory created time is 17/02/2019 12:31:11 PM
Directory last modified time is 10/03/2019 3:04:55 PM
Directory Name is Chapter 9
Directory created time is 2/03/2019 5:55:50 PM
Directory last modified time is 10/03/2019 3:04:55 PM
Directory Name is Chapter10
```

There are additional operations available with the `DirectoryInfo` object.

Checking whether the directory exists

Using a particular directory path, we can identify if any directory with that path exists in the filesystem or not. In the code implementation, we are creating a `DirectoryInfo` object and then using the `Exists` property to check whether the directory exists in the filesystem:

```
DirectoryInfo directoryInfoExists = new DirectoryInfo("C:\\UCN Code
Base\\Programming-in-C-Exam-70-483-MCSD-Guide\\Book70483Samples\\Chapter
20");
if (directoryInfoExists.Exists)
{
    Console.WriteLine("It exists");
}
else
{
    Directory.CreateDirectory("Does not exist");
}
```

If we execute the code using the path mentioned during the creation of the `DirectoryInfo` object, the program execution will determine whether there is a directory in the filesystem in the specified path. Thus, when the program is executed, as we do not currently have a sub-folder called `Chapter 20` in the `Book70483Samples` base folder we will see **Does not exists** in the console output window. The following is globally the relevant output on the console window:

```
Does not exists
```

In the next section, we will look at how to create a directory in a filesystem using C#.

Creating a directory

Using the `DirectoryInfo` class, we can also create new directories in the filesystem. The following code illustrates how we create a new directory in the system:

```
Directory.CreateDirectory("C:\\UCN Code Base\\Programming-in-C-Exam-70-483-
MCSD-Guide\\Book70483Samples\\Chapter 20");
```

If the preceding code is executed, it will create a subdirectory called `Chapter 20` in the root folder.

In the preceding code, we are passing an absolute path to create the directory. However, if we need to create a subdirectory in a particular directory, we can just execute the following code:

```
DirectoryInfo subDirectory =
parentDirectory.CreateSubdirectory("NameChildDirectory");
```

In the preceding code, `parentDirectory` is the parent directory in which we want to create the subdirectory. `NameChildDirectory` is the name that we want to give to the child directory.

Looping through the files

Using the `DirectoryInfo` class, we can also loop through the files present in the directory. The following code shows how we can loop through the files and access their properties:

```
DirectoryInfo chapter20 = new DirectoryInfo("C:\\UCN Code
Base\\Programming-in-C-Exam-70-483-MCSD-Guide\\Book70483Samples\\Chapter
20");
foreach (FileInfo f in chapter20.GetFiles())
{
    Console.WriteLine("File Name is " + f.FullName);
    Console.WriteLine("Directory created time is " + f.CreationTime);
    Console.WriteLine("Directory last modified time is " +
f.LastAccessTime);
}
```

In the preceding code snippet, we are looping through the files present in the `Chapter 20` directory and showing the information present in it. In the `Chapter 20` folder, we have only one file: `dynamics365eula.txt`. Thus, when the program is executed, it will pick up the file and will read the file information present in it. To illustrate this, we are displaying the filename, the time the file was created, and the time the file was last accessed. So when the code is executed, we will get the following output:

```
File Name is C:\UCN Code Base\Programming-in-C-Exam-70-483-MCSD-Guide\Book70483Samples\Chapter 20\dynamics365eula.txt
File created time is 10/03/2019 5:19:09 PM
File last modified time is 10/03/2019 5:19:09 PM
```

Now that we have some knowledge about drives and `DirectoryInfo`, we will explore some helper classes that allow us to do operations on files.

Working with files

In this section, we will go through the helper classes that allow us to do operations on the files present in a directory. C# provides the `File` and `FileInfo` helper classes to do operations on files. While going through the following code snippets, we will be looking at some of the typical operations that we can do with file objects.

Checking whether a file exists

This basically involves checking whether a file with the given path exists or not. This can help us write fail-safe code in such a way that we read a file only after establishing that it exists in the given path:

```
string file = "C:\\UCN Code Base\\Programming-in-C-Exam-70-483-MCSD-
Guide\\Book70483Samples\\Chapter 20\\IO Operations.txt";
if(File.Exists(file))
{
    Console.WriteLine("File Exists in the mentioned path");
}
else
{
    Console.WriteLine("File does not exists in the mentioned path");
}
```

`File` is a static class available in the `System.IO` namespace. This class provides operations that we can use to execute functionalities related to file access. In the preceding code, we have declared a file path and, using the static `File` class, we are checking whether the file indeed exists in the given path.

Moving a file from one location to another

In this operation, we basically cut the file from one location and paste it into another. The following code snippet shows how this can be done:

```
string sourceFileLocation = "C:\\UCN Code Base\\Programming-in-C-
Exam-70-483-MCSD-Guide\\Book70483Samples\\Chapter 20\\IO Operations.txt";
 string targetFileLocation = "C:\\UCN Code Base\\Programming-in-C-
Exam-70-483-MCSD-Guide\\Book70483Samples\\Chapter 21\\New File.txt";
if (File.Exists(sourceFileLocation))
{
    File.Move(sourceFileLocation, targetFileLocation);
}
else
{
    Console.WriteLine("File does not exists in the mentioned path");
}
```

In the preceding code snippet, we are first checking whether the file exists in a particular location. If the file is present in the location, we are copying it into another location.

Once the code is executed, we will notice that the file is cut from the source location and is pasted in to the target location.

Copying a file from one location to another

In this operation, we basically copy the file from one location and paste it into another. Please note the Move operation will delete the file present in the source folder. However, the Copy operation will copy the file present in the source folder to the destination folder. The following code snippet shows how this can be done:

```
if (File.Exists(targetFileLocation))
{
    File.Copy(targetFileLocation, sourceFileLocation);
}
else
{
    Console.WriteLine("File does not exists in the mentioned path");
}
```

When the code is executed, we will see that the file is copied from the source file location and pasted in to the target file location path.

Deleting a file

In this operation, we delete a file present in the specified location:

```
File.Delete(sourceFileLocation);
```

When the code is executed, we will see that the file is deleted from the source file location. Once the code is executed, we will see that the file specified in the sourceFileLocation path has been deleted.

 Please note that operations that work with the File class work the same way with the FileInfo class. The same implementations that we have done with the File class can be done via the FileInfo class as well.

In all the preceding examples, we have been hard-coding the path property of the file. This is not a recommended practice as it is error-prone. For example, if you look at the actual path of any file and compare it to what we need to supply in the program, you will notice a difference:

- Actual path: C:\File Location\Chapter 20\Sample.txt
- Path which we need to specify in the program: C:\\File Location\\Chapter 20\\Sample.txt

We need to provide some extra slashes in the path. Also, when we are combining the folder path with the file path, we need to concatenate them with an extra \ as well. For these reasons, hardcoding the path is not a recommended practice. A better approach is to use the `Path` helper class. The following code shows how to use it:

```
string sourceFileLocation = @"C:\UCN Code Base\Programming-in-C-
Exam-70-483-MCSD-Guide\Book70483Samples\Chapter 20";
string fileName = @"IO Operations.txt";
string properFilePath = Path.Combine(sourceFileLocation, fileName);
Console.WriteLine(Path.GetDirectoryName(properFilePath));
Console.WriteLine(Path.GetExtension(properFilePath));
Console.WriteLine(Path.GetFileName(properFilePath));
Console.WriteLine(Path.GetPathRoot(properFilePath));
```

In the preceding code implementation, we have declared a folder path. Please also note the use of `&` before the filename. This is an escape character that allows us to not specify an extra \ in the folder path structure. We have also declared a filename and are now combining the two together using the helper static class: `Path`. Once we have combined them, we retrieve the properties in the resulting file path. If the code is executed, we get the following output:

```
File Existis in the mentioned path
C:\UCN Code Base\Programming-in-C-Exam-70-483-MCSD-Guide\Book70483Samples\Chapter 20
.txt
IO Operations.txt
C:\
```

Let's examine the output:

- `Path.GetDirectoryName`: This returns the directory name of the combined path file. Note that it has the complete absolute directory path.
- `Path.GetExtension`: This returns the file extension of the combined path file. In this case, it's a `.txt` file.
- `Path.GetFileName`: This returns the name of the file.
- `Path.GetPathRoot`: This returns the root of the filepath. In this case, it's `C:`, hence it's mentioned in the output.

Now that we are aware of basic operations on files, we will look at how to access and modify the contents of a file. For this, we will look at the operations available in `FileStream`.

Stream object

The main operations with files are related to reading, writing, retrieving, and updating text present in file. In .NET, these operations are performed using an exchange of bytes in I/O operations. This sequence of bytes is a stream, and in .NET, it's represented using the abstract `Stream` class. This class forms the basis of all I/O operations in .NET such as `FileStream` and `MemoryStream`.

With stream we can perform the following operations in .NET:

- Reading data in the stream object
- Writing data into the stream object
- Searching for or finding relevant information from the stream object

Let's take a look at the different operations that are implemented using stream objects. In the next section, we will go through the `FileStream` object, which aids operations on the file object.

FileStream

Using the `FileStream` object, we can read and write information back to the file in the directory. It's done using the `File` and `FileInfo` object we discussed in the previous section in this chapter.

Lets go through the following code example, in which we are writing information to a file:

```
string sourceFileLocation = @"C:\UCN Code Base\Programming-in-C-
Exam-70-483-MCSD-Guide\Book70483Samples\Chapter 20\Sample.txt";
using (FileStream fileStream = File.Create(sourceFileLocation))
{
    string myValue = "MyValue";
    byte[] data = Encoding.UTF8.GetBytes(myValue);
    fileStream.Write(data, 0, data.Length);
}
```

In the preceding code implementation, we are doing the following:

- Opening the `Sample.txt` file that's present in the specified location
- Creating a `File` object from it and then converting the data present in the file to a `FileStream` object
- Writing data to the file using the `Write` operation available in the `FileStream` object

Please note that we are using the `using` block for the `FileStream` object. Due to this, the `Dispose` method will be automatically called for the `FileStream` object. Therefore, the memory from unmanaged resources will be reclaimed automatically.

Please note that in the preceding implementation, we are encoding the string value before we are writing that data to the `FileStream` object.

Another way of handling the same functionality is to use the `StreamWriter` helper class. The following code implementation shows how it can be handled using the `StreamWriter` helper class:

```
string sourceFileLocation = @"C:\UCN Code Base\Programming-in-C-
Exam-70-483-MCSD-Guide\Book70483Samples\Chapter 20\Sample.txt";
using (StreamWriter streamWriter = File.CreateText(sourceFileLocation))
{
    string myValue = "MyValue";
    streamWriter.Write(myValue);
}
```

While choosing between the two helper classes, we need to consider the data we are dealing with. A `FileStream` object deals with an array of bytes. However, the `StreamWriter` class implements `TextWriter`. It only deals with string data and automatically encodes it into bytes so that we don't have to explicitly do it. However, in cases when we use the `FileStream` class, we must encode and decode the bytes to data into the string representation.

In the next section, we will look at some best practices relating to exception handling while dealing with file I/O operations.

Exception handling

In any real-world scenario, multiple people might be working with the same file concurrently. Using threading in C#, we can lock objects while a particular operation is happening on a resource. However, such locking is not available on files present in the filesystem.

So, it's quite possible that files that are being accessed in the program have been moved or even deleted altogether by a different application or user. C# provides some exceptions with which we can handle such scenarios in a better way. Please refer to the following code implementation, where we are handling an exception:

```
private static string ReadFileText()
{
    string path =@"C:\UCN Code Base\Programming-in-C-Exam-70-483-MCSD-
Guide\Book70483Samples\Chapter 20\Sample.txt";
    if (File.Exists(path))
    {
        try
        {
            return File.ReadAllText(path);
        }
        catch (DirectoryNotFoundException)
        {
            return string.Empty;
        }
        catch (FileNotFoundException)
        {
            return string.Empty;
        }
    }
    return string.Empty;
}
```

From a functionality perspective, in the preceding code we are reading file present in the given location. We are retrieving all the text present in the file and then passing it back to the calling function. Please also note the following best practices that we are using in the code implementation:

- In the code, we are first checking whether the file exists in the directory location using the `Exists` method. If the file exists, we proceed to extract data from the file.
- Even though we have checked that the file exists before we proceed, there are still some circumstances in which the file is removed, deleted, or becomes inaccessible after the code moves to the next block. To handle such scenarios, we are catching the `DirectoryNotFoundException` and `FileNotFoundException` exceptions. `DirectoryNotFoundException` is thrown when the directory specified in the path no longer exists. `FileNotFoundException` is thrown when the file specified in the path no longer exists.

Now that we have a fair understanding of how to execute I/O operations on a file, we will look at examples of calling external web services to get a response from them.

Reading data from a network

While developing applications in .NET Framework, we will encounter several scenarios where we need to call external APIs to get the required data. .NET Framework provides a `System.Net` namespace that provides a large number of helper classes that allow us to execute these operations.

In this section, we will go through an example in which we will use the `WebRequest` and `WebResponse` classes to call the external APIs and process their responses. We will be calling an external page, and we also process the response that we will get from the call. We will also be looking at code examples in which we will learn how to make asynchronous calls to an external web server.

WebRequest and WebResponse

`WebRequest` is an abstract base class provided by .NET Framework for accessing data from the internet. Using this class, we send a request to a particular URL, such as `www.google.com`.

On the other hand, `WebResponse` is an abstract class that provides a response from the URL called by the `WebRequest` class.

The `WebRequest` object is created by calling the static `Create` method. In the method, we pass the address URL that we want to call in the request. The request inspects the address we are passing to it and selects a protocol implementation, for example, HTTP or FTP. Based upon the web address passed, an appropriate instance of the derived class, such as `HttpWebRequest` for HTTP or `FtpWebRequest` for FTP, is returned when the `WebRequest` object is created. The `WebRequest` class also allows us to specify some other properties, such as the authentication and content type. Let's go through the following code implementation, which will help us learn more about this class:

```
WebRequest request = null;
HttpWebResponse response = null;
Stream dataStream = null;
StreamReader reader = null;
try
{
    request = WebRequest.Create("http://www.google.com/search?q=c#");
```

```
        request.Method = "GET";
        response = (HttpWebResponse)request.GetResponse();
        dataStream = response.GetResponseStream();
        reader = new StreamReader(dataStream);
        Console.WriteLine(reader.ReadToEnd());
    }
    catch(Exception ex)
    {
        Console.WriteLine(ex.ToString());
    }
    finally
    {
        reader.Close();
        dataStream.Close();
        response.Close();
    }
```

In the preceding code implementation, we are creating a `WebRequest` object for `http://google.com`. We are using a `GET` method in the `HTTP` request and passing parameters embedded in the URL itself. As the protocol is `HTTP`, we are converting the `WebResponse` object to `httpWebResponse`.

Once we have captured the response, we are retrieving the stream of bytes into a `Stream` object and are then using a `StreamReader` object to retrieve the response from `google.com`.

A very important thing to note here is that in the `finally` block, we are closing all the response, stream, and reader objects that have been created in the `try...catch` block. This is essential: as we are dealing with unmanaged resources, it's important to reclaim the memory for better performance.

 For further reading, please refer to the following blog from Microsoft, which discusses the different parameters that we can set in the `WebRequest` object when we are making a call: `https://docs.microsoft.com/en-us/dotnet/api/system.net.webrequest?view=netframework-4.7.2`.

In the preceding code, we were making synchronous calls to the external web service and waiting for a response. However, in a real-world scenario, this may not be the ideal implementation.

The external server to which we are making a call may take some time to send us the response. Therefore, if our application continues to wait for a response during this time, the responsiveness of the application will be challenged. To avoid such scenarios, we can make I/O calls asynchronous. In the next section, we will learn why we need to look at making asynchronous I/O calls and how they're implemented in code.

Asynchronous I/O operations

When we were going through the `WebRequest` and `WebResponse` section, we wrote a program in which we made a call to `google.com`. In very crude terms, when the request is made, it's picked up by the Google server, which then assigns a thread to cater to this request. The thread then sends the response to the calling machine.

Theoretically, however, there is always a possibility that fewer free threads are available on the server. Also, there is the possibility that the server may take a long time to complete the request and send the response to the caller.

The challenge here is that we must design communication between the caller and the server is such a way that the performance and responsiveness of the application are not compromised. We do that by making the calls asynchronous.

If we make these operations asynchronous, we can rest assured that, while the server is processing the request and sending us the response, our application remains responsive and users can continue using the application. We do this using the `async/await` keywords.

Any method that is written asynchronously in C# must have the following characteristics:

- The method definition must have the `async` keyword to indicate that the method is executed asynchronously.
- The method must have one of the following return types:
  - `Task`: If the function has no return statements
  - `Task<TResult>`: If the function has a return statement in which the object being returned is of type `TResult`
  - `Void`: If the function is an event handler
- In the function, we execute an asynchronous call to an external web server.
- The function may have an `await` statement. The `await` statement basically tells the compiler that the application must wait at that statement for the asynchronous process executed by the external web server to finish.

Let's go through all these points in the following code implementation:

```
async Task<int> ExecuteOperationAsync()
{
    using (HttpClient client = new HttpClient())
    {
            Task<string> getStringTask =
    client.GetStringAsync("http://google.com");
            ExecuteParallelWork();
            string urlContents = await getStringTask;
            return urlContents.Length;
    }
}
```

Please refer to the following in the preceding code:

- We have defined a function called `ExecuteOperationAsync`. To indicate the asynchronous behavior of the function, we have used the `async` keyword in the function definition.
- We have declared the return type of the function as `Task<int>`, which indicates that the function will return an object of type `int`.
- We have declared an object of the `HttpClient` helper class and are making a call to `http://google.com`. We are making the request call asynchronously.
- To ensure that the application carries on doing other work, we are calling the `ExecuteParallelWork` function so that, until the response arrives, the application does not stop processing.
- We have used an `await` statement so that the compiler stops at that point and waits for the response for a asynchronous request call. Once the response is received, it checks the length of the response string and returns the result to the calling function.

Now that we have a fair understanding of how asynchronous calls work in I/O operations, we will look at how to use them in I/O operations.

In the next section, we will look at how different I/O operations can be made asynchronous using this keyword.

Async operations on file

In this section, we will learn how to perform I/O operations on a file asynchronously. This can be helpful in scenarios when the data that we are writing to the file is large.

The following code implementation shows how to write data to a file asynchronously. Please note that we must use the `FileStream` object to execute file I/O operations asynchronously:

```
public async Task CreateFile()
{
    string path =@"C:\UCN Code Base\Programming-in-C-Exam-70-483-MCSD-
Guide\Book70483Samples\Chapter 20\New.txt";
    using (FileStream stream = new FileStream(path,FileMode.Create,
    FileAccess.Write, FileShare.None, 4096, true))
    {
        byte[] data = new byte[100000];
        new Random().NextBytes(data);
        await stream.WriteAsync(data, 0, data.Length);
    }
}
```

In the preceding code implementation, we are creating a new file in a given directory location. The calling function does not require a value to be returned, so we have just set the return type as `Task`. To create the file and write data to it, we have used a `FileStream` object. For a detailed analysis of the properties passed in the constructor of the class, please refer to the following link: `https://docs.microsoft.com/en-us/dotnet/api/system.io.filestream?view=netframework-4.7.2`.

After creating the object, we are generating a random sequence of bytes and are then writing it asynchronously to the `FileStream` object.

For a code implementation related to calling web requests asynchronously, we can refer to the implementation in the previous example where we created an object called `HttpClient` and made a call asynchronously.

In the next section, we will learn how to execute multiple I/O operations asynchronously and in a parallel manner.

This is quite useful in scenarios where the application must wait for the completion of different functions that are executing in parallel.

Using the await statement for parallel asynchronous calls

While writing programs, we often come across situations in which we must wait for results from different asynchronous calls. This is required when the processing is dependent upon multiple responses from an external medium, such as web services. Let's look at the following code example:

```
public async Task ExecuteMultipleRequestsInParallel()
{
    HttpClient client = new HttpClient();
    Task google = client.GetStringAsync("http://www.google.com");
    Task bing = client.GetStringAsync("http://www.bing.com");
    Task yahoo = client.GetStringAsync("http://yahoo.com/");
    await Task.WhenAll(google, bing, yahoo);
}
```

In the preceding code, we are executing asynchronous calls to different servers. Suppose we have to wait for the output from all of them before we can proceed; we can use the `WhenAll` statement. The `WhenAll` statement will ensure that the execution waits for responses from all three asynchronous calls before the processing can move ahead.

Summary

In this chapter, we learned how to execute I/O operations related to files and networks in C#. We went over namespaces that provide helper classes for executing I/O operations. We started with the basic operations that we can perform on drives and directories. We looked at code that we can use to loop through files in directories.

Then we looked at the helper classes that help us with I/O operations on files. We looked at the `File` and `FileInfo` classes, which help us create, copy, move, and delete files. We looked at best practices for dealing with directory and file paths. We then looked at *streams*, or sequences of bytes, which allow us to edit information present in files. We then looked at best practices for exception handling in files.

After that, we looked at helper classes for dealing with I/O operations over networks. We looked at a code example in which we made HTTP calls over the internet. We then looked at a code implementation in which we made asynchronous I/O calls. Whenever possible, it's always beneficial to use asynchronous operations because it's better for the overall performance of the application. We went over code examples for executing asynchronous operations on both I/O and over the internet.

In the next chapter, we will look at how LINQ queries can we used in C# to work efficiently when we are querying different data sources, such as XML and SQL. Working with code examples, we will explore the different components of LINQ, along with the different operators that we can use while working with LINQ queries.

Questions

1. Which syntax should we use to append text to a file?
    1. `File.CreateText`
    2. `FileInfo.Create`
    3. `File.Create`
    4. `File.AppendText`

2. Which syntax should we use if the application needs to wait for asynchronous calls from multiple sources?
    1. `async`
    2. `await`
    3. `Task`
    4. `Task.WhenAll`

3. Which one of the following statements is incorrect?
    1. `StreamWriter` only works with text; however, `FileStream` works with bytes.
    2. We can lock files in .NET.
    3. If we have an asynchronous function, it can have one of three return types: `Task`, `Task<TResult>`, and `Void`.
    4. `DirectoryNotFoundException` is thrown when the directory in the file path is no longer available.

Answers

1. **File.AppendText.**
2. **Task.WhenAll.**
3. **Except "B" that is we can lock files, all other statements are true.**

15
Using LINQ Queries

In .NET, we often need to query data from different sources, such as XML, SQL, and web services. In earlier versions of .NET, we performed these operations using simple strings. The main issue with this approach is that it lacks any IntelliSense and is quite cumbersome in implementation. These queries also differ from one another as to the source from which we are querying the data, thereby increasing the code complexity.

To overcome these issues, LINQ was firstly introduced in .NET 3.5. Compared to conventional data access methods, LINQ introduces an easy and consistent approach for the querying and modification of data across different types of data sources such as XML and even in-memory data structures such as arrays. In LINQ, we query data using a query expression. The query expression enables us to perform filtering, ordering, and grouping of operations on the data using minimal code.

In this chapter, we will look at the following topics:

- Introducing LINQ
- Understanding the language features that make LINQ possible
- Understanding LINQ query operators
- Understanding LINQ behind the scenes
- Using LINQ to XML

By the end of this chapter, we will have learned how we can use LINQ queries while performing operations on an XML file. We will look at how LINQ queries can help us write, query, and modify XML files.

Technical requirements

Like in the previous chapters covered in this book, the programs explained in this book will be developed in Visual Studio 2017.

The sample code for this chapter can be found on GitHub in `Chapter 15` (`https://github.com/PacktPublishing/Programming-in-C-Sharp-Exam-70-483-MCSD-Guide/tree/master/Book70483Samples`).

Introducing LINQ

In this section, we will learn the basics of LINQ. We can use LINQ queries against any collection of objects, with the only condition being that the object must support the `IEnumerable` or generic `IEnumerable<T>` interface.

Along with that, the target framework of the project in which we are planning to use LINQ must be version 3.5 or more recent.

In the next section, we will look at queries, which form the basis of LINQ operations. We will be looking at the different components of a query and understand how they are constructed in .NET.

Queries

A query is a string expression that retrieves data from a data source. The expression is usually related to a particular data source such as SQL or XML and will generally be expressed in that respective data source language. However, with LINQ, we can develop a reusable coding pattern that works on different data sources. The pattern is divided into three parts:

- Obtaining the data source
- Creating the query
- Executing the query

The following code that illustrates the three operations in their simplest forms:

```
// 1. Obtaining the data source.
 int[] numbers = new int[3] { 0, 1, 2};
// 2. Query creation.
var numQuery =
from num in numbers
where (num % 2) == 0
select num;
// 3. Query execution.
foreach (int num in numQuery)
{
    Console.Write("{0,1} ", num);
}
```

In the preceding code example, we created an array of integers whose size is 3. As it implements the `IEnumerable<int>` interface, we will be able to implement LINQ on the array. In the next step, we created a query in which we are filtering even numbers present in the array. Finally, in the third step, we are looping through the results of the query execution and printing it.

In the preceding example, we used an array as the source of data. The array already supports the `IEnumerable` or `IEnumerable <T>` interface. However, in some cases, that may not always be the case. For example, when we read the data source from sources such as XML files, we need LINQ to load the data in memory as a queryable type. In this case, we can use the `XElement` type. The following is the syntax for this:

```
// Create a data source from an XML document. //
using System.Xml.Linq;
XElement students = XElement.Load(@"c:\students.xml");
```

In the preceding code example, we have loaded the data from the XML file in the `XElement` object, which implements an `IQuerable` interface. Now, on this, we can easily write LINQ queries to execute any operation.

Before we move ahead and understand more around LINQ, we must understand the built-in features of C# that help us implement LINQ queries. In the next section, we will discuss some of these features.

Understanding language features that make LINQ possible

There are several features available in C# that are either necessary for the implementation of LINQ or that help us effectively use LINQ queries. These are some of the topics that we will be going through in this chapter:

- Implicitly typed variables
- Object initialization syntax
- Lambda expressions
- Extension methods
- Anonymous types

Implicitly typed variables

In C#, we generally use statically typed variables. This implies that the compiler knows the type of variable at compile time. Due to this, if it finds any operation that may result in an error, it will highlight it at compile time. For example, refer to the following code:

```
int i = 1;
FileStream f = new FileStream("test.txt", FileMode.Open);
string s = i + f; // This line gives a compile error
```

We will observe that the compiler will give us a compile-time error. The following is the screenshot this:

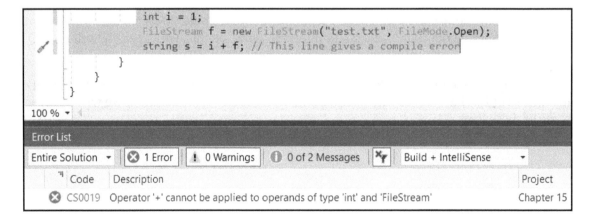

As illustrated by the error description, the compiler identifies that the operation is not supported in terms of the type of the two variables, hence, it throws this error. This is referred to as explicit typing.

Implicit typing was added to C# in version 3.0. In implicit typing, the compiler automatically identifies the variable type at compile time. The compiler does this based on the value that is assigned to the variable during declaration. The compiler then strongly types the variable to that particular type.

In C#, we use implicit typing by using the `var` keyword. The following shows the same code written earlier, albeit with implicit typing:

```
var i = 1;
FileStream f = new FileStream("test.txt", FileMode.Open);
string s = i + f; // This line gives a compile error
```

Please note that even though we have not implicitly specified the type of the variable as `int`, based upon the value 1 assigned to it, the compiler will infer that the type of the variable must be `int`. In this case, it will give us the same compile-time error. The following is the screenshot for this:

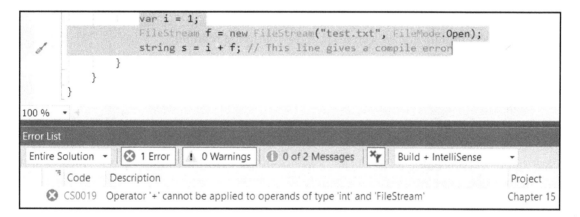

Implicit `Type` helps in the LINQ query in circumstances when the return type is determined at compile time. In addition to being a mandatory declaration, implicit typing also improves code readability. To illustrate this example, refer to the following declaration in the code.

Note that, instead of declaring the actual type, we have used the `Type` variable in the declaration, hence improving code readability:

```
Dictionary<string, IEnumerable<Tuple<Type, int>>> implicitData = new
Dictionary<string, IEnumerable<Tuple<Type, int>>>();
var implicitData = new Dictionary<string, IEnumerable<Tuple<Type, int>>>();
```

In the next section, we will look at initializers and how they can improve code readability.

Object initialization syntax

Initializers in C# help us combine the creation of objects and set their properties. Let's refer to the following code example. Let's assume we have a `Student` class that has the following declaration:

```
public class Student
{
    public int rollNum { get; set; }
    public string Name { get; set; }
}
```

Now, suppose we need to declare an object for this class. In a conventional way, without the use of object initializers, we can do it in the following manner:

```
Student p = new Student();
p.rollNum = 1;
p.Name = "James";
Student p2 = new Student();
p2.rollNum = 2;
p2.Name = "Donohoe";
```

Note that in the preceding code, we have to specify the creation of the p and p2 objects and set up their respective properties separately.

Using object initialization syntax, we will be able to combine the creation of the object and the setting up of its properties in one statement. As an example, if we use object initialization to execute the same functionality that we did earlier, we can use the following syntax:

```
// Creating and initializing a new object in a single step
Person p = new Person
{
    FirstName ="James",
    LastName = "Doe"
};
```

Please note that even though usage of object initialization is not necessary and doesn't provide any additional capability or feature to us, it can improve the readability of our code. The code can also be enhanced if there is a requirement for creating a collection of the same objects. The following is the syntax for this:

```
var students = new List<Student>
{
    new Student
    {
        rollNum = 1,
        Name = "James"
    },
    new Student
    {
        rollNum = 2,
        Name = "Donohoe"
    }
};
```

Note that object initialization syntax makes the code much more readable and, in cases where we are working with anonymous types, it is actually required. In the next section, we will look at lambda expressions.

Lambda expressions

Lambda expressions were introduced to C# in 3.0 version. Lambda expressions are based upon anonymous functions and a lambda expression is a shorter way to represent an anonymous method.

In `Chapter 5`, *Creating and Implementing Events and Callbacks*, in the *Initiate delegate using anonymous functions* section, we looked at how we can create anonymous functions in C# using the `delegate` keyword. In a nutshell, just to recap, using anonymous methods, we can create an inline method in some code, assign it to a variable, and pass it around.

In Chapter 5, *Creating and Implementing Events and Callbacks*, in the *Lambda expressions* section, we looked at how we can convert an anonymous function into its equivalent lambda expression. However, just to recap, let's go through the following code example, in which we will first create an anonymous function and then create a lambda expression for the same:

```
Func<int, int> anonymousFunc = delegate (int y)
{
    return y * 5;
};
Console.WriteLine(anonymousFunc(1));'.
```

In the preceding code, we declared a delegate function of the Func<T, T> format. This implies that this function takes an input of int and returns an integer output. Hence, the output for the preceding operation would be *1 * 5*, that is, *5*.

Now, if we need to write the same code using a lambda expression, we can use the following code syntax:

```
Func<int, int> anonymousFuncLambda = y => y * 5;
Console.WriteLine(anonymousFuncLambda(1));
```

Please also note the usage of the => notation in a lambda expression. This notation translates into *becomes* or *for which*.

If we execute the two code blocks, we will notice that the results of the operations are the same. However, with lambda expressions, we end up with much cleaner code and avoid a lot of code typing. In the next section, we will look at extension methods.

Extension methods

Extension methods in C# allow us to add methods to an existing type without altering them or using inheritance. The extension methods are defined in the System.Linq.Enumerables namespace.

An extension method is always defined in a static class and as a static method. Along with that, it also uses the this keyword to qualify itself as an extension method. The following is a code example in which we have declared an extension method multiple on the int type. To identify the calling object as the first parameter being passed to the function, we have used the this keyword:

```
public static class IntExtensions
{
```

```
    public static int MultiplyExtension(this int x, int y)
    {
        return x * y;
    }
}
int z = 6;
Console.WriteLine(z.MultiplyExtension(5));
Console.ReadLine();
```

Once the preceding code is executed, we get the output of 30, which is the output when the calling object, 6, is multiplied by 5, which is declared in the extension method. In the next section, we will look at anonymous types.

Anonymous types

An anonymous type is a combination of both object initializers and implicit typing. An anonymous type is a type that doesn't have a name. Using anonymous types, using the var and new keyword, we create an object without defining its type or class. The type of anonymous type variable is inferred based on the value with which it's initialized. Along with that, the properties of an anonymous variable are read-only, which means we cannot change their values after the variable has been initialized.

The following is some sample code syntax where we have declared an object of an anonymous type. In the object, we have specified three properties, PropertyNum1, PropertyNum2, and PropertyNum3:

```
var anonymousType = new
{
    PropertyNum1 = "One",
    PropertyNum2 = 2,
    PropertyNum3 = true
};
Console.WriteLine(anonymousType.GetType().ToString());
```

Once the code is executed, we get the following output:

```
<>f__AnonymousType0`3[System.String,System.Int32,System.Boolean]
```

Note that, as we are displaying the type of the anonymous type, for each of its respective properties, the execution is displaying the type based upon the value that is assigned to the property. Hence, the output that we see is `String`, `Int32`, and `Boolean`.

In the next section, we will look at some standard LINQ operators that we use often while writing LINQ queries.

Understanding LINQ query operators

As described in the *Queries* section, each LINQ operation is divided into three parts. In the first part, we obtain data from a data source. In the second part, we do operations on the data and finally, in the last part, we extract the data.

While doing the second part, that is, performing operations on the data, there are some standard operators that we can use. These operators help us to achieve a consistent experience and a code base that can be easily adapted to different data sources.

Some of the standard query operators are `Select`, `SelectMany`, `Join`, `OrderBy`, `Average`, `GroupBy`, `Max`, `Min`, and `Where`. In the following sections, let's see some code and learn how some of these operators work.

Select and SelectMany

We use `Select` in LINQ when we need to select some values from a collection. For example, in the following code syntax, we have declared an array of integers and are selecting all of the numbers present in the array:

```
int[] numbers = new int[3] { 0, 1, 2 };
var numQuery =
from num in numbers
select num;

foreach(var n in numQuery)
{
    Console.Write(n);
}
```

Therefore, if the preceding code is executed, it will print all of the numbers present in the array. The following is the output of the preceding code snippet:

```
012
```

We use `Select` when we need to select a value from a collection. However, in scenarios where we need to select values from nested collections, that is, a collection of collections, we use the `SelectMany` operator. Refer to the following code example, in which we are using the `SelectMany` operator to retrieve individual characters from string objects present in a string array:

```
string[] array =
{
    "Introduction",
    "In",
    "C#"
};
var result = array.SelectMany(element => element.ToCharArray());
foreach (char letter in result)
{
    Console.Write(letter);
}
```

The following would be the output of the program:

```
IntroductionInC#
```

In the preceding program, the source of data is an array of strings. Now, strings are again an array of characters. Using `SelectMany`, we have directly looped through the characters present in the `Introduction`, `In`, and `C#` strings. Hence, using `SelectMany`, we can perform actions using fewer statements than it would take otherwise.

In the next section, we will look at the `Join` operator, which helps us join two collections.

The join operator

The `join` operators in LINQ help us join two collections that could be linked to each other by a common attribute. Refer to the following code example, which will provide a better explanation of this. Consider that we have two class objects, one representing `ClassDetail` and another representing `Students` that are studying in the class:

```
public class Student
{
    public int rollNum { get; set; }
    public string Name { get; set; }
    public string classID { get; set; }
}
public class ClassDetail
{
    public string classID { get; set; }
    public string className { get; set; }
}
```

Please note that in the `ClassDetail` class, we have details specific to the class in itself such as `ClassID` and `ClassName`. In the `Student` class, we have details specific to the student such as `rollNum`, `Name`, and `ClassID`. In the `Student` class, `ClassID` attribute refers to the class in which the student is currently studying. We will use this attribute to link the collections of `ClassDetail` and `Student`.

The following code indicates how we make a join between the two collection items of `Student` and `Class`:

```
List<ClassDetail> classNames = new List<ClassDetail>();
classNames.Add(new ClassDetail { classID = "1", className = "First
Standard" });
classNames.Add(new ClassDetail { classID = "2", className = "Second
Standard" });
classNames.Add(new ClassDetail { classID = "3", className = "Third
Standard" });
List<Student> students = new List<Student>();
students.Add(new Student { rollNum = 1, classID = "1", Name = "Sia Bhalla"
});
students.Add(new Student { rollNum = 2, classID = "2", Name = "James
Donohoe" });
students.Add(new Student { rollNum = 3, classID = "1", Name = "Myra
Thareja" });
var list = (from s in students
join d in classNames on s.classID equals d.classID
select new
{
```

```
        StudentName = s.Name,
        ClassName = d.className
    });
    foreach (var e in list)
    {
        Console.WriteLine("Student Name = {0} , Class Name = {1}",
    e.StudentName, e.ClassName);
    }
```

In the preceding code, we have created two collections lists, one each of `Student` and `ClassDetail`. Then, using a `join` operator, we are combining the two lists based on a common attribute, `ClassID`. In the resultant items, we are then saving the name of the student and the name of the class. If the code is executed, we will get the following output:

```
Student Name = Sia Bhalla , Class Name = First Standard
Student Name = James Donohoe , Class Name = Second Standard
Student Name = Myra  Thareja , Class Name = First Standard
```

In the next section, we will look at the `orderby` operator.

The orderby operator

The `orderby` operator is used to sort your data in ascending or descending order. The following code shows how to sort the data in descending order:

```
int[] dataElements = { 8, 11, 6, 3, 9 };
var resultOrder = from dataElement in dataElements
                  where dataElement > 5
                  orderby dataElement descending
                  select dataElement;
Console.WriteLine(string.Join(", ", resultOrder));
```

In the preceding code, we have declared an array of integers. Now, from this array, we select all numbers that are greater than 5. After selecting them, we sort them in descending order using the `orderby` clause. Finally, we print them. The following is the output of the program when it's executed:

```
11, 9, 8, 6
```

Note that, in the preceding output, the numbers are in descending order and all are greater than 5. In the next section, we will look at the `Average` operator in LINQ.

Average

In LINQ, we sometimes need to calculate the `Average` value of any numeric item present in the collection. To execute this operation, we can use the `Average` operator. Let's go through the following code example to see how it works. Let's assume we have the following class:

```
public class Student
{
    public int rollNum { get; set; }
    public string Name { get; set; }
    public string classID { get; set; }
    public int age { get; set; }
}
```

Now, we have created the following objects for the student class:

```
List<Student> students = new List<Student>();
students.Add(new Student { rollNum = 1, classID = "1", Name = "Sia Bhalla",
age = 1 });
students.Add(new Student { rollNum = 2, classID = "2", Name = "James
Donohoe", age = 35 });
students.Add(new Student { rollNum = 3, classID = "1", Name = "Myra
Thareja", age = 8 });
```

To calculate the average age of the students, we can use the following code statement:

```
var avg = students.Average(s => s.age);
```

If we execute the code, we get the following output:

```
14.6666666666667
```

In the next section, we will look at the `GroupBy` operator.

GroupBy

We use the `GroupBy` clause in LINQ when we need to group elements based upon some key value. Each group is represented by a respective key and a collection of grouped elements.

To explain this operator, we will consider the same `Class` and `Student` example we have been discussing throughout this chapter. Let's consider a scenario wherein we need to group students based upon the classes they are currently enrolled in.

To recap, the following is the structure of the `Student` class:

```
public class Student
{
    public int rollNum { get; set; }
    public string Name { get; set; }
    public string classID { get; set; }
    public int age { get; set; }
}
```

Let's assume that we have the following objects in the `Student` class:

```
List<Student> students = new List<Student>();
students.Add(new Student { rollNum = 1, classID = "1", Name = "Sia Bhalla",
age = 1 });
students.Add(new Student { rollNum = 2, classID = "2", Name = "James
Donohoe", age = 35 });
students.Add(new Student { rollNum = 3, classID = "1", Name = "Myra
Thareja", age = 8 });
students.Add(new Student { rollNum = 4, classID = "3", Name = "Simaranjit
Bhalla", age = 33 });
students.Add(new Student { rollNum = 5, classID = "3", Name = "Jimmy
Bhalla", age = 33 });
students.Add(new Student { rollNum = 6, classID = "2", Name = "Misha
Thareja", age = 35 });
```

To group the students in terms of class ID, we use the following code:

```
 List<Student> students = new List<Student>();
 students.Add(new Student { rollNum = 1, classID = "1", Name = "Sia
Bhalla", age = 1 });
 students.Add(new Student { rollNum = 2, classID = "2", Name = "James
Donohoe", age = 35 });
 students.Add(new Student { rollNum = 3, classID = "1", Name = "Myra
Thareja", age = 8 });
 students.Add(new Student { rollNum = 4, classID = "3", Name = "Simaranjit
Bhalla", age = 33 });
 students.Add(new Student { rollNum = 5, classID = "3", Name = "Jimmy
Bhalla", age = 33 });
 students.Add(new Student { rollNum = 6, classID = "2", Name = "Misha
Thareja", age = 35 });
 var groupedResult = from s in students
 group s by s.classID;
 //iterate each group
 foreach (var classGroup in groupedResult)
 {
     Console.WriteLine("Class Group: {0}", classGroup.Key);
     foreach (Student s in classGroup)
```

```
            Console.WriteLine("Student Name: {0}", s.Name);
    }
```

In the preceding code, we have created six objects of student class and are then trying to group them by `ClassID`. After the grouping is complete, we are looping through the groups that have been created. We are printing `Key`, which is, in this case, the class ID and the name of the student.

If we execute the code, we get the following output:

```
Class Group: 1
Student Name: Sia Bhalla
Student Name: Myra  Thareja
Class Group: 2
Student Name: James Donohoe
Student Name: Misha Thareja
Class Group: 3
Student Name: Simaranjit Bhalla
Student Name: Jimmy Bhalla
```

In the preceding code, the students are grouped with different classes. It shows the different students present in each class.

With this, we have seen how operators work in LINQ. In the next section, we will look at the behind-the-scenes interfaces that make LINQ queries possible.

Understanding LINQ behind the scenes

Now that we have a fair understanding of LINQ queries, let's consider a scenario in which we need to alter the way LINQ works. For the sake of explanation, let's consider a scenario in which we need to change the built-in implementation of the `Where` clause in the query.

To do that, we first need to understand how the `Where` clause works in LINQ queries. We can do this by looking at the definition of the `Where` clause in Visual Studio. The following is how the definition of the `Where` clause would appear:

```
public static IEnumerable<TSource> Where(
    this IEnumerable<TSource> source,
    Func<TSource, bool> predicate)
```

Now, to create our own implementation of the `Where` clause, we will need to create an extension method with the same signature.

Once this is done, we can remove the `using` statement for `System.Linq` in the respective class and, instead, use our own method. The following is the complete code in which we have altered the built-in implementation of the `Where` clause without its own custom implementation:

```
public static class LinqExtensions
{
    public static IEnumerable<TSource> Where<TSource>(
        this IEnumerable<TSource> source,
        Func<TSource, bool> predicate)
    {
        foreach (TSource item in source)
        {
            if (predicate(item))
            {
                yield return item;
            }
        }
    }
}
```

Please note that in the preceding example, we have used the `Yield` keyword. The `Yield` keyword was introduced in C# in 2.0. Using this keyword, the execution will basically remember the item that was returned from the previous execution of the `Where` function and will return the next item in the iteration.

This is particularly important when we working using LINQ queries on data providers such as SQL. Due to the usage of `Yield`, the query won't be sent to the database until the result is iterated over. However, this would also mean if we execute the query multiple times, each time it will hit the database and hence have a negative effect on the performance of the system.

In the next section, we will look at how LINQ queries are used on an XML data source.

Using LINQ to XML

While working with XML files, we generally use the `XmlWriter`, `XmlReader`, and `XmlDocument` classes. Apart from these classes, we can also LINQ to execute operations on the XML file. One of the main advantages of using LINQ to execute XML operations is that we can use a consistent query experience that LINQ provides with other data providers.

Using LINQ, we can create, edit, and parse XML files. Apart from providing a consistent query experience, LINQ also helps us in writing much more powerful queries that are more compact than other XML classes. Let's look at the operations that we can perform on XML and understand how we can execute them via LINQ.

Querying XML

While using LINQ on an XML file, we use the XDocument class to load the XML as a string in the memory.

Until LINQ was introduced in .NET, developers used to work with the XmlDocument helper class to do operations on the XML file. XDocument is a similar helper class that we use in LINQ for doing operations on the XML file. Using LINQ for such xml operations not only helps to provide a consistent query experience but also increases the overall performance of the application. The XDocument class contains the following elements:

- XDeclaration: This component signifies information in regards to XmlDeclaration and contains information such as XML version and the encoding used.
- XElement: This component signifies the root node or object present in the XML class.
- XProcessingInstruction: This component contains relevant information for the application that will ultimately be consuming the XML file.
- XComments: This component contains any additional information apart from the XElement component that we want to add in the XML class.

All of the preceding components derive from a common abstract class, XNode, and any operation executed using XDocument is based upon this XNode class. While working with XDocument, we can use XNode in several ways. For example, using the XDocument.Nodes syntax, we can loop through all of the nodes present in the XML file.

Similarly, if we have a scenario to search for a specific element or node, we can also use the XDocument.Descendants or XDocument.Elements syntax. Using XNode, we can also directly reach a particular element or a node that's present in the XML file. This can greatly enhance the performance of the application as we no longer need to loop through the entire XML file rather than just straightway jumping to the required node.

Please note that in an XML file, attributes are not considered nodes; instead, they are key-value pairs that belong to a node.

The following code sample shows a sample XML containing a set of students who all have the attributes of `Name`, `rollNum`, and contact information:

```
String xml = @"<?xml version=""1.0"" encoding=""utf-8"" ?>
                <Students>
                    <Student Name=""Simaranjit"" rollNum=""1"">
                        <contactdetails>
                            <emailaddress>sbhalla@gmail.com</emailaddress>
                            <phoneNumber>0416274824</phoneNumber>
                        </contactdetails>
                    </Student>
                    <Student Name=""James"" rollNum=""2"">
                        <contactdetails>
<emailaddress>jamesdonohoe@gmail.com</emailaddress>
                        </contactdetails>
                    </Student>
                </Students>";
```

Suppose we need to loop through all of the student records that are present in this XML file. Using LINQ, we can execute queries that would load all of the names of the students present in the XML file as a string. To use LINQ on an XML file, we first need to add a reference to the `System.Xml.Linq` namespace. The following code syntax shows how we can use the `Descendants` method and the `Attribute` method to load this data:

```
XDocument doc = XDocument.Parse(xml);
IEnumerable<string> studentNames = from p in doc.Descendants("Student")
                                   select (string)p.Attribute("Name")
                                   + " " + (string)p.Attribute("rollNum");
foreach (string s in studentNames)
{
        Console.WriteLine(s);
}
```

The following is the output of the preceding code:

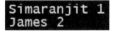

In the preceding program, using a LINQ query, we are retrieving all of the child nodes present in the `Student` descendant in the XML file. Once we have retrieved all of the nodes, we are selecting the values in the attribute nodes, `Name` and `rollNum`. To select the respective element present in the node, we are using the `.Attribute` syntax. The method returns an instance of an `XAttribute` object. Even though `XAttribute` has a `Value` property of the string type, we can always use explicit operators to cast the value to other data types in C#.

While using LINQ on XML files, we can also use operators such as `Where` and `OrderBy` in the queries. The following code syntax shows how we can filter all students to only those with a phone number:

```
XDocument docFil = XDocument.Parse(xml);
IEnumerable<string> studentNamesFilter = from p in
docFil.Descendants("Student")
                                        where
p.Descendants("phoneNumber").Any()
                                        select (string)p.Attribute("Name")
                                        + " " +
(string)p.Attribute("rollNum");
foreach (string s in studentNamesFilter)
{
        Console.WriteLine(s);
}
```

In the preceding code, we have added a `where` clause, in which we have added a condition on the phone number. Note that, in the XML string, only one child node has a phone number. When the preceding code is executed, we get the following output:

```
Simaranjit 1
```

In the preceding XML file, only one student record has a phone number, hence it's filtering out that particular record. In the next section, we will look at how we can create an XML file using LINQ.

Creating XML

Apart from querying XML, we can also use LINQ to create XML files. To do this, we can use the `XElement` class. There is an `ADD` method available in the class that we can use to construct an XML file. The following code syntax shows how we can create some XML:

```
XElement root = new XElement("Student",
new List<XElement>
{
    new XElement("Marks"),
    new XElement("Attendance")
},
new XAttribute("Roll Number", 1));
root.Save("StudentTestResults.xml");
```

In the preceding code, we have defined an element by the name `Student`. In the root element, we have added a child node of `Marks` to represent the marks the student has earned. We have also added a child node of `Attendance` to represent the attendance of `Student`. Finally, we have added a `"Roll Number"` attribute to represent the unique identifier of `Student`.

Once the code is executed, we will observe that it has created an XML file with the following structure:

```
<?xml version="1.0" encoding="utf-8"?>
    <Student RollNumber="1">
        <Marks />
        <Attendance />
    </Student>
```

In the next section, we will look at how we can use LINQ to update XML.

Updating XML

In this section, we will look at how we can modify an XML file using LINQ. With LINQ, we can modify the XML file by doing the following:

- Removing existing nodes in the XML file
- Inserting new nodes in the XML file
- Changing the content of existing nodes
- Saving the XML file back once the operation finishes

For the sake of explanation, we will work on the same XML file that we created in the previous section. We will be writing a code that would add a mobile number element for all of the students. We will add this element in the node element of `ContactDetails`:

```
XElement rootUpd = XElement.Parse(xml);
foreach (XElement p in rootUpd.Descendants("Student"))
{
    XElement contactDetails = p.Element("contactdetails");
    contactDetails.Add(new XElement("MobileNumber", "12345678"));
}
rootUpd.Save("testupd.xml");
```

In the preceding code, we are looping through all `Students` present in the XML and are then looping through the child element of `ChildDetails`. In that node, we are adding the element of `MobileNumber`. Once the code is executed, we will get the following output in the XML file:

```
<?xml version="1.0" encoding="utf-8"?>
<Students>
    <Student Name="Simaranjit" rollNum="1">
        <contactdetails>
            <emailaddress>sbhalla@gmail.com</emailaddress>
            <phoneNumber>0416274824</phoneNumber>
            <MobileNumber>12345678</MobileNumber>
        </contactdetails>
    </Student>
    <Student Name="James" rollNum="2">
        <contactdetails>
            <emailaddress>jamesdonohoe@gmail.com</emailaddress>
            <MobileNumber>12345678</MobileNumber>
        </contactdetails>
    </Student>
</Students>
```

In the preceding XML, we have added a `MobileNumber` element in the `ContactDetails` node of `Student`.

Summary

In this chapter, we learned how we can use LINQ to write consistent queries against multiple data sources. We learned about the different components of a LINQ query and understood how we can construct them in a query. We then looked at the features in a C# language that allows us to work with LINQ such as implicit typing, object initialization syntax, lambda expressions, extension methods, and anonymous types.

We then looked at the different operators available in LINQ such as `Select`, `SelectMany`, `Where`, `join`, and `Average`. Using code scenarios, we looked at different situations in which we should use each of them.

We then looked at the different interfaces that LINQ queries are based on. Finally, we looked at how we can use LINQ queries to perform an operation on XML files. Using code examples, we looked at how we perform, create, update, and query operations on LINQ.

In the next chapter, we will look at the serialization and deserialization of data. We will look at the different collection items, such as arrays, lists, and dictionaries, which are available in C#.

Questions

1. Which LINQ code can be used to extract customers that have made sales of over 5,000 dollars and whose name starts with A?

    a.
    ```
    FROM p IN db.Purchases
    WHERE p.Customer.Name.StartsWith("A")
    WHERE p.PurchaseItems.Sum (pi => pi.SaleAmount) = 5000
    SELECT p
    ```

    b.
    ```
    FROM p IN db.Purchases
    WHERE p.Customer.Name.StartsWith("A")
    WHERE p.PurchaseItems.Sum (pi => pi.SaleAmount) > 5000
    SELECT p
    ```

    c.
    ```
    FROM p IN db.Purchases
    WHERE p.Customer.Name.EndsWith("A")
    WHERE p.PurchaseItems.Sum (pi => pi.SaleAmount) < 1000
    SELECT p
    ```

    d.
    ```
    FROM p IN db.Purchases
    WHERE p.Customer.Name.StartsWith("A")
    WHERE p.PurchaseItems.Sum (pi => pi.SaleAmount) >= 1000
    SELECT p
    ```

2. Which of the following statements in regards to LINQ is incorrect?

    a. Compared to languages such as SQL, LINQ is more complex to code.

    b. LINQ supports `Join`.

    c. LINQ can be used to do operations on XML files.

    d. All of the above.

3. Which of the following supports LINQ queries?
   a. Object Collection
   b. Entity Framework
   c. XML Document
   d. All of the above

Answers

1. **b**
2. **a**
3. **d**

16
Serialization, Deserialization, and Collections

When a .NET application interacts with an external network, the data being exchanged must be transformed into a flat or binary format. Similarly, when the data is retrieved from external applications, binary data needs to be formatted to objects on which they can then be worked upon. This is done via the serialization and deserialization of data using different approaches. The process of changing objects into binary format is referred to as serialization. Deserialization is the reverse of serialization. In involves transforming binary data into its object representation so that it can be used in the application.

In this chapter, we will work on different serialization and deserialization approaches available in the .NET Framework. We will look into XML serialization, JSON serialization, and binary serialization. We will also look at how we define data contracts in web services to inform the consuming application of the format of the data that is to be exchanged between different applications.

We will then look at how we can use different collections objects such as arrays, lists, dictionary, queues, and stacks and we'll learn how they can be used for storing and consuming data. Finally, we will look at different things that help us choose collection objects while working with .NET applications.

We will cover the following topics in this chapter:

- Serialization and deserialization
- Working with collections
- Choosing a collection

Technical requirements

The programs explained in this book will be developed in Visual Studio 2017. The sample code for this chapter can be found at GitHub at `https://github.com/` `PacktPublishing/Programming-in-C-Sharp-Exam-70-483-MCSD-Guide/tree/master/` `Book70483Samples`.

Serialization and deserialization

While working with objects, we often find a need to either save them in different mediums such as a database or file or, in some cases, transfer them to other applications over a network. To do this, we must first convert the object into a stream of bytes—this process is known as **serialization**.

Deserialization is the process of converting bytes received from the external application into objects that can be then used inside the application. With serialization, we can transform an object into bytes and save information related to its state, attributes, assembly version, and so on in external mediums such as databases, or we can exchange them on a network to external applications. An important thing to note here is that we can only apply serialization to objects and their attributes but not to their methods.

.NET Framework provides us with the `System.Runtime.Serialization` namespace, which has got helper classes that help us serialize and deserialize the data. .NET provides us with three mechanisms for achieving this: XML serialization, JSON serialization, and data contract serialization.

In the next section, we will learn how we do serialization using `XMLSerializer`.

XmlSerializer

In `XMLSerialization`, we convert the data into the format of an XML document, which can then be transferred easily across the network.

During deserialization, we can render an object from the same XML document format. `XMLSerializer` is based upon **Simple Object Access Protocol** (**SOAP**), a protocol for exchanging information with web services.

While working with XmLSerlializer, we must mark our classes with the Serializable tag to inform the compiler that this class is serializable. Please refer to the following code implementation wherein we are using this tag against our class to inform the compiler that the class is Serializable:

```
[Serializable]
public class Student
{
    public string FirstName { get; set; }
    public string LastName { get; set; }
    public int ID { get; set; }
    public Student()
    {
    }
    public Student(string firstName, string lastName, int Id)
    {
        this.FirstName = firstName;
        this.LastName = lastName;
        this.ID = Id;
    }
}
```

In the preceding code implementation, we declared a Student class and specified it with the FirstName, LastName, and ID attributes. To inform the compiler that the class is serializable, we have used the Serializable tag on the class.

Sometimes, we need to pick and choose the attributes that we would like to be serialized. In these cases, we can use the NonSerialized tag on the attribute and convey to the compiler that the attribute will not be serializable. Following is the code implementation for this:

```
[Serializable]
public class Student
{
    public string FirstName { get; set; }
    public string LastName { get; set; }
    [NonSerialized()]
    public int ID;
}
```

We used the Serializable tag on the class name but used the NonSerialized tag to indicate that the ID attribute cannot be serialized.

Let's go through a code implementation scenario where we will look at a code base in which we will serialize a class object using `XmlSerializer` and will save the file on the filesystem. This file can then be transferred across the network:

```
XmlSerializer serializer = new XmlSerializer(typeof(Student));
string fileName = "StudentData";
using (TextWriter writer = new StreamWriter(fileName))
{
    Student stu = new Student("Jacob", "Almeida", 78);
    serializer.Serialize(writer, stu);
}
```

In the preceding code example, we are using the same `Student` class we used in the previous example. We have created a dummy `Student` object and are then serializing the object into bytes. The bytes are then converted into a file using the `TextWriter` object.

Once the preceding code gets executed, a file with the name `StudentData` gets created in the system:

| Windows (C:) > UCN Code Base > Programming-in-C-Exam-70-483-MCSD-Guide > Book70483Samples > Chapter 16 > bin > Debug |

Name	Date modified	Type	Size
Chapter 16	24/03/2019 5:09 PM	Application	6 KB
Chapter 16.exe	24/03/2019 1:47 PM	XML Configuration...	1 KB
Chapter 16.pdb	24/03/2019 5:09 PM	Program Debug D...	18 KB
☑ StudentData	24/03/2019 5:09 PM	File	1 KB

If we open the file in Internet Explorer, we will see the student data in XML format:

```
<?xml version="1.0" encoding="utf-8"?>
<Student xmlns:xsi="http://www.w3.org/2001/XMLSchema-instance" xmlns:xsd="http://www.w3.org/2001/XMLSchema">
  <ID>78</ID>
  <FirstName>Jacob</FirstName>
  <LastName>Almeida</LastName>
</Student>
```

In the preceding code example, there was no hierarchy in the data. All of the data is represented as an element in the XML file. However, in most situations, we will need to represent data that is following some sort of hierarchy. Using the preceding example, let's try to represent the course scores for each of the students as well. Let's say there are five courses: English, Maths, Physics, Chemistry, and Computers. Now, let's try to represent the scores for each of the courses for the student using the following code implementation:

```
[Serializable]
public class Student
```

```
{
 public string FirstName { get; set; }
 public string LastName { get; set; }
 public int ID;
 [XmlIgnore]
 public string Feedback { get; set; }
 [XmlArray("CourseScores")]
 [XmlArrayItem("Course")]
 public List<CourseScore> CoursePerformance { get; set; }
 public void CreateCoursePerformance()
 {
        Course phy = new Course { Name = "Physics", Description =
                                  "Physics Subject" };
        CourseScore phyScore = new CourseScore { Course = phy,
                                                  Score = 80 };
        List<CourseScore> scores = new List<CourseScore>();
        scores.Add(phyScore);
        this.CoursePerformance = scores;
 }
}
[Serializable]
public class CourseScore
{
 [XmlElement("Course")]
 public Course Course;
 [XmlAttribute]
 public int Score;
}
[Serializable]
public class Course
{
 [XmlAttribute]
 public string Name;
 public string Description;
}
```

 The preceding complete code can be found in the GitHub repository for this chapter.

In the preceding code implementation, we declared three classes:

- Course: To represent the subject along with the description
- CourseScore: To represent the score that a student is getting in that particular course

- Student: Has a list of CourseScore to represent the score the student gets in each subject

Please note the following tags we used in the classes:

- XmlIgnore: We use this tag against attributes that we don't want to be saved in the generated XML class. In the preceding class example, we have used XmlIgnore against the Feedback class. This will ensure that the Feedback attribute will not be present in the generated XML file.
- XmlElement: We can use this tag if we want to represent an element in the generated XML. The element can then have attributes. In the preceding example, we used the XmlElement tag for the Course attribute. This will then enable us to add attributes of Course Name and Course Description in the generated XML file.
- XMLArray: We use this tag when there can be multiple child records in this element. In the preceding example, we used the XMLArray tag for the CourseScores attribute to indicate that this is an element in the XML that can have multiple child records.
- XMLArrayItem: We use this tag to represent the individual child records in the XMLArray record. In the preceding example, we used the XMLArrayItem tag to represent individual records in the list collection variable, CourseScores.

If we need to serialize the data using XMLSerialization, we can use the following code. Once the code is executed, it will generate an XML file based on the data structure and tags used in the preceding declaration of the class:

```
XmlSerializer serializer = new XmlSerializer(typeof(Student));
string fileName = "StudentDataWithScores";
using (TextWriter writer = new StreamWriter(fileName))
{
        Student stu = new Student("Jacob", "Almeida", 78, "Passed");
        stu.CreateCoursePerformance();
        serializer.Serialize(writer, stu);
        writer.Close();
}
```

Once the program is generated, note that an XML file, `StudentDataWithScores`, is generated. Now, open the XML file and review the following:

```
<?xml version="1.0" encoding="utf-8"?>
<Student xmlns:xsi="http://www.w3.org/2001/XMLSchema-instance" xmlns:xsd="http://www.w3.org/2001/XMLSchema">
  <ID>78</ID>
  <FirstName>Jacob</FirstName>
  <LastName>Almeida</LastName>
  <CourseScores>
    <Course Score="80">
      <CoursePerformance Name="Physics">
        <Description>Physics Subject</Description>
      </CoursePerformance>
    </Course>
    <Course Score="80">
      <CoursePerformance Name="Chemistry">
        <Description>Chemistry Subject</Description>
      </CoursePerformance>
    </Course>
    <Course Score="80">
      <CoursePerformance Name="Maths">
        <Description>Mathsmetics Subject</Description>
      </CoursePerformance>
    </Course>
    <Course Score="80">
      <CoursePerformance Name="Computers">
        <Description>Computers Subject</Description>
      </CoursePerformance>
    </Course>
    <Course Score="80">
      <CoursePerformance Name="English">
        <Description>English Subject</Description>
      </CoursePerformance>
    </Course>
  </CourseScores>
</Student>
```

Please note the following points in the structure of the XML file that is generated:

- In the XML file, there is no node for `Feedback` as it has been marked with the `XmlIgnore` tag in the `Student` class file.
- In the `Student` node, there is a `CourseScores` element node in line with the `XmlArray` tag that we used in the `CourseScore` list collection.
- In the element node, `CourseScores`, we have an individual node item element, `Course`, in line with `XmlArrayItem`, which we declared for each element in the `CourseScores` collection.

Each of the child item nodes has a `Score` attribute. It is in line with the tag—`XmlElement`—that we used for `CoursePerformance`; note that the XML also shows the name and description of the course.

Even though we're using `XMLSerialization`, we can produce data that we can easily read, but there are certain issues with regard to `XmlSerialization`:

- It consumes more space. If we are sharing XML files, they will ultimately end up saving space on the filesystem, which might not be ideal.
- In addition to that, if we declare an attribute with the access modifier of `private`, it will not be picked during the XML serialization. For example, if we set the access modifier of the `LastName` attribute in the preceding example, we will see that the generated XML file will not have the attribute.

The following code is the updated set of access modifiers for the attributes in the `Student` class:

```
public string FirstName { get; set; }
private string LastName { get; set; }
public int ID;
[XmlIgnore]
public string Feedback { get; set; }
[XmlArray("CourseScores")]
[XmlArrayItem("Course")]
public List<CourseScore> CoursePerformance { get; set; }
```

The access modifier for the `LastName` attribute has been changed from `public` to `private`. If we execute the project and open the XML file, we will observe that the `LastName` attribute no longer exists in the generated XML file:

```
<?xml version="1.0" encoding="utf-8"?>
<Student xmlns:xsi="http://www.w3.org/2001/XMLSchema-instance" xmlns:xsd="http://www.w3.org/2001/XMLSchema">
  <ID>78</ID>
  <FirstName>Jacob</FirstName>
  <CourseScores>
    <Course Score="80">
      <Course Name="Physics">
        <Description>Physics Subject</Description>
      </Course>
    </Course>
  </CourseScores>
```

In the next section, we will go through the binary serialization approach in C#.

Binary serialization

In `XmlSerialization`, the output of the serialization is an XML file that can be easily opened by Notepad. However, as explained previously, creating a file adds to the overall storage space required by the application, which may not be desirable in all circumstances.

We also observed that if we marked any attribute with the access modifier of `private`, it was not copied across to the generated XML file. This may also be an issue in many cases.

In this section, we will look at an alternative approach in which we will serialize the data to a stream of bytes. This data will not be viewable like the XML file but will save us space and will deal with `private` attributes in a much better way.

.NET Framework provides us with the `System.Runtime.Serialization` and `System.Runtime.Serialization.Formatters.Binary` namespaces, which provide us with helper classes for dealing with binary serialization.

To understand how binary serialization works, let's look at the following example. We will work with `Student`, a similar class to what we created while we were working on XML serialization:

```
[Serializable]
public class StudentBinary
{
    public string FirstName;
    public string LastName;
    public int ID;
    public string Feedback;

    public StudentBinary(string firstName, string lastName, int Id, string
feedback)
    {
        this.FirstName = firstName;
        this.LastName = lastName;
        this.ID = Id;
        this.Feedback = feedback;
    }
}
```

Please note that in the class declaration, just like in `XmlSerialization`, we used a `Serializable` tag in the declaration of the `StudentBinary` class. This indicates to the compiler that the `StudentBinary` class can be serialized.

We can use the following code to serialize and deserialize an object of this class:

```
StudentBinary stu = new StudentBinary("Jacob", "Almeida", 78, "Passed");
IFormatter formatter = new BinaryFormatter();
using (Stream stream = new FileStream("StudentBinaryData.bin",
FileMode.Create))
{
    formatter.Serialize(stream, stu);
}
```

```
using (Stream stream = new FileStream("StudentBinaryData.bin",
FileMode.Open))
{
    StudentBinary studeseria =
(StudentBinary)formatter.Deserialize(stream);
}
```

In the code example, we created an object of the StudentBinary class and then used a helper class, BinaryFormatter, to serialize the data into binary data. Once the data is serialized, using the FileStream helper class, we saved this binary data in a binary file, StudentBinaryData.bin.

In the next step, we open the file we created in the previous step and deserialize it back to the StudentBinary class. If we try to debug the application and do a quick watch on the studeseria variable, we will see the following output:

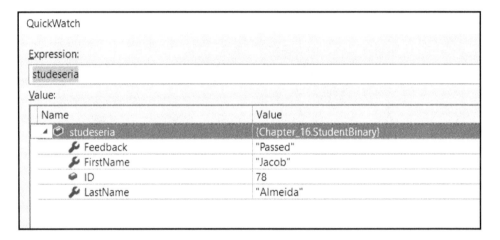

Now let's make one change to the preceding class: let's mark the LastName attribute as private. When we used XmlSerialization, we saw that any attribute marked with the private access modifier was excluded from the attribute. Let's do the same with binary serialization and observe the difference:

```
[Serializable]
public class StudentBinary
{
    public string FirstName;
    private string LastName;
    public int ID;
    public string Feedback;
    public StudentBinary(string firstName, string lastName, int Id, string
feedback)
```

```
        {
            this.FirstName = firstName;
            this.LastName = lastName;
            this.ID = Id;
            this.Feedback = feedback;
        }
    }
```

If we now try to debug an application and do a QuickWatch on the `studeseria` variable, we will get the following output:

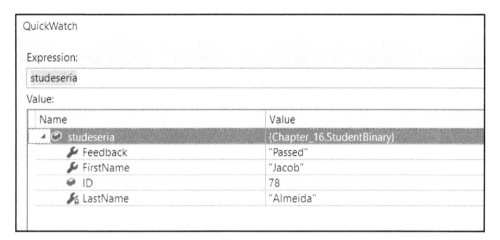

Note that even though we made `LastName` as `private`, it has no impact on the output. This illustrates the advantage binary serialization has on `XmlSerialization`.

Just with `XmlSerialization`, we can also set tags on an attribute that would ensure that that attribute is ignored during the serialization. We can do it with the `NonSerialized` tag. In the following code implementation, we are using this tag for the `Feedback` attribute:

```
[Serializable]
public class StudentBinary
{
    public string FirstName;
    private string LastName;
    public int ID;
    [NonSerialized]
    public string Feedback;

    public StudentBinary(string firstName, string lastName, int Id, string
feedback)
    {
```

```
            this.FirstName = firstName;
            this.LastName = lastName;
            this.ID = Id;
            this.Feedback = feedback;
        }
    }
```

Even though binary serialization allows us to overcome the restriction around any attribute that is marked with the `private` access modifier, there are still some scenarios when we would deliberately want to restrict the exchange of certain data, especially those attributes that are sensitive and that we would like to restrict anyhow. We can do this by using the `ISerializable` interface.

In the following implemented code, we used a similar class, `StudentBinaryInterface`, and have implemented an `ISerializable` interface in it. As part of this interface, we must implement a `GetObjectData` method in this class. This method is classed when the class gets serialized. In this method, we will do encapsulation and not add any sensitive attributes to the serialized stream. Let's have a look at how to do this:

```
[Serializable]
public class StudentBinary:ISerializable
{
    public string FirstName;
    private string LastName;
    public int ID;
    public string Feedback;
    protected StudentBinary(SerializationInfo info,
                            StreamingContext context)
    {
        FirstName = info.GetString("Value1");
        Feedback = info.GetString("Value2");
        ID = info.GetInt32("Value3");
    }
    public StudentBinary(string firstName, string lastName,
                    int Id, string feedback)
    {
        this.FirstName = firstName;
        this.LastName = lastName;
        this.ID = Id;
        this.Feedback = feedback;
    }
    [System.Security.Permissions.SecurityPermission(
        SecurityAction.Demand, SerializationFormatter = true)]
    public void GetObjectData(SerializationInfo info,
                            StreamingContext context)
    {
        info.AddValue("Value1", FirstName);
```

```
          info.AddValue("Value2", Feedback);
          info.AddValue("Value3", ID);
    }
}
```

In the preceding code example, we declared the `LastName` attribute as `private`. Through this code, we will try to exclude this attribute from being serialized.

There are two important functions in this class:

- `GetObjectData`: As illustrated previously, this function is called when the class gets serialized. In this method, we will serialize the data present in `Firstname`, `Feedback`, and `ID`. Note that `LastName` is not present in this. This has been to make sure that the data in the `LastName` attribute will not be added to the stream.
- Constructor: As the class implements the `ISerializable` interface, it must implement the following constructor with the parameters of `SerializationInfo` and `StreamingContext`:

```
StudentBinary(SerializationInfo info, StreamingContext context)
```

This constructor will be called when the data will be deserialized into this class object. Note that in the constructor, we are accessing the values in the `Value1`, `Value2`, and `Value3` attributes and converting them into their respective mapped attributes:

```
StudentBinary stu = new StudentBinary("Jacob", "Almeida", 78, "Passed");
IFormatter formatter = new BinaryFormatter();
using (Stream stream = new FileStream("StudentBinaryData.bin",
FileMode.Create))
{
    formatter.Serialize(stream, stu);
}
using (Stream stream = new FileStream("StudentBinaryData.bin",
FileMode.Open))
{
    StudentBinary studeseria =
(StudentBinary)formatter.Deserialize(stream);
}
```

If we debug this code and do a QuickWatch on the `studeseria` variable, we get the following output:

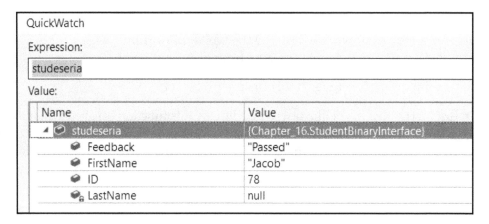

Note that no value is present in the `LastName` attribute. In the next section, we will learn how to work with collections.

Working with collections

A collection in .NET defines a group of related data or elements. Elements can be variables of simple data types such as `int`, `float`, or `String` or can be complex data variables such as a class or structure. While working with .NET applications, we often need to work with such collections. We can execute operations such as these:

- Creating a collection
- Adding an element to a collection
- Reading elements present in the collection
- Removing elements present in the collection

In this section, we will understand what the different types of collections available in .NET are and how programmers can execute operations on them.

Arrays

Arrays are the most basic collection variable available in .NET Framework. Arrays are used to store a group of data variables that are of the same type as `int`, `String`, and many more.

Let's go through a code implementation in which we will create an array collection of `int` variables and then loop through them:

```
public static void CollectionOperations()
{
    int[] arrayOfInt = new int[10];
    for (int x = 0; x < arrayOfInt.Length; x++)
    {
        arrayOfInt[x] = x;
    }
    foreach (int i in arrayOfInt)
    {
        Console.Write(i);
    }
}
```

Please note the following in the code implementation:

- An array is declared by the `[]` syntax after the data type. In the implemented code, we are declaring an array of the `int` type.
- While declaring the array collection, we must define the length of the array collection. In the code, we are declaring that the length of the array is `10`. This basically implies that the array can contain `10` elements of the `int` type.
- The index of the array starts at `0`. This implies that, in the preceding case, the first element will start at index `0` and will end at index `9`. If we need to refer to the elements present in the ith index in the array, we can use the `array[i]` declaration.
- Each array has a `length` property. This attribute indicates the maximum number of elements that can be present in the array. In the code, we are doing a `for` loop from `0` to `9` that is of the length -1 and are setting the value in each element present in that index.
- Array implements the `IEnumerable` interface. Due to this, we can loop through the array using the `foreach` loop.

On executing the preceding code, we get the following output:

C:\UCN Code Base\Programming-in-C-Exam-70-483-MCSD-Guide\Chapter16\bin\Debug\Chapter 16.exe

0123456789

In the code, we are setting values in each index of the array—the same value as the index in itself. Before we move ahead and start looking at the code examples, we need to understand two important concepts regarding arrays:

- Multidimensional arrays: These are arrays in which we store elements in a matrix structure that has both rows and columns. For example, we can use the following code for declaring a multidimensional array:

```
int[,] arrayInt = new int[3,2] { { 1, 2 }, { 3, 4 }, { 5, 6 } };
```

- The use of a single , mark during the array declaration indicates that this is a two-dimensional array. In the case of a two-dimensional array, the first dimension indicates the number of rows, while the second indicates the number of columns present in the array. Also, note that by using 3, 2, we are basically indicating that the number of rows in the array should be 3 while the number of columns should be 2.

Just like in a normal array, in a multidimensional array, the index for both dimensions starts at 0. Therefore, the first element will be present at index {0,0}, while the last element will be present at index {2,1}.

Let's look at the following code implementation, in which we will look at the code to loop through this multidimensional array and read each number present in the array:

```
int[,] arrayInt = new int[3,2] { { 1, 2 }, { 3, 4 }, { 5, 6 } };
for (int i=0; i < 3; i++)
{
    for (int j = 0; j < 2; j++)
    {
        Console.WriteLine(arrayInt[i, j]);
    }
}
```

In the preceding code implementation, we are doing two nested loops. In the first loop, we are looping through the number of rows present in the multidimensional array. In the second loop, we are looping through the number of columns present in the multidimensional array. Using the arrayInt[i, j] syntax, we are printing the element present in that combination of rows and columns in the array.

When we execute the code, we get the following result. As we have to loop through the two-dimensional array using a nested loop, at each step, we will access elements present at position {i, j}. For each iteration of the i variable, the j variable will iterate from 0 to 1. Hence, it will start at {0,0}, which will be 1 and will end at {2,1}, which will be 6, hence generating the following output:

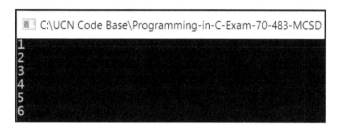

In the next section, we will look at another collection type: lists.

Lists

While working on arrays, we learned that the length of an array must be specified when the array is declared. Also, we cannot increase the length of an array collection.

To overcome these issues, we can use the list collection. Lists provide us with several helper methods that help us to add and remove items in a list, sort a list, search in a list, and more. A list collection is declared by the following index:

```
List<int> vs = new List<int>();
```

If we go to the definition of a list, we will realize that, internally, it implements many interfaces, such as IEnumerable, ICollection, and IList. Due to these different interfaces, list collections are extremely powerful and provide different operations. The following screenshot shows what the definition of a list collection looks like in .NET:

```
namespace System.Collections.Generic
{
    public class List<T> : IList<T>, ICollection<T>, IEnumerable<T>, IEnumerable, IList, ICollection, IReadOnlyList<T>,
    {
        public List();
        public List(int capacity);
        public List(IEnumerable<T> collection);

        public T this[int index] { get; set; }
```

The `IEnumerable` interface allows us to loop through the list collection using the `foreach` loop just as we did for arrays. The `ICollection` interface allows us to do operations such as count length, add a new element, and remove an element.

Let's look at the following code implementation, in which we will execute all of these operations on the list:

```
public static void ListCollectionOperations()
{
    List<int> vs = new List<int> { 1, 2, 3, 4, 5, 6 };
    for (int x = 0; x < vs.Count; x++)
    Console.Write(vs[x]);
    vs.Remove(1);
    Console.WriteLine(vs[0]);
    vs.Add(7);
    Console.WriteLine(vs.Count);
    bool doesExist = vs.Contains(4);
    Console.WriteLine(doesExist);
}
```

Let's look at what we did in the preceding code:

- We have created a list of `int` and added the elements 1-6.
- We are looping across the list using a `for` loop and we are printing the values present in it. To find the length or the number of elements present in a list, we are using the `Count` property.
- To remove an element from a particular index, we can use the `Remove` method. In the preceding code implementation, we are removing the element present at index `1`.
- To add a new element in the list, we use the `Add` method. In the preceding code implementation, we are adding an element, `7`, to the list.
- To check whether an element is present in the list, we use the `Contains` method. In the preceding code implementation, we are checking whether a `4` element is present in the list.

If we execute this, we get the following output:

```
C:\UCN Code Base\Programming-in-C-Exam-70-483-MCSD-Guide\Chapter16\bin\Debug\Chapter 16.exe
1234562
6
True
```

One potential issue with a list collection is that we can have duplicate values in the list. For example, in the preceding example, it's possible to have two elements with the same value as 1 in the list.

Due to this issue, we cannot use list collection in scenarios where we must ensure the uniqueness of values. In the next section, we will look at another collection dictionary that overcomes this issue with a list object.

Dictionary

The dictionary collection can be used in scenarios when we need to maintain uniqueness in values that are being saved. A dictionary collection is comprised of two parts: a key and a value. Together, they are referred to as a key-value pair in .NET. When a dictionary collection is created, it ensures that the key-value is unique and no duplicate keys are present in the collection. Retrieval is also based upon the key, making the operation extremely fast. A dictionary collection is declared by the following index:

```
Dictionary<int, int> vs = new Dictionary<int, int>();
```

In the preceding code implementation, we are declaring a dictionary collection where both key and value are of the int format.

Let's right-click on the Dictionary class and click on **Go to Definition**. On doing this, we will be taken to the definition of the dictionary. Upon doing so, we will realize that it implements several interfaces such as IEnumerable, ICollection<KeyValuePair<Tkey, and TValue>>. Please refer to the following definition of the Dictionary class:

```
public class Dictionary<TKey, TValue> : IDictionary<TKey, TValue>, ICollection<KeyValuePair<TKey, TValue>>
{
    public Dictionary();
    public Dictionary(int capacity);
    public Dictionary(IEqualityComparer<TKey> comparer);
    public Dictionary(IDictionary<TKey, TValue> dictionary);
    public Dictionary(int capacity, IEqualityComparer<TKey> comparer);
```

Due to the implementation of the ICollection interface based on KeyValuePair, it ensures that the uniqueness is maintained based on the key.

In the code implementation, we will look at a code example wherein we will implement operations on the Dictionary object:

```
public static void DictionaryCollectionOperations()
{
    Dictionary<int, int> vs = new Dictionary<int, int>();
```

```
        for (int x = 0; x < 5; x++)
        {
            KeyValuePair<int, int> pair = new KeyValuePair<int, int>(x, x *
100);
        }
        foreach(KeyValuePair<int, int> keyValue in vs)
        {
            Console.WriteLine(keyValue.Key + " " + keyValue.Value);
        }
        vs.Remove(1);
        Console.WriteLine(vs[0]);
        vs.Add(5, 500);
        Console.WriteLine(vs.Count);
        bool hasKey = vs.ContainsKey(4);
        bool hasValue = vs.ContainsValue(900);
        Console.WriteLine(hasKey);
        Console.WriteLine(hasValue);
    }
```

Please note the following in the preceding code implementation:

- We have declared a dictionary collection variable. We have implemented a `for` loop that runs five times. In the loop, we are creating `KeyValuePair` and adding it to the dictionary object.
- After we have added elements to the dictionary object, we are looping through the dictionary. We are doing it via a `foreach` loop on `KeyValuePair` present in the dictionary.
- To remove a particular element from the dictionary, we can use the `Remove` method. The method takes the input of a key and, based on a key, deletes the respective `KeyValuePair` present in the dictionary.
- To add a particular element in the dictionary, we can use the `Add` method. The method has two parameters, one of the key and another of the value.
- To check whether a particular key is present in the dictionary, we can use the `ContainsKey` method. The method returns whether the given key exists in the dictionary. If the key exists, it returns `true` and, in other cases, it returns `false`.
- To check whether a particular value is present in the dictionary, we can use the `ContainsValue` method. The method returns whether the given value exists in the dictionary. If the value exists, it returns `true` and, in other cases, it returns `false`.

If the preceding code is executed, we get the following output:

Please note the following points in the output of the code:

- The values (0, 0), (1, 100), (2, 200), (3, 300), and (4, 400) indicate the key-value pairs that are added in the dictionary.
- 5 indicates the length or number of elements present in the dictionary.
- True indicates that the dictionary contains KeyValuePair with the key 4.
- False indicates that the dictionary does not contain KeyValuePair with the value 900.

Before we move to the next section, let's try what would happen if we try to add KeyValuePair in the same dictionary in which the key already exists in the dictionary. For the sake of an example, we will add KeyValue of (1, 1000). Please note that the key 1 is already present in the dictionary. When the code is executed, we get the following exception. The exception indicates that if we try to add a value with the same key in the dictionary, it will throw an error:

In the next section, we will go over another set of collection objects: queues and stacks.

Queues and stacks

Queues and stacks are collection items that allow us to save data temporarily during the execution of the program. These collections are very similar to the other collections, such as lists, with the major difference being how elements are added and removed from the collection.

A queue is a first-in, first-out type of collection. It basically implies that elements are accessed from the queue in the same order they are added to the collection. When the items are accessed, they can also be removed in the same operation. A queue has three main operations:

- Adding a new element to the queue: It's executed by the `Enqueue` method.
- Removing an existing element from the queue: It's executed by the `Dequeue` method.
- Peeking or retrieving the value of an element in the queue: It's executed by the `Peek` method.

This diagram shows how the queue works:

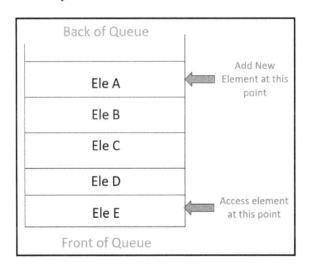

In the preceding diagram, the block indicates a queue collection. In the collection, we have added five elements: element A, element B, element C, element D, and element E. Element E was the first element added to the queue and it's at the front of the queue. Element A was the last element added to the queue and it's at the back of the queue.

The green arrows indicate the indexes in the queue at which the different operations will take place. The addition of a new element will always take place at the back of the queue. Removal of an element will take place at the front of the queue.

Let's look at a code implementation to show how it's done programmatically. In the following code, we have created a queue collection object. We will then add elements to the object and execute different operations on it:

```csharp
public static void QueueOperations()
{
    Queue<string> que = new Queue<string>();
    que.Enqueue("E");
    que.Enqueue("D");
    que.Enqueue("C");
    que.Enqueue("B");
    que.Enqueue("A");
    int index = 0;
    foreach(string s in que)
    {
        Console.WriteLine("Queue Element at index " + index + " is " + s);
        index++;
    }
    Console.WriteLine("Queue Element at top of the queue is "
                        + que.Peek());
    que.Dequeue();
    index = 0;
    foreach (string s in que)
    {
        Console.WriteLine("Queue Element at index " + index + " is " + s);
        index++;
    }
}
```

When the preceding code is executed, we get the following output:

```
C:\UCN Code Base\Programming-in-C-Exam-70-483-MCSD-Guide\Chapter16\bin\Debug\Chapter 16.exe
Queue Element at index 0 is E
Queue Element at index 1 is D
Queue Element at index 2 is C
Queue Element at index 3 is B
Queue Element at index 4 is A
Queue Element at top of the queue is E
Queue Element at index 0 is D
Queue Element at index 1 is C
Queue Element at index 2 is B
Queue Element at index 3 is A
```

As illustrated by the queue diagram, when we add elements to the queue, they are always added to the end. Therefore, when we add the E, D, C, B, and A elements in the same order, A will always be at the back of the queue and E will be at the front of the queue. The indexes in the preceding output indicate the position in the queue where each respective element is present.

A peek operation in a queue is always done on the front index, that is, the 0 index of the queue. A removal operation in a queue is always done on the front index, that is, the 0 index of the queue. Therefore in the preceding output, both of these operations are executed on the element E.

Once these operations are done and we reiterate through the queue, we find that, owing to the remove operation, element E is no longer present in the queue. Now that we have an understanding of the queue, let's look at how a stack works in .NET Framework.

Just like a queue, the stack also provides temporary storage with the only difference being in terms of how the operations are executed on a stack. Stack follows the LIFO model, which implies that the last element added to the stack will be the first one to be removed. The following are the three main operations that we can do on a stack:

- Add a new element to the stack. It's executed by the Push method.
- Remove an existing element from the stack. It's executed by the Pop method.
- Peek or retrieve the value of an element in the stack. It's executed by the Peek method.

The following diagram shows how the stack works:

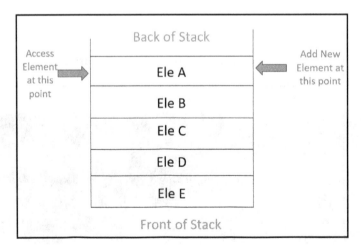

In the diagram, the block indicates a stack collection. In the collection, we have added five elements: element A, element B, element C, element D, and element E. Element E was the first element added to the stack and it's at the front of the stack. Element A was the last element added to the stack and it's at the back of the stack.

The green arrows indicate the indexes in the stack at which the different operations will take place. The addition of a new element will always take place at the bottom of the stack. The removal of an element will take place at the top of the stack.

Let's look at a code implementation to show how it's done programmatically. In the following code, we have created a stack collection object. We will then add elements in the object and execute different operations on it:

```
public static void StackOperations()
{
    Stack<string> sta = new Stack<string>();
    sta.Push("E");
    sta.Push("D");
    sta.Push("C");
    sta.Push("B");
    sta.Push("A");
    int index = 0;
    foreach (string s in sta)
    {
        Console.WriteLine("Stack Element at index " + index + " is " + s);
        index++;
    }
    Console.WriteLine("Stack Element at top of the stack is "
                    + sta.Peek());
    sta.Pop();
    index = 0;
    foreach (string s in sta)
    {
        Console.WriteLine("Stack Element at index " + index + " is " + s);
        index++;
    }
}
```

When the preceding code is executed, we get the following output:

```
C:\UCN Code Base\Programming-in-C-Exam-70-483-MCSD-Guide\Chapter16\bin\Debug\Chapter 16.exe
Stack Element at index 0 is A
Stack Element at index 1 is B
Stack Element at index 2 is C
Stack Element at index 3 is D
Stack Element at index 4 is E
Stack Element at top of the stack is A
Stack Element at index 0 is B
Stack Element at index 1 is C
Stack Element at index 2 is D
Stack Element at index 3 is E
```

A `Peek` operation on a stack is always done on the last element added on the stack. Element A was the last element to be added to the stack. Therefore, when a `Peek` operation is done on the stack, it gives an output of A. Similarly, when a `Pop` operation is executed on the stack, it removes the element A.

With this, we have gone through the different collections that are available in .NET. Each of these collection items has some properties that make them usable in some scenarios and not in others. These criteria need to be evaluated when we are trying to select a collection item to use.

In the next section, we will look at some of the criteria that help us to select the right collection item for each scenario.

Choosing a collection

While choosing a collection type, we have to analyze the scenarios in the application in which we want to use them. The primary difference between these collection types is the way we access elements in them:

- The array collection needs to have a definite size or length while declaring itself. On the other hand, all other collection types can have their sizes increased dynamically. Also, arrays support random access to the data. This basically implies that as long as the element exists at the specified index in the array, we can access that element without needing to loop through the entire array.
- Queues and stacks allow us access the elements in a definite manner. While the queue works in a FIFO manner, the stack works in a LIFO manner.

- On the other hand, the list and dictionary collection types allow us to configure random access to the elements. Please note that, conceptually, the list does not support random access; however, in C#, the list is maintained as an array. Due to this, it supports random access.
- One important difference between a list and dictionary is the way they save data as well as the performance. In the dictionary collection, we save data in `KeyValuePair`. This allows us to maintain the uniqueness of the keys that are present in the dictionary. On the other hand, a list does not provide us with that feature.

Summary

In this chapter, we learned about how we serialize and deserialize data while exchanging it over a network. We looked at the different techniques available for serialization and deserialization. We started with `XmlSerialization` and saw how we serialize the data to XML files. We also looked at different attribute tags, such as `XmlArray`, `XmlArrayItem`, and `XmlIgnore`, which we can place in the class object when it's being converted into an XML file. We then looked at binary serialization and learned the advantages it has compared to `XmlSerialization`. We also looked at the `ISerializable` interface and learned how it provides security while exchanging data over the network.

We then looked at different collection types available in C# and the scenarios in which we should use each of them. We looked at arrays and their restrictions in terms of the length or size of the array, which we must declare during the declaration of the array. We then looked at some other complex collection types, such as list and dictionary. Both of these collection items allow us to increase the collection size during execution but differ in the way they access data. A dictionary saves the data in `KeyValuePair` and enforces the uniqueness of the keys that are present in the collection type.

Then, we looked at queues and stack collection types. As opposed to lists and dictionaries, which allow random access to the data, stacks and queues allow us to access to data in a particular order. Queues follow the FIFO model, while stacks follow the FILO model.

Questions

1. Which of the following statements are true?
   a. During serialization, XmlSerialization automatically includes private attributes in the generated XML class.
   b. In XmlSerialization, the XmlIgnore tag can be used to exclude any attribute that we don't want to include in the generated XML class.
   c. In binary serialization, private marked attributes are not serialized.
   d. Using the ISerializable interface, we can select the attributes and their tags that we want to be present in serialization.

2. Which of the following statements are true?
   a. We can increase the size of an array collection type during program execution.
   b. Queues follow the LIFO model for accessing elements.
   c. A dictionary saves data in KeyValuePair, ensuring the uniqueness of key-value pairs present in the collection item.
   d. Both a list and dictionary allow random access to the data elements.

3. You are working with a large group of student objects. You need to remove all duplicates and then group them by studentid. Which collections should we use?
   a. List
   b. Stack
   c. Dictionary
   d. Queue

Answers

1. **b and d**
2. **c and d**
3. **c**

17
Mock Test 1

1. We have a class called `LogException`. The class implements a `CaptureException` method using the following code segment: `public static void CaptureException(Exception ex)`. Pick one of the following syntaxes to make sure all exceptions in the class are captured and rethrow the original exception, including the stack:

   a.
   ```
   catch (Exception ex)
   {
       LogException.CaptureException(ex);
       throw;
   }
   ```

   b.
   ```
   catch (Exception ex)
   {
       LogException.CaptureException(ex);
       throw ex;
   }
   ```

   c.
   ```
   catch
   {
       LogException(new Exception());
   }
   ```

   d.
   ```
   catch
   {
       var ex = new Exception();
       throw ex;
   }
   ```

2. You are creating a class named `Store`, which should have a `Store Type` member that meets the following requirements:
   - The member must be accessible publicly.
   - The member must only acquire a restricted set of values.
   - While setting the value, the member must ensure that it validates the input set in the member.

In which form should you implement the score member?

a. `public string storeType;`

b.
```
protected String StoreType
{
    get{}
    set{}
}
```

c.
```
private enum StoreType { Department, Store, Warehouse}
public StoreType  StoreTypeProperty
{
    get{}
    set{}
}
```

d.
```
private enum StoreType { Department, Store, Warehouse}
private StoreType  StoreTypeProperty
{
    get{}
    set{}
}
```

3. Write an extension method for a string; it should have an `IsEmail` method . The method should check whether the string is a valid email. Select the syntax and map it to the places where it should be placed:

```
--------------------/*Line which needs to be filled*/
{
    ------------------/*Line which needs to be filled*/
    {
        Regex regex = new Regex(@"^([\w\.\-]+)@([\w\-
]+)((\.(\w){2,3})+)$");
        return regex.IsMatch(str);
    }
}
```

     a. `protected static class StringExtensions`

     b. `public static class StringExtensions`

     c. `public static bool IsEmail(this String str)`

     d. `public static bool IsEmail(String str)`

     e. `public class StringExtensions`

4. You need to write an application in which we ensure that the garbage collector does not release an object's resources until the process completes. Which of the following syntaxes would you use?

     a. `WaitForFullGCComplete()`

     b. `RemoveMemoryPressure()`

     c. `SuppressFinalize()`

     d. `collect()`

5. For a list collection, someone has written the following code:

```
static void Main(string[] args)
{
    List<string> states = new List<string>()
    {
        "Delhi", "Haryana", "Assam", "Punjab", "Madhya Pradesh"
    };
}

private bool GetMatchingStates(List<string> states, string
stateName)
{
    var findState = states.Exists(delegate(
    string stateNameToSearch)
    {
```

```
            return states.Equals(stateNameToSearch);
    });
    return findState;
}
```

Which of the following code segments is the correct representation of the corresponding Lambda expression?

a. `var findState = states.First(x => x == stateName);`

b. `var findState = states.Where(x => x == stateName);`

c. `var findState = states.Exists(x =>
   x.Equals(stateName));`

d. `var findState = states.Where(x => x.Equals(stateName));`

6. Which of the following collection objects would fulfill the following requirements?
   - It must internally store a key and value pair for each item.
   - It must allow us to iterate over the collection in order of the key.
   - It allows us to access the objects using the key.

   The collection objects are as follows:

   a. Dictionary
   b. Stack
   c. List
   d. SortedList

7. You are creating an application that has a `Student` class. The application must have a `Save` method that should satisfy the following:
   - It must be strongly typed.
   - The method must only accept types inherited from the `Animal` class that use a constructor that accepts no parameters.

The options are as follows:

```
a. public static void Save(Student target)
   {
   }
b. public static void Save<T>(T target) where T : Student
   , new()
   {
   }
c. public static void Save<T>(T target) where T : new(),
   Student
   {
   }
d. public static void Save<T>(T target) where T : Student
   {
   }
```

8. We are writing an application that is receives a JSON input from another application in the following format:

```
{
  "StudentFirstName" : "James",
  "StudentLastName" : "Donohoe",
  "StudentScores" : [45, 80, 68]
}
```

We have written the following code in our application to process the input. What would be the correct syntax in the `ConvertFromJSON` method to ensure that we convert the input to its equivalent student format?

```
public class Student
{
    public string StudentFirstName {get; set;}
    public string StudentLastName {get; set;}
    public int[] StudentScores {get; set;}
}

public static Student ConvertFromJSON(string json)
{
    var ser = new JavaScriptSerializer();
    ----------------/*Insert a line here*/
}
```

The options are as follows:

   a. `Return ser.Desenalize (json, typeof(Student));`

   b. `Return ser.ConvertToType<Student>(json);`

   c. `Return ser.Deserialize<Student>(json);`

   d. `Return ser.ConvertToType (json, typeof (Student));`

9. You have an array of integers with `studentId` values in them. Which code logic would you use to do the following?
   - Only select the unique `studentID`
   - Remove a particular `studentID` from the array
   - Sort the result in descending order into another array

Your options are as follows:

   a.
```
int[] filteredStudentIDs =
studentIDs.Distinct().Where(value => value !=
studentIDToRemove).OrderByDescending(x => x).ToArray();
```

   b.
```
int[] filteredStudentIDs = studentIDs.Where(value =>
value != studentIDToRemove).OrderBy(x => x).ToArray();
```

   c.
```
int[] filteredStudentIDs = studentIDs.Where(value =>
value != studentIDToRemove).OrderByDescending(x =>
x).ToArray();
```

   d.
```
int[] filteredStudentIDs =
studentIDs.Distinct().OrderByDescending(x =>
x).ToArray();
```

10. Identify the missing line in the following line of code:

```
private static IEnumerable<Country> ReadCountriesFromDB(string
sqlConnectionString)
{
    List countries = new List<Country>();
    SqlConnection conn = new SqlConnection();
    using (sqlConnectionString)
    {
        SqlCommand sqlCmd = new SqlCommand("Select name, continent
        from Counties", sqlConnectionString);
        conn.Open();
        using (SqlDataReader reader = sqlCmd.ExecuteReader())
        {
            // Insert the Line Here
```

```
        {
            Country con = new Country();
            con.CountryName = (String)reader["name"];
            con.ContinentName = (String)reader["continent"];
            counties.Add(con);
        }
    }
}
return countries;
}
```

a. while (reader.Read())

b. while (reader.NextResult())

c. while (reader.Being())

d. while (reader.Exists())

11. Write the following StudentCollection class in such a way that you can process each object in the collection using a foreach loop:

```
public class StudentCollection //Insert Code Here
{
    private Student[] students;
    public StudentCollection(Student[] student)
    {
        students = new Student[student.Length];

        for (int i=0; i< student.Length; i++)
        {
            students[i] = student[i];
        }
    }
    //Insert Code Here
    {
        //Insert Code Here
    }
}
```

a. : IComparable

b. : IEnumerable

c. : IDisposable

d. public void Dispose()

e. return students.GetEnumerator();

f. return obj == null ? 1: students.Length;

g. public IEnumerator GetEnumerator()

12. Which of the following lines of code would you use if you are writing code to open a file in line with the following conditions?
    - No changes should be made to the file.
    - The application should throw an error if the file does not exist.
    - No other processes should be allowed to update this file while the operation is in progress.

    a. ```
       var fs = File.Open(Filename, FileMode.OpenOrCreate,
       FileAccess.Read, FileShare.ReadWrite);
       ```

    b. ```
       var fs = File.Open(Filename, FileMode.Open,
       FileAccess.Read, FileShare.ReadWrite);
       ```

    c. ```
       var fs = File.Open(Filename, FileMode.Open,
       FileAccess.Read, FileShare.Read);
       ```

    d. ```
       var fs = File.Open(Filename, FileMode.Open,
       FileAccess.ReadWrite, FileShare.Read);
       ```

13. Which of the following lines of code would you use while converting a float to an int? You need to ensure that the conversion will not throw the `Float floatPercentage;` exception:

    a. `int roundPercentage = (int)floatPercentage;`

    b. `int roundPercentage = (int)(double)floatPercentage;`

    c. `int roundPercentage = floatPercentage;`

    d. `int roundPercentage = (int)(float)floatPercentage;`

14. Which of the following lines of code would you use while converting a float to an int? You need to ensure that the conversion will not throw the `Float floatPercentage;` exception:

    a. `int roundPercentage = (int)floatPercentage;`

    b. `int roundPercentage = (int)(double)floatPercentage;`

    c. `int roundPercentage = floatPercentage;`

    d. `int roundPercentage = (int)(float)floatPercentage;`

15. We are creating a `Student` class with a `StudentType` attribute. We need to ensure that the `StudentType` property can only be accessed within the `Student` class or by a class inheriting from the the `Student` class. Which of the following implementations would you use?

    a. ```
       public class Student
       {
           protected string StudentType
           {
               get;
       ```
       ```

```
                        set;
                }
        }
  b. public class Student
        {
                internal string StudentType
                {
                        get;
                        set;
                }
        }
  c. public class Student
        {
                private string StudentType
                {
                        get;
                        set;
                }
        }
  d. public class Student
        {
                public string StudentType
                {
                        get;
                        set;
                }
        }
```

16. We are writing an application in which we have declared a Car class that has two attributes, CarCategory and CarName. In the execution, we need to convert the class to its JSON string representation. Refer to the following code snippet:

```
public enum CarCategory
{
    Luxury,
    Sports,
    Family,
    CountryDrive
}

[DataContract]
public class Car
{
    [DataMember]
```

```
     public string CarName { get; set; }
     [DataMember]
     public enum CarCategory { get; set; }
}

void ShareCareDetails()
{
     var car = new Car { CarName = "Mazda", CarCategory =
CarCategory.Family };
     var serializedCar = /// Insert the code here
}
```

Which of the following lines of code would you use to get the correct structure for the JSON representation?

a. new DataContractSerializer(typeof(Car))

b. new XmlSerializer(typeof(Car))

c. new NetDataContractSerializer()

d. new DataContractJsonSerializer(typeof(Car))

17. We are writing an application for a bank in which we use the following code to find out the interest amount for a specified number of months, and the initial amount deposited in the bank:

```
1    private static decimal CalculateBankAccountInterest(decimal
initialAmount, int numberOfMonths)
2    {
3         decimal interestAmount;
4         decimal interest;
5         if(numberOfMonths > 0 && numberOfMonths < 6 &&
initialAmount < 5000)
6         {
7              interest = 0.05m;
8         }
9         else if(numberOfMonths > 6 && initialAmount > 5000)
10        {
11             interest = 0.065m;
12        }
13        else
14        {
15             interest = 0.06m;
16        }
17
18        interestAmount = interest * initialAmount * numberOfMonths
/ 12;
19        return interestAmount;
```

```
20  }
```

We've learned that the application is calculating incorrect interest amounts if the number of months is 6. If the number of months is 6, the interest rate should be 6.2%. Which of the lines of code would you change?

  a. Replace line 7 with `interest = 0.062m`

  b. Replace line 11 with `interest = 0.06m`

  c. Replace line 4 with `decimal interest = 0.062m`

  d. Replace line 15 with `interest = 0.062m`

18. We are writing an application in which we are making asynchronous calls to three different services, as described in the following example:

```
public async Task ExecuteMultipleRequestsInParallel()
{
    HttpClient client = new HttpClient();
    Task task1 = client.GetStringAsync("ServiceUrlA");
    Task task2 = client.GetStringAsync("ServiceUrlB");
    Task task3 = client.GetStringAsync("ServiceUrlC");
    // Insert the call here
}
```

Which of the following lines would you insert if you need to wait for the results from all three preceding services before control can be transferred back to the calling function?

  a. `await Task.Yield();`

  b. `await Task.WhenAll(task1, task2, task3);`

  c. `await Task.WaitForCompletion(task1, task2, task3);`

  d. `await Task.WaitAll();`

19. We are writing an application in which we are executing multiple operations, such as assigning, modifying, and replacing on string variables. Which of the following keywords would you use to make sure the operations consume as little memory as possible?

  a. `String.Concat`

  b. `+ operator`

  c. `StringBuilder`

  d. `String.Add`

20. We are writing an application in which we are maintaining students scores in a list, as shown in the following code block. We need to write a statement to filter out scores greater that 75. Which of the statements would you use?

```
List<int> scores = new List<int>()
{
    90,
    55,
    80,
    65
};
```

    a. `var filteredScores = scores.Skip(75);`

    b. `var filteredScores = scores.Where(i => i > 75);`

    c. `var filteredScores = scores.Take(75);`

    d.
```
var filteredScores = from i in scores
groupby i into tempList
where tempList.Key > 75
select i;
```

18
Mock Test 2

1. You need to write an application in which you create a class that establishes a connection with SQL Server and reads records in a certain table. We need to ensure the following in the class:

    - The class should automatically release all the connections after the operation is complete.
    - The class should support iteration.

    Which of the following interfaces would you implement in the class?

    a. `IEnumerator`

    b. `IEquatable`

    c. `IComparable`

    d. `IDisposable`

2. If you need to write a function that could be called with a varying number of parameters, what would you use?

    a. Interface

    b. Method overriding

    c. Method overloading

    d. Lamda expressions

3. You are writing an application in which you need to reverse a string. Which of the following code snippets would you use?

a.
```
char[] characters = str.ToCharArray();
for (int start = 0, end = str.Length - 1; start < end;
start++, end--)
{
    characters[end] = str[start];
    characters[start] = str[end];
}
string reversedstring = new string(characters);
Console.WriteLine(reversedstring);
```

b.
```
char[] characters = str.ToCharArray();
for (int start = 0, end = str.Length - 1; start < end;
start++, end--)
{
    characters[start] = str[end];
    characters[end] = str[start];
}
string reversedstring = new string(characters);
Console.WriteLine(reversedstring);
```

c.
```
char[] characters = str.ToCharArray();
for (int start = 0, end = str.Length; start < end;
start++, end--)
{
    characters[start] = str[end];
    characters[end] = str[start];
}
string reversedstring = new string(characters);
Console.WriteLine(reversedstring);
```

d.
```
char[] characters = str.ToCharArray();
for (int start = 0, end = str.Length; start < end;
++start, end--)
{
    characters[start] = str[end];
    characters[end] = str[start];
}
string reversedstring = new string(characters);
Console.WriteLine(reversedstring);
```

4. Which of the following features of Visual Studio would you use if you needed to compare the memory usage of different builds of the application?

    a. IntelliSense

    b. Use the CPU usage from the performance profiler

    c. Use the memory usage from the performance profiler

    d. Use UI analysis from the performance profiler

5. Which of the following regex expressions would you use to ensure that the input being validated is a non-negative decimal number?

    a. `^(?!\D+$)\+?\d*?(?:\.\d*)?$`

    b. `^(?:[1-9]\d*|0)?(?:\.\d+)?$`

    c. `^\d+(\.\d\d)?$`

    d. `^(-)?\d+(\.\d\d)?$`

6. We are developing an application in which we are using an assembly called X. If we need to debug the code in the assembly, which of the following should we do?

    a. For the application, in **Project Build Properties**, set the **Allow unsafe code** property.

    b. For the application, in the **Debug** pane, in **Debugging**, set **Enable native code** and **Continue**.

    c. For the application, in the **Debug** pane, in **Debugging**, uncheck **Enable Just My Code**.

    d. For the application, in **Project Debug Properties**, select the **Start external program** radio button and select assembly X.

7. We are creating an application with a `Student` class. We also have a variable called `students` declared in the application. Which of the following statements would you use to check whether the `students` variable is of a List of objects of type `Student`?

    a. `if(students.GetType() is List<Student>[])`

    b. `if(students.GetType() is List<Student>)`

    c. `if(students is List<Student>[])`

    d. `if(students is List<Student>)`

8. Which of the following code segments will not result in any loss of data?

   a.
   ```
   public void AddDeposit(float deposit)
   {
       AddToActBalance(Convert.ToDouble(deposit));
   }
   public void AddToActBalance(Double deposit)
   {
   }
   ```

   b.
   ```
   public void AddDeposit(float deposit)
   {
       AddToActBalance(Convert.ToDecimal(deposit));
   }
   public void AddToActBalance(Decimal deposit)
   {
   }
   ```

   c.
   ```
   public void AddDeposit(float deposit)
   {
       AddToActBalance(Convert.ToInt32(deposit));
   }
   public void AddToActBalance(int deposit)
   {
   }
   ```

   d.
   ```
   public void AddDeposit(float deposit)
   {
       AddToActBalance((Decimal)(deposit));
   }
   public void AddToActBalance(Decimal deposit)
   {
   }
   ```

9. We are writing an application in which we need to write some text to a file. The code syntax for this is as follows:

```
public async void PerformFileWriteOperation()
{
    string path = @"InputFile.txt";
    string text = "Text to read\r\n"
    await PerformFileUpdateAsync(path, text);
}
private async Task PerformFileUpdateAsync(string path, string
textToUpdate)
{
    byte[] encodedBits = Encoding.Unicode.GetBytes(textToUpdate);
    using(FileStream stream = new FileStream(
```

```
            path, FileMode.Append, FileAccess.Write, FileShare.None,
    bufferSize: 4096, useAsync: true))
        {
            /// Insert the code here
        }
    }
```

Which of the following lines would you insert in the preceding code to ensure the execution is not stopped until the file operation is in progress?

a. `async stream.Write(encodedBits, 0, encodedBits.Length);`

b. `await stream.Write(encodedBits,0, encodedBits.Length);`

c. `async stream.WriteAsync(encodedBits,0, encodedBits.Length);`

d. `await stream.WriteAsync(encodedBits,0, encodedBits.Length);`

10. We are writing an application in which we have written the following code:

```
public class Car
{
    public Car()
    {
        Console.WriteLine("Inside Car");
    }
    public void Accelerate()
    {
        Console.WriteLine("Inside Acceleration of Car");
    }
}
public class Ferrari : Car
{
    public Ferrari()
    {
        Console.WriteLine("Inside Ferrari");
    }
    public void Accelerate()
    {
        Console.WriteLine("Inside Acceleration of Ferrari");
    }
}

class Program
{
    static void Main(string[] args)
    {
```

```
            Car b = new Ferrari();
            b.Accelerate();
        }
    }
```

What would be the output of the program?

     a. Compile-time error

     b. Runtime error

     c. `Inside Acceleration of Ferrari`

     d. `Inside Acceleration of Car`

11. We have an application in which we have written the following logic in a `while` loop:

```
int i = 1;
while(i < 10)
{
    Console.WriteLine(i);
    ++i;
}
```

What would you do to convert it into the equivalent of a `for` loop?

     a.
```
for (int i = 0; i < 10 ; i++)
{
    Console.WriteLine(i);
}
```

     b.
```
for (int i = 1; i < 10 ; i++)
{
    Console.WriteLine(i);
}
```

     c.
```
for (int i = 1; i < 10 ; ++i)
{
    Console.WriteLine(i);
}
```

     d.
```
for (int i = 1; i <= 10 ; i++)
{
    Console.WriteLine(i);
}
```

12. What would be the output of the following program?

```
try
{
    int[] input = new int[5] { 0, 1, 2, 3, 4 };
    for (int i = 1; i <= 5; i++)
    {
            Console.Write(input[i]);
    }
}
catch (System.IndexOutOfRangeException e)
{
    System.Console.WriteLine("An error has occured in collection
operation");
    throw;
}
catch (System.NullReferenceException e)
{
    System.Console.WriteLine("An error has occured in null
reference operation");
    throw;
}
catch (Exception e)
{
    System.Console.WriteLine("Error logged for the application");
}
```

    a. 01234

    b. 1234
       An error has occurred in collection operation

    c. 1234
       An error has occurred in collection operation
       Error logged for the application

    d. 1234
       An error has occurred in collection operation
       An error has occurred in null reference operation
       Error logged for the application

13. Delegates can be instantiated by:
    a. Anonymous methods
    b. Lambda expressions
    c. Named methods
    d. All of the above

14. What action needs to be performed to move a thread to the run state when suspended?
    a. Resume
    b. Interrupt
    c. Abort
    d. Suspended

15. What would be the output of the following program?

```
public class DisposeImplementation : IDisposable
{
    private bool isDisposed = false;
    public DisposeImplementation()
    {
        Console.WriteLine("Creating object of
DisposeImplementation");
    }
    ~DisposeImplementation()
    {
        if(!isDisposed)
        {
            Console.WriteLine("Inside the finalizer of class
DisposeImplementation");
            this.Dispose();
        }
    }
    public void Dispose()
    {
        isDisposed = true;
        Console.WriteLine("Inside the dispose of class
DisposeImplementation");
    }
}

DisposeImplementation d = new DisposeImplementation();
d.Dispose();
d = null;
GC.Collect();
Console.ReadLine();
```

a. Creating object of DisposeImplementation
   Inside the dispose of class DisposeImplementation
   Inside the finalizer of class DisposeImplementation

b. Creating object of DisposeImplementation
   Inside the dispose of class DisposeImplementation

c. Runtime error in the application

d. Creating object of DisposeImplementation
   Inside the finalizer of class DisposeImplementation
   Inside the dispose of class DisposeImplementation

16. Look at the following program:

```
static int CalculateResult(int parameterA, int parameterB, int
parameterC, int parameterD = 0)
{
    int result = ((parameterA + parameterB) / (parameterC -
parameterD));
    return result;
}
```

What would be the output when it is called using the following syntax?

```
CalculateResult(parameterA: 20, 15, 5)
```

    a. −7

    b. 1

    c. 7

    d. Run time error

17. Which of these can be used to authenticate user input?
    a. Symmetric algorithm
    b. Asymmetric algorithm
    c. Hash values
    d. Digital signatures

17. We are working with a large group of student objects. You need to use a data structure that allows access to elements in any order and also allows duplicate values without needing to group them under a particular key. What would you choose?

    a. List

    b. Stack

    c. Dictionary

    d. Queue

18. Your application is running multiple worker threads. How do you make sure your application waits for all threads to complete their execution?

    a. `Thread.Sleep()`

    b. `Thread.WaitAll()`

    c. `Thread.Join()`

    d. None

19. In an application, we are writing a method in a class that should be accessible to classes in the same class and in classes that are present in the same assembly that inherit from the class. What do you need?

    a. Private protected

    b. Protected internal

    c. Protected

    d. Internal

19
Mock Test 3

1. In your application, you have implemented the `LogException(string message)` method to log exceptions. When an exception is thrown from your application, you want to log and rethrow the original exception. How do you achieve this?

    a. `catch(Exception ex){LogException(ex.Message); throw;}`

    b. `catch(Exception ex){LogException(ex.Message); throw ex;}`

    c. `catch{LogException(ex.Message); throw new Exception();}`

    d. `catch{LogException(ex.Message); rethrow;}`

2. You have created an application where you have implemented custom exception types and have also implemented multiple log methods, as follows:

```
public class CustomException1 : System.Exception{}
public class CustomException2 : CustomException1 {}
public class CustomException3 : CustomException1{}

void Log(Exception ex){}
void Log(CustomException2 ex) {}
void Log(CustomException3 ex) {}
```

You have a method that can throw one of the preceding exceptions. You need to make sure that, when the exception is caught, a log exception message by the log method accepts the exception; when `CustomException2` is caught, a log message by the log method accepts `CustomException2`; and the same for `CustomException3`. How do you want to achieve this? Please specify the order of catch statements:

```
a. catch(CustomException1 ex){...}
   catch(CustomExceotion2 ex){...}
   catch(CustomException3 ex){...}
b. catch(Exception ex){...}
   catch(CustomExceotion2 ex){...}
   catch(CustomException3 ex){...}
c. catch(Exception ex){...}
   catch(CustomExceotion1 ex){...}
d. catch(CustomException3 ex){...}
   catch(CustomExceotion2 ex){...}
   catch(Exception ex){...}
```

3. Your application is running multiple tasks using a task factory. However, a customer has requested you to run a specific task when its parent task throws an exception. How do you achieve this?

    a. `task.when()`

    b. `task.whenany()`

    c. `task.continuewhenany()`

    d. None of the above

4. Your application is running multiple worker threads. How do you make sure that your application waits for all the threads to complete their execution?

    a. `Thread.Sleep()`

    b. `Thread.WiatALL()`

    c. `Thread.Join()`

    d. None of the above

5. Secret key encryption is also known as asymmetric encryption.

    a. `True`

    b. `False`

6. In public-key encryption, anyone with the public key can process the message.
   a. True
   b. False

7. When using RSACryptoServiceProvider in your sample application, how would you get your public and private keys?

   a. ```
   RSACryptoServiceProvider rsa = new
   RSACryptoServiceProvider();
   string publicKey = rsa.ToXmlString(false);
   string pricateKey = rsa.ToXmlString(true);
   ```

   b. ```
   RSACryptoServiceProvider rsa = new
   RSACryptoServiceProvider();
   string publicKey = rsa.ToXmlString(true);
   string pricateKey = rsa.ToXmlString(false);
   ```

   c. ```
   RSACryptoServiceProvider rsa = new
   RSACryptoServiceProvider();
   string publicKey = rsa.ToXmlString(public);
   string pricateKey = rsa.ToXmlString(private);
   ```

   d. ```
   RSACryptoServiceProvider rsa = new
   RSACryptoServiceProvider();
   string publicKey = rsa.ToXmlString("public");
   string pricateKey = rsa.ToXmlString("private");
   ```

8. What is the best way to authenticate a sender?
   a. Encrypt your message.
   b. Sign your message.
   c. Use digital signatures.
   d. All of the above.

9. When you apply the hash algorithm on a string, what will the output be?
   a. The string gets encrypted.
   b. Each character gets hashed into a different binary string.
   c. The string gets hashed as a whole.
   d. None of the above.

10. You are adding new features to an existing application for your customers. When you deploy them, you get an assembly manifest mismatch error. What is the best possible solution to resolve this issue?

    a. Update all major and minor assembly versions of the current and dependent assemblies, then rebuild and deploy.

    b. Check all assembly versions of the current and dependent assemblies and make sure the configurations or policies are updated to reflect the change in assembly versions, then rebuild and deploy.

    c. Update the `machine.config` file to ignore such errors.

    d. Update `web.config` and set the custom error mode to `off`.

11. You create a release package and deploy your application into a production environment. When users start using the application, they receive an error. You are unable to reproduce it in any lower-level environments, so you decide to debug your application in the production environment. However, the application never stops at the breakpoint. Why is this?

    a. You don't have local admin permissions on the system.

    b. Visual Studio's debugging module is not loaded.

    c. The release version doesn't allow us to debug.

    d. All of the above.

12. You create an application and you want to monitor it while it is executing. So, you decide to implement tracing. How do you trace your application so that you can see your trace messages in the output window?

    a. Use `Console.WriteLine()`.

    b. Use `tracelistener` to add the output window and use `trace.write`.

    c. `Debug.WriteLine()`.

    d. `Output.WriteLine()`.

13. You are creating an application where you have an `if` statement and an `else` statement. In the `if` statement, you have two conditions. You want both of these conditions to be validated before executing the code block. How do you achieve this?

    a. Use the `&&` operator.

    b. Use the `&` operator.

    c. Use the `|` operator.

    d. User the `||` operator.

14. How do you return a default value into a variable when your expression returns a null value?
    a. Use the `ternary` operator.
    b. Use the `binary` operator.
    c. Use the conditional `OR`.
    d. Use the `null` coalescing operator.

15. You have multiple versions of the same method in your code. Your customer has requested you to make sure that all dependent applications use a specific version of the method. How do you make sure that no one invokes any other methods which may cause other exceptions?
    a. Change the access modifiers for all other methods.
    b. Throw an exception from these methods.
    c. Use the `Obsolete` attribute to let users know the correct method to use.
    d. All of the above.

16. You are creating a C# application where you need to output multiple lines with a line break between them. How do you achieve this?
    a. `var sb = new StringBuilder();sb.AppendLine(Line1);`
       `sb.AppendLine(Environment.NewLine);`
    b. `var sb = new StringBuilder();foreach(string line in`
       `strList){sb.AppendLine(Line1);`
       `sb.AppendLine(Environment.NewLine); }`
    c. `var sb = new StringBuilder();sb.Append(Line1);`
       `sb.Append('\t');`
    d. All of the above

17. How would you make sure a parent class method is not accessible in inherited classes? Which access modifier would you use?
    a. Private
    b. Internal
    c. Protected
    d. Abstract

18. Specify the code to load an assembly at runtime:
    a. `Assembly.Load()`
    b. `Assembly.Create("A1.dll");Assembly.Load();`
    c. `Assembly.Load("a.dll");`
    d. `Assembly.GetType().Load();`

19. When you create a C# console application, which files do you see in the solution explorer?

   a. Project, `App.Config`, `Program.cs`, Solution, Properties, and References
   b. `App.Config`, `Program.cs`
   c. Project, `App.Config`, `Program.cs`, Solution, Properties
   d. `App.Config`, `Program.cs`, Properties

20. When you create a console application and change the `static Main(string[] args)` to `static main(string[] args)`, what will happen?

   a. A compile-time error is raised.
   b. A runtime error is raised.
   c. Both **a** and **b**.
   d. None of the above.

21. A class or a class member that is declared as internal can only be accessed by classes in the same assembly but not by outside assemblies.

   a. True
   b. False

22. Consider the following statements. **Statement 1**: A value type maintains the address of the variable. **Statement 2**: Two reference type variables pointing at address 1 reflect the updated value.

   a. Both are true.
   b. Statement 1 is true, statement 2 is false.
   c. Statement 1 is false, statement 2 is true.
   d. Both are false.

23. While defining an interface, it is good practice to have access modifiers for the methods.

   a. True
   b. False

24. How do you define an optional parameter?

   a. `void AddNumbers(int a=1, int b)`
   b. `void AddNumbers(int a, int b  optional)`
   c. `void AddNumbers(int a, int b=4)`
   d. `void Add numbers(int a, optional int b)`

25. What is the keyword that you use in a program function where you are using a pointer declaration?

    a. Sealed

    b. Safe

    c. Internal

    d. Unsafe

26. What syntax do we use to append text to a file?

    a. `File.CreateText`

    b. `FileInfo.Create`

    c. `File.Create`

    d. `File.AppendText`

27. Which collection type can be used to create a strongly typed, zero-based index to process objects in a FIFO manner?

    a. `Queue<T>`

    b. `List<T>`

    c. `Array`

    d. `Dictionary`

28. You are creating an application that manages information. You define a save method in the class and you want to ensure that only this class and any inherited classes can invoke the method. You want to define the save method as a strongly typed method. How do you achieve this?

    a. `public static void Save<T>(T target) where T : new(), ParentClass {}`

    b. `public static void Save<T>(T target) where T : ParentClass,new() {}`

    c. `public static void Save<T>(T target) where T : ParentClass {}`

    d. `public static void Save(ParentClass target) {}`

29. You are developing an assembly that will be used by multiple applications. You need to install it in GAC. Which actions would you perform to achieve this?

    a. Sign the assembly and use the Gacutil tool to install the assembly in GAC.

    b. Version assembly and use the Regsvr32 tool to install the assembly in GAC.

    c. Drag and drop to the Windows assembly folder.

    d. All of the above.

30. When two parties need to communicate using the asymmetric algorithm, which key do they need to share?

    a. Private key

    b. Public key

    c. Both

    d. None

Assessments

Chapter 17 – Mock Test 1

1. b
2. c
3. b in the first line , c in the second line
4. c
5. c
6. d
7. c
8. c
9. a
10. a
11. b, g, e
12. c
13. d
14. a
15. a
16. a
17. d
18. b
19. c
20. b

Chapter 18 – Mock Test 2

1. a, d
2. c
3. b
4. c
5. a
6. d
7. b
8. a
9. d
10. c
11. b
12. c
13. d
14. a
15. b
16. c
17. b, d
18. a
19. b
20. a

Chapter 19 – Mock Test 3

1. a
2. d
3. d
4. b
5. a
6. b
7. a
8. c
9. b
10. a
11. c
12. c
13. b
14. d
15. c
16. b
17. a
18. c
19. a
20. a
21. a
22. c
23. b
24. c
25. d
26. d
27. a
28. b
29. a
30. c

Other Books You May Enjoy

If you enjoyed this book, you may be interested in these other books by Packt:

Hands-On Design Patterns with C# and .NET Core
Gaurav Aroraa, Jeffrey Chilberto

ISBN: 978-1-78913-364-6

- Make your code more flexible by applying SOLID principles
- Follow the **test-driven development** (**TDD**) approach in your .NET Core projects
- Get to grips with efficient database migration, data persistence, and testing techniques
- Convert a console application to a web application using the right MVP
- Write asynchronous, multithreaded, and parallel code
- Implement MVVM and work with RxJS and AngularJS to deal with changes in databases
- Explore the features of microservices, serverless programming, and cloud computing

Hands-On Network Programming with C# and .NET Core
Sean Burns

ISBN: 978-1-78934-076-1

- Understand the breadth of C#'s network programming utility classes
- Utilize network-layer architecture and organizational strategies
- Implement various communication and transport protocols within C#
- Discover hands-on examples of distributed application development
- Gain hands-on experience with asynchronous socket programming and streams
- Learn how C# and the .NET Core runtime interact with a hosting network
- Understand a full suite of network programming tools and features

Leave a review - let other readers know what you think

Please share your thoughts on this book with others by leaving a review on the site that you bought it from. If you purchased the book from Amazon, please leave us an honest review on this book's Amazon page. This is vital so that other potential readers can see and use your unbiased opinion to make purchasing decisions, we can understand what our customers think about our products, and our authors can see your feedback on the title that they have worked with Packt to create. It will only take a few minutes of your time, but is valuable to other potential customers, our authors, and Packt. Thank you!

Index

await statement
    used, for parallel asynchronous calls 329

B

background threads 129, 130, 131
binary serialization 362, 363, 368
block ciphers 271
boxing 190, 192, 193
break statement 94
built-in delegates 114
business-defined integrity 253
ByteCode 14

C

C# application
    debugging 295, 296, 297, 298, 299, 300, 301,
        302, 303, 304, 305
C#
    basic program, creating 25, 27
    boxing 192, 193
    data types 31
    data types, consuming 192
    features 11, 13
    input parameters 25
    interface 47, 48, 49, 50, 51
    Microsoft Visual Studio 19
    program, creating 22, 24, 25
    programming syntax 20, 21, 22
    return type 25
    type conversions 193
    unboxing 192, 193
    versus C 11
    versus C++ 11, 12, 14
C++, compilers
    Linux 14
    Windows 14
C++
    features 13
    versus C# 11, 12, 14
C, compilers
    Linux 14
    Windows 14
C
    features 11
    versus C# 11

caller information attribute 242
ChapterInfo attribute 244
cipher-text 269
class functions
    constructor 367
    GetObjectData 367
class library 17
class, components
    data attributes 20
    methods 20
class
    feature 40
    versus struct 34, 36, 38, 39, 40
classes 20
code block 91
collection, types
    array 368, 369, 370, 371
    dictionary 373, 375
    list 371, 372, 373
    queue 376, 377, 378, 379, 380
    stack 376, 377, 378, 379, 380
collection
    selecting 380, 381
    working with 368
Common Language Runtime (CLR) 14, 17, 18,
        176, 178, 212, 246
Common Language Runtime (CLR), features
    exception handling 18
    memory management 17
compile-time polymorphism 73, 74
compiler-generated exceptions 171
condition section 97
conditional AND (&&) operator 87
conditional attribute 241
conditional operator
    about 87, 88
    conditional AND (&&) operator 87
    conditional OR (||) operator 87
conditional OR (||) operator 87
conditional/selection statements
    about 90
    break statement 94
    continue statement 95
    goto statement 94
    if...else statement 90, 91, 92

while statement 99

J

join operator 342
JSON 263, 264, 265, 266, 267
Just in Time (JIT) 14, 15

L

Lambda expressions 107, 108, 109
Lambda operator 107
language features, LINQ
  about 334
  anonymous type 339, 340
  extension methods 338
  implicitly typed variables 334, 335, 336
  Lambda expressions 337, 338
  object initialization syntax 336, 337
Language-Integrated Query (LINQ)
  about 16, 151, 332
  queries 332, 333
  reference link 151
  used, for working with XML 347, 348
  working 346, 347
LINQ query operators
  about 340
  Average operator 344
  GroupBy operator 344, 346
  join operator 342
  orderby operator 343
  Select operator 340, 341
  SelectMany operator 340, 341
list 371, 372, 373
logical AND (&) operator 87
logical operator
  about 87, 88
  logical AND (&) operator 87
  logical OR (|) 87
  logical XOR (^) operator 87
logical OR (|) operator 87
logical XOR (^) operator 87

M

managed code
  versus unmanaged code 212
managed heap 215, 216

mark-compact algorithm
  about 219, 220
  compacting phase 219
  mark phase 219
  relocating phase 219
memory management
  about 17
  memory, allocating 17
  memory, releasing 18
metadata
  retrieving 244
method overriding
  about 64, 67
  override keyword 64
  virtual method 64
Microsoft Visual Studio
  features 20
  for C# 19
  URL 20
MoveNext method 99
multicast delegates 114, 115
multicasting 114
multithreading
  about 143
  asynchronous programming, with async 157, 158
  asynchronous programming, with await 157, 158
  data, synchronizing 138, 139, 142
  Parallel Language-Integrated Query (PLINQ) 151
  parallel programming 143, 144
  Task Parallel Library (TPL) 144, 145

N

named parameters 186
NamedMethod
  used, for initiating delegate 105, 107
namespaces 17, 22
network
  data, reading from 324
null coalescing (??) operator 87
null operator
  about 87, 88
  null coalescing (??) operator 87
  ternary operator (?) 87

O

object-oriented programming
  about 56, 58
  categories 12
  disadvantages 56
obsolete attribute 240, 241
operand 82
operator
  about 82
  conditional operator 87, 88
  equality operator 85, 86
  logical operator 87, 88
  null operator 87, 88
  relational operator 84
  shift operator 85
  unary operator 82, 83, 84
optional parameters 187
orderby operator 343
override keyword 64

P

parallel asynchronous calls
  await statement, using 329
Parallel FX 16
Parallel Language-Integrated Query (PLINQ) 143,
  151
parallel programming 143, 144
parameterized threads 128
parameterless constructor 185
parsing 256, 257, 259, 260, 261
pointer type
  about 31
  usage 177, 178, 179, 180
polymorphism
  about 72, 73
  compile-time polymorphism 73, 74
  runtime polymorphism 75, 77
  static polymorphism 73, 74
portable executable (PE) 288
public-key encryption (asymmetric encryption) 271

Q

queue
  about 376, 377, 378, 379, 380

operations 376
  working 376
queues, finalization mechanism
  finalization queue 222
  fReachable queue 222

R

reference type 177
reference type variable
  about 34
  class 35
  dynamic 35
  interface 35
  object 35
  string 35
referential integrity 253
reflection
  about 175, 245, 246
  methods, invoking 246, 247
  overview 206, 207
  properties, using 246, 247
regular expressions 261, 262, 263
relational operator
  about 84
  expression 84
runtime polymorphism 75, 77

S

scalability 42
sealed classes 71
Select operator 340, 341
SelectMany operator 340, 341
serialization
  about 356
  binary serialization 362, 363, 368
  XmlSerializer, using 356, 357, 358, 360, 361,
    362
shift operator
  about 85
  expression 85
Simple Object Access Protocol (SOAP) 356
simple types 32
stack
  about 376, 377, 378, 379, 380
  working 378

unmanaged code
  versus managed code 212
unmanaged resources
  finalization mechanism 222, 223, 224, 225, 227
  managing 220, 221
unsafe code 177, 178, 179
  about 180
Unstarted state 131
user-defined integrity 253
using block 231, 232, 233

V

value type 176
value type variable
  about 32
  enum types 32, 33
  simple types 32
  struct types 34
variable type
  creating 176
  in C# 176
  pointer type 177
  reference type 177
  selecting 180, 181, 182, 183
  value type 176
virtual method 64
Visual Studio

used, for signing assemblies 292, 293, 294

W

Wait/Join Sleep state 132
WebRequest 324, 325, 326
WebResponse 324, 325, 326
while statement 99
Windows Communication Foundation 16
Windows Forms applications 16
Windows Presentation Foundation 16
worker threads 124

X

XDeclaration
  XComments 348
XDocument class
  XDeclaration 348
  XElement 348
  XProcessingInstruction 348
XML
  about 263, 264, 265, 266, 267
  creating 351
  querying 348, 349, 350
  updating 351, 352
  working with, LINQ 347, 348
XmlSerializer
  using 356, 357, 358, 360, 361, 362

www.ingramcontent.com/pod-product-compliance
Lightning Source LLC
Chambersburg PA
CBHW060647060326
40690CB00020B/4545